DEATH IS FOR THE LIVING

DEATH IS FOR
THE LIVING

Anne Gordon

Paul Harris Publishing

Edinburgh

First published 1984 by
Paul Harris Publishing
40 York Place
Edinburgh

ISBN 0 86228 089 3

The publishers gratefully acknowledge the financial assistance of the Scottish Arts Council in the publication of this volume.

Typeset by Jo Kennedy, Edinburgh
Printed by Billings Bookplan, Worcester

Acknowledgements

I am greatly indebted to the following people for the generous help they have given in answer to my queries and especially to those who have, in addition, taken time to look up records, to send photostats and pamphlets and to get in touch with other people on my behalf:

Rev. Duane Armistead, Udny.
Berwickshire District Burial Grounds Department.
Rev. W. Campbell, Tain (Caithness).
Rev. C. Cowie, Isle of Whithorn.
G.N.M. Collins, Free Church of Scotland.
Country Life Section staff, Museum of Antiquities.
Miss Davidson, Thurso.
Rev. Dunlop, Church of Scotland Offices.
Rev. Robert Fraser, Lauder.
Mr C. Gibson, Monifieth.
Dr I. Grant, General Register Office for Scotland.
John Goudie (Lerwick) Ltd.
Mrs Henderson, Nigg (Caithness).
Mrs Henderson, Spean Bridge.
Hamilton & Inches, Edinburgh.
William Jardine, Funeral Directors, Dumfries.
Miss Lawrie, St Boswells.
Library staffs in Roxburghshire, Aberdeen and Inverness and the Royal Bank of Scotland, Edinburgh.
Mrs R. Mackenzie, Tain.
Mr Macdonald, Balintore (Benbecula).
Mrs Macdonald, Balintore.
Rev. D. McCuish, Caddonfoot (Harris, Barra, Iona, Bute).
Mr L. Morrison, St Boswells (Shetland).
Rev. Nigel Mackenzie, Lauder (Skye).
Mrs J. Murray, Castle Douglas.
Rev. W. Moore, Daviot.
Mr Frank Maclennan, Brora.
Mr William Munro, Alness.
Mr Plenderleith, Kelso.
Mr W. Robertson, Tannadice.
Mr U. Ross, Tain.
Mr and Mrs Macdonald Scott, Kelso.
Miss E. Scott, Tain.
Ms Sally Smith, Edinburgh.
Mr and Mrs G. Tinline, Lilliesleaf.
Rev. D. A. Tosh, Ancrum.
Rev. K. Thomson, Newtown St Boswells (Orkney, Shetland).

Note

Scots money went out of use officially in 1707 but in spite of that it continued to be used for long thereafter. In some cases, accounts appear in both Scots money and sterling, as in the Kirk Session records of Rayne, Aberdeenshire, in 1765 when the price of a new mortcloth is shown in the accounts in Scots money and the minutes in sterling. After changing to sterling, there was sometimes a reversion to Scots money, as in Melrose Kirk Session records which use sterling in 1745 and Scots money in 1746.

Scots money = one-twelfth of sterling.

merk = 13/4 Scots = 13⅓ sterling.

rix (rex) dollar = silver coin worth between 2/3 and 4/6.

By and large, this book only cover the post-Reformation years and does not include deaths by war or witchcraft.

CONTENTS

Weep not for them,
They weep no more.
Sorrow not for them
For their sorrows are o'er.
Sweet is their sleep
Though cold and hard
Their pillows lie low
In the old kirkyard.

From 'The Churchyard', quoted in the
History of Channelkirk, by
Rev. Archibald Allan.

Preparations

D eath was part of life. This is made very clear in John Galt's *Annals of the Parish* in which he describes how a young woman who was far from right in the head still knew just what to do when her mother died. There was a routine to go through and through it she went.

When someone was dying – or 'his friends were looking on him' as they said in the Borders – there was much to be seen to and many preparations to be made. There were variations from district to district but the basics were the same country-wide. In fishing villages it was believed that the spirit of a dying person would only depart on an outgoing tide and that if it missed one tide it would have to wait until the next. But on the coast or inland, when death was imminent no one in the house was allowed to sleep and neighbours and friends gathered round the death-bed. In some areas, such as Hawick in the mid-19th century, the assembled watchers sang psalms during the mortal struggle and a song of triumph and praise when it was over. Immediately death occurred one of the first things to be done was to open all doors and windows. Old people still remember this custom but usually think it was to let in fresh air, having long since lost sight of the real reason which was to let the spirit escape, something which was done not just in Scotland but all over Europe. The clock was stopped at the moment of death and not restarted until the burial was over.

In great houses, the walls were draped in black for funerals. Lesser establishments had the walls painted white or draped with white sheets and all furniture, pictures and clocks, as well as the deathbed, were also covered in white sheets, often specially kept for this purpose, and napkins were often used to cover smaller items in the house.

Mirrors were covered too or else turned to the wall. Writing in 1961, I.F. Grant said that it was still customary in some places then to cover mirrors and the glass of pictures in this way. The original and largely-lost-sight-of reason for this was to prevent the spirit catching sight of itself which might mislead it as it tried to escape from the house, because however much loved the dead person had been, it was essential that the spirit should go and not come back. The same reason lies behind the custom of taking a corpse out of the house feet foremost – to prevent it seeing the way back. The old custom of not taking it out the door had the same origin and was sometimes carried to the length of taking it out through the smoke-hole or through a specially-made opening which was closed immediately afterwards to prevent it finding its way back. Gradually this came to be confined to those who died 'bad deaths' such as suicide. Chairs or benches on which a coffin was laid used to be thrown over when the cortège set out and left that way until everyone returned from the graveyard. Although this was widely said to indicate the disorder caused in the house by death, it originated in the necessity to perplex the spirit and prevent its return.

In spite of this desire to see the spirit go and stay away, in some parts of Scotland there was a custom which seems contradictory. This was 'receiving the breath' of a dying person, a custom which probably explains an illustration of the word, *Deo*, breath, given in *McAlpine's Gaelic Dictionary*, '*Glacaibh mo Dheo*, lay hold on my departing spirit, on my ghost.' This appears to be the continuance of a very ancient custom. The Romans thought it essential that the nearest relative should catch the last breath of the dying to ensure the continued existence of the spirit while primitive people believed that the soul of a dying person might be passed on to his successor by the successor catching in his mouth or in a bag the last breath and with it the soul. There is hardly a reference anywhere to this custom in Scotland although it continued to be remembered in Ross and Cromarty in the early 20th century and in Caithness some time later; unfortunately those who remember the fact of it do not remember the details. There was much superstition to do with breath and where this custom occurred in later years it seems very possible that it fell into this category.

There was a belief that death caused defilement, something supported by the categorical Biblical statement in *Numbers* 19. 14 which says, 'This is the law, when a man dieth in a tent (i.e. indoors) all that come into the tent and all that is in the tent, shall be unclean seven days.' Thus all foodstuffs in a house of death were thought to be unclean but because they were far too precious to be wasted they were purified. Iron was a metal thought to have powerful qualities and to be an influence against evil, and so a piece of iron was often thrust into each item of food and drink in the house to make them fit for human consumption once more. In fishing villages, onions and butter – specifically those two commodities – were removed from the house when someone was dying or put out after the death.

Water in a house of death was also thought to be unclean. The verse following the quotation from *Numbers* already given says, 'And every open vessel, which hath no covering bound upon it, is unclean', which explains why in some areas all water containers were emptied. In some places water was thrown out after the funeral procession left the house; sometimes water from all the houses along a funeral route was thrown out after the procession passed which, in view of the difficulties involved in the fetching and carrying of water in earlier days, can only have been for some strong reason such as fear of corruption by death, or else to prevent the return of the spirit because the dead do not like to cross water. In spite of this, water was sometimes provided for the spirit to drink while the body lay in the house, perhaps as a final form of nourishment, although there was always a fear that it might drown itself which is, of course, another explanation of putting out water.

In the 18th century there was a custom of laying iron, cheese, a plate of salt and perhaps a green turf on the chest of the deceased. By the mid-to-late 18th century, a platter of salt and earth was placed upon the corpse. These were in the one dish but kept apart from one another on it although in time, or perhaps in different areas, they were mixed together and also in time the use of earth died out and salt was used alone. People now in their seventies, from the Borders to the Highlands, can still remember seeing a dish of salt placed on or beside a corpse. The value of iron has already been mentioned; cheese seems most surprising for this purpose; earth or turf were believed to represent the earthly and corruptible body and salt the immortal spirit. Latterly salt was regarded as a hygienic precaution and was thought to prevent the body swelling although it is hard to see how that could be. It seems likely that in later years the use of salt was simply folk memory in action, something being done long after the real reason was forgotten, the reason most probably being because salt has a saving and preserving quality and blessed salt has been used for liturgical purposes throughout the ages.

In some places, and in Aberdeenshire certainly, one or perhaps two lighted candles were placed beside the corpse. Even though this happened into the first half of the 19th century, it seems almost certainly a survival of Roman Catholic usage, over and above the obvious reason of giving light. Sometimes a bell was placed below the head of the corpse, bells being thought a most effective way of warding off the devil. A surprisingly late example of this primitive and instinctive desire to ward off evil appeared as late as 1914 or 1915 at the death of an old man in Fearn, Ross and Cromarty. His daughter placed a bowl of oatmeal on his breast and beside him a glass of either milk or water. While water might of course be provided for the spirit to drink, the explanation given to two visitors was something different. This was an old, old custom, said the old man's daughter; it was for the devil who would eat and drink and take away evil spirits. By way of another slant on this, in some fishing villages, bread and water was placed in the room where the body had lain, on the night after the funeral.

Laying out and dressing a corpse was usually a job for the howdy, that invaluable local woman who specialized in birth and death, but if no howdy was available, the womenfolk of the household managed themselves. The body was 'straiked' – stretched – on a board or plank or even on a table. In the 18th century in some parts another board was suspended from the roof above and a piece of cloth thrown over it to hang down like a canopy. When darkness fell, candles were set on the upper board. This old custom explains a phrase which was used 'on the borders of the low country' for an unburied corpse, 'that he is under the board'.

In later years, after stretching, the body was laid in bed. In a cottage this might be in a box bed in the kitchen, or in the best room, while in a larger house there was often a 'dead room', the best bedroom, used only on the occasions of marriage and death and called after the less cheerful of these uses.

People of importance used to be embalmed, a necessary precaution when a considerable delay might elapse between death and burial. Lack of it explains a letter written by the Laird of Newton, Morayshire, in 1734 about his wife's funeral in which he said, 'I am determined to bury her Tuesday next since the body can keep no longer.' Embalming required not only a howdy but a medical man. A surgeon's account in 1562 shows '. . . spices, vainagre . . . pulderis, odouris . . . and for his labours in handeling of the said Erle of Huntleis bodie that it should not putrefie . . .' Well into the 18th century, when means allowed, bodies were half-embalmed and wrapped in a special winding sheet which was a cloth dipped in melted wax, known as a 'cere cloth'. The putting on of the cere cloth became one of the pre-burial ceremonies often accompanied by the serving of alcohol. In 1692 a 'schar cloth for inrolling of the corpse' of Lady Mey cost £33 Scots and the charge for the surgeon's attendance to wrap her in it, along with the necessary oils, powders and perfumes came to a further £24 Scots. William Strogg, a surgeon from Miltown, Ross and Cromarty, charged £120 Scots for 'imbowelling . . . and sheer cloth' for the Laird of Balnagown's funeral in 1711. These perfumes included frankincense and incense, the former also being used 'for Corpse and coffin' at the funeral of a Perth minister who died in 1719. By the 19th century embalming had died out but *The Scotsman* of 22 December 1827 reported that a new method had been discovered by Sir George Stewart Mackenzie, saying '. . . should embalming ever become popular this new method will supersede all others.' In fact, at the present day, a simple method has been introduced of injecting a fluid which delays decomposition of the body.

Grave clothes could be very splendid. The Act anent Burying in Scots Linen in 1686 made it plain just how elaborate they could be if means permitted because it forbade the use of lace or point, silk, hair, woollen, gold and silver materials for that purpose. In general, however, a corpse was dressed more simply in dead clothes made by a local sempstress. Elizabeth Grant in her *Memoirs of a Highland Lady* describes a corpse, lying in bed with a well ruffled shirt and a nightcap, an elegant simplicity. For those in humble circumstances a decent burial was always in the forefront of their minds and one of the first tasks of a bride was to prepare dead linen for herself and her husband. This was said to remind her of mortality, but surely such a reminder cannot have been necessary when death was ever present. She was simply being provident because people realized that if they were to be decent corpses at the end, they must do something about it ahead of time. Preparing those dead clothes might mean spinning and weaving a coarse winding sheet; it might mean buying material and sewing it; or it might require the careful stitching of special white nightwear, but whichever was done the results were carefully kept, along with sheets, in a kist or drawer and only taken out for an annual airing. According to Captain Burt who travelled in Scotland in the 1730s, a husband who sold or pawned the dead linen prepared by his wife was 'esteemed among all men one of the most profligate'.

As time went on and communications improved, such requirements became available in the shops. In 1755 James Rose of Inverness supplied '1 sute Fine grave Flannels' for £2. 16/- stg. as well as a pair of white gloves for a corpse. In Glasgow a Miss Christian Brown started a shop at the west side of Hutcheson Street where she carried on the 'business of making dead flannels and getting up burial crapes'. But fashion being what fashion is, refinement crept in in this sphere and in 1809 the *Inverness Courier* carried the following advertisement: 'Mrs. Fraser, next door to Fraser's Hotel, has just got on hand from London a variety of ready-made graveclothes, all sizes and prices. They surpass in quality and elegance anything of the kind ever offered to the attention of the public (desirous of paying all necessary respect to the deceased) in this quarter. Mrs. Fraser has also small shrouds for children.'

A former doctor on Barra told of how women who came to keep the bereaved company before the burial, also made the shroud. Without using any patterns or formal instructions, they cut a large white sheet into intricate designs, giving a final effect of lace work but with no stitching involved.

It was not so easy for country people to get to shops for 'deid claes' but pedlars sometimes obliged by fetching them if asked to do so. A story is told of a pedlar in the Forfar area who brought a shroud to an old woman only to be told by her on his next visit that it was no use at all, it was far too tight and she couldn't draw breath in it. People who are now in their sixties and seventies still remember the days of the special nightdress and the shroud kept in the kist, although one such memory tells of the time when it was finally decided that keeping a shroud was no longer necessary. The housewife made it into handkerchiefs and very stiff they were and consequently most unpopular with the family. Even in 1978 a Caithness woman who often laid out the dead though she was neither howdy nor nurse, insisted on using a sheet 'as in the old days' as well as a shroud. She always kept in a bottom drawer at least one pair of sheets which, though just ordinary cotton or linen ones, were special and always referred to as 'white sheets' and her children were always admonished with 'Now don't touch these white sheets.' People not only provided dead clothes before death, they liked to put by a little money for their burials. Some bought or made coffins in advance and I.F. Grant tells of an old woman, dying in a lonely glen who laid herself out lest no one should do this for her. 'Be Prepared' was undoubtedly the watchword.

In many cottages, animals and poultry lived in such close proximity to humans that it was easy for them to jump on or walk over a corpse, especially when it lay in the kitchen. This was considered very ominous; in some places it was thought that if a cat walked across a body, then the first person to see it thereafter would lose their sight. The result was that any dog or cat doing so was killed at once and so a first essential at a time of death was to shut up all dogs and cats, as well as hens. The straw or heather which had been the dead person's bed was always burnt but there were differences as to when this was done. It could happen just after death, often on some nearby raised ground, when it was regarded as a signal of death and as a summons, or it could be burnt during the funeral. In some places, after the cortège had gone a little way the bedding was taken out and burnt where no animals could get at it and examined next morning for signs of any footprints which might indicate who was going to die next in the family. If the reek of it blew over a house someone was expected to die in that house before the year was out.

The womenfolk of a bereaved family were immediately involved in all the domestic preparations for a funeral except in some east coast fishing areas where the matrons customarily took to their beds on the occasion of bereavement and there received expressions of sympathy. In small communities when a death occurred all everyday work stopped for the men: during the 'dead days' until the body was buried not a spadeful of earth was turned, all fishing boats were beached, no crops cultivated or harvested, as a mark of respect, one which could mean real hardship when life was lived at subsistence level.

It was normal practice for a corpse to lie before burial in his or her own home but in the Episcopal periods of the 17th century it might lie in a church and at one stage it seems to have been permissible to lay bodies in the Session House of the parish church. The Kirk Session records of Inverness about 1703 state that Kirk Officers were to be allowed half a dollar for every corpse laid there 'for their attendance upon the said corpse and friends therein concerned'. An exception to this was in the Highlands where no one would bring the body of a drowned person into the house; it was put instead in some outbuilding. This may have had something to do with the Gael's belief that the sea will search as far as necessary for what it regards as its own. On the subject of drowning, there was an extraordinary panic all over the country in 1777 about the risk of people being buried before they were dead, especially in cases of drowning. Lawrie & Co, a firm of druggists in Niddry's Wynd, Edinburgh, advertized a terrifying list of instruments which might be used to revive people and the public concern about this is evident from the fact that the Board of Police sent this advertisement to the Presbytery of Ayr. As a result at least one Kirk Session, Mauchline, bought a set, justifying the extravagance by saying that the instruments could also be used for people who had been frozen, suffocated or hanged.

Even though certain procedures were considered essential prior to a funeral, occasionally things were not done just as they might be and Hugh Miller tells of two girls being so upset at the manner in which an orphan's body was dressed for burial that they made a pact agreeing that whichever of them survived the other would prepare her friend's corpse.

With so much to be done at such times, people had to be practical which could lead to prelimary arrangements being overdone. Dean Ramsay tells of a dying man being asked whether he would like the bannocks for his burial meal to be square or round. An Aberdeenshire writer tells of a burial letter which must have been printed before the death occurred; of a dying man and his son discussing what day the funeral should be and deciding to avoid the day of Huntly market; and of a man who was told by the doctor that his wife could not last the week and swept out the barn and set out seats for the mourners, only to find that she lived longer and he had to undo all his good work in order to do some essential threshing. There is a story, perhaps apocryphal, of a dying man reviving somewhat and asking for some of the handsome ham he saw prepared, only to be told that he couldn't have any because it was for his funeral, and another story, worse still, tells of an old dying man seeing his young wife getting out the stretching board . . .

The Tolling of Church Bells

Bells have played a long standing part in funeral proceedings. In Roman Catholic days, when anyone was dying the passing bell was tolled so that people knew to pray for the departing soul as the priest went to perform his last duties. After death the 'soul bell' was rung for people to give thanks for the deceased's deliverance and the tolling of bells at funerals called people to pray for the departed soul. Superstition overtook this ancient religious reason for funeral bell ringing, however, as people believed that the ringing of bells was one of the best ways of frightening off evil spirits which were thought to be everywhere. They were also thought to daunt the devil who had a natural loathing of them because they called people to prayer.

At the time of the Reformation any sort of burial service or prayers for the dead were forbidden and so the tolling of church and steeple bells in connection with deaths and funerals was prohibited. Nevertheless the custom seems to have persisted in places and this 'superstitious rite' had to be specifically discharged in Aberdeen in 1643. But old customs die hard and a mere twelve years later, in 1658, the Burgh Records stated that 'the foresaid abuses are piece and piece creeping in again within this town'. In 1666 the Kirk Officer of Aberdeen received £8 Scots for tolling the kirk bells of the town at the funeral of Sir Robert Farquhar of Mouny (a former Provost) and £1. 10/- Scots was paid to have the tolbooth bell rung too. Elsewhere, as in Mauchline, Ayrshire, the funeral tolling of bells was 'not unusual' in the 17th century in spite of the Reformers' attitude to them but it seems as if it was the desperate need for money to support the poor during the Seven Years Famine (1694-1701) which decided burghs and Kirk Sessions that ringing of bells at burials was something which should be accepted and put to good use for the poor.

It was in 1695 that the Magistrates and Council of Stirling laid down charges for this – kirk bells could be rung at the death of a burgess or any member of his family for £4 Scots while any stranger or non-burgess must pay 10 merks (£6. 13. 4 Scots) but a careful recommendation was included that payment should be received before any ringing was done. In 1696 the Kirk Session of Mauchline, Ayrshire, started to charge for bell ringing, considering it 'reasonable that whoever desired the tolling of the bell, at the funeral of their relations, should pay some small quantity of money to the Kirk Treasurer to be disposed for the poors' use.' Thereafter the number of entries of bell-penny in the treasurer's accounts show that from then until about the 1880s the tolling of the church bell became a common part of funeral solemnities.

It was in 1698, also during these famine years, that it was ordained in Fenwick,

Ayrshire, 'that any persons who desire to have the church bell rung at the burials of their dead shall pay in to the Treasurer 14/- Scots for the poor and 6/- to the bellman', and similar decrees were passed about the same date by other Kirk Sessions. In time, the big bell, as the church bell was called, was used only for the burials of the better-off. In Kilmarnock, Ayrshire, for instance, it was tolled only seven times between October 1731 and October 1732, the fees coming to £21 Scots. People of quality were expected to pay generously for the tolling of the church bell and in the Burial Register of Inverness the words 'big bells' appear after the names of such people. There is no doubt that their use must have been sombre and impressive and even more so when rung on a large scale. An account of the burial in 1711 of a Provost of Edinburgh who died in office gives the details of his imposing funeral procession and adds, 'And all the time the Citie bells were tolled'.

Where they had any rights in bells, craft guilds greatly valued 'the privilege of the ringing of the great bell at the burial of their dead'. That these guilds might make some financial contribution towards the expenses of the bells seems implicit in the Kelso Glovers' Book which gives a list of forty glovers 'haveing an intrest in the belles' in 1663. In fact, anyone who contributed towards bells claimed a special right to their use. This happened, for instance, in the parish of Tough, Aberdeenshire, where forty-two principal parishioners bought a new church bell in 1734 with the stipulation that when a member of their families died, it should be rung when the Kirk Officer first got word of the death and then again on the day of burial, from morning until the coffin was laid in the ground 'in the manner that bells should be rung at funerals' adding 'and that by no other person than the officer' thus preventing him from delegating this long task to anyone else.

In time, the money from funeral bell-ringing was found useful for other objects than the poor, and an Act of Council in Inverness appointed money for such bell-ringing to be used for repair of churchyard dykes and in 1764 the Kirk Session decided that what there was of this money should be used in this way. In general, funeral bell-ringing died out about the time of the 1914-18 War but it is still occasionally to be heard at Roman Catholic churches, with varying numbers of peals. Church bells were not always in the church belfry. Although the First Book of Discipline had specified in 1560 that a church bell was an essential for every parish church to call people to Sunday worship many churches had neither bell nor belfry till the 17th century. In some places they never had a belfry at all and simply tied the bell to a tree and rang it from there, something still to be seen in the parish of Ewes, Dumfriesshire, in 1983.

3

The Mort Bell

M uch had to be done however before that stage of tolling the bells was reached and one of the first essentials was to let everyone know of the death. Although this might occasionally be done in the 17th century by beat of drum, it was normally announced by the mort bell, a hand bell of fairly standard type, much the same as that of Nigg, Ross and Cromarty, which is 5½ inches high and 7½ inches across the mouth, made of good bell metal with an iron clapper and an iron stirrup handle, now somewhat rusted. It has a pleasant clear tone. As soon as a death occurred, the bellman or beadle was told so that he might publicize the fact by walking slowly through the streets of the parish, tinkling the mort bell as he went, and stopping at intervals to make his announcement. Very often the death announcement and the general invitation to attend the funeral were made simultaneously but sometimes he made two trips.

The basic wording used on these occasions appears on a gravestone in Jedburgh, Roxburghshire, in memory of a man named Adam Wilson who was the last person to perform this function in that town and who died in 1812 or 1816 – the final figure is difficult to read. His announcement went as follows, 'A our brethren and sisters, we let ye to wit that we hae a brother departed at the pleasure of Almighty God yestreen at ten o'clock and ye are invited to attend the funeral at eleven o'clock.' With slight variations, that was the standard funeral notification all round the country. The name and address of the dead person were also given and all and sundry regarded this public intimation as an invitation to attend the burial itself and the lykewake as well. The bellman or beadle sometimes went bare-headed on this mission but sometimes just doffed his hat when he came to the words 'at the pleasure of Almighty God'. The mort bell belonged to burghs and to Kirk Sessions and was used only in connection with funerals. It had three functions: it was hired by bereaved families to announce a death; it was rung by the beadle at the head of the funeral procession; and its hire for these purposes brought in money to the burgh or Kirk Session.

In many towns the keeper of the mort bell was the town bellman although in Glasgow where the Council bought an old bell in 1577, it was initially put in charge of a man who had to hand it back at the end of each year. By 1612 this system changed and after a period 'for tryell of his aptness and sufficiencie in the said office' the keeper of the mort bell was admitted to the office 'during the town's will'. The prices that he might charge were laid down, for an adult 13/4 and for a child 6/8, both Scots, and he was ordered to wear black to suit his office.

The town bellman was mainly responsible for ringing the steeple bell at certain hours and for keeping the steeple in good order but he sometimes was given other duties as well, as in Edinburgh in 1597 when he had to keep a register of all who died of pestilence. Burgh records have fairly frequent references to bellmen being dismissed but this was usually for failure to carry out tasks to do with the steeple bell. Occasionally, however, bellmen misused the mort bell itself. At one point, Thomas Wallace in Anstruther, Fife, not only became very careless about the five and eight o'clock bells but he also used the mort bell for a quite unsuitable purpose, in fact as a 'clap', which was a small iron box with a handle, the clinking of which announced the sale of goods, not funerals.

Burgh bellmen quite commonly had a substitute to go round the streets ringing the mort bell for them. This custom is referred to in Edinburgh Burgh Records in 1591 when the Council gave the post of ringer of the mort bell temporarily – 'till further order be taken' – to the boy who rang the bell for Thomas Boncle, bellman of Leith, who was dismissed because for some unspecified reason he was 'not admitted by the toun'.

The use of the mort bell to lead the funeral procession to the grave is of long standing: in Chaucer's *Pardoner's Tale* written about 1370, there is a description of three young roisterers sitting in a tavern when they heard,

. . . . a hand bell clink
Before a corpse being carried to his grave.

At Mauchline and at Galston, both in Ayrshire, and presumably elsewhere too, a hand bell was used to indicate a change of bearers in the funeral procession but this is thought to be a later development in the use of the mort bell, not altering its original purpose. Hiring the mort bell was one thing, paying for it another. When little education was available, keeping accounts was not easy and during times of famine and destitution, with many deaths and great poverty, enforcing payment was very hard. In 1698, right in the middle of the Seven Years' Famine, the Kirk Session of Nigg, Ross and Cromarty, laid down prices for use of the mort bell, only to discover in 1708 that no account could be found of any income from it since then, the Kirk Officer stoutly denying that he had received any payment. To put things on a proper footing, the Kirk Session revived their order of 1698 and instructed the clerk to make a list of everyone who had the bell, both in and outside the parish, and forbade the officer to use it unless he was paid for it.

When the mort bell belonged to a burgh the income from its hire, less a fee to the bellman, went to good causes within the burgh. When it belonged to the Kirk Session the income went to the Session's funds and was used largely for the poor, with the beadle or Kirk Officer receiving a share of the charge as his fee. At Nigg, Ross and Cromarty, in 1698 the charge was one merk (13/4 Scots) outside the parish and half a merk inside it, of which the beadle received half. At Galston, Ayrshire, the grave-digger, who was also beadle, was given permission in 1762 to charge '3d a mile going in ringing the small bell' and was ordered never to ring it for less than 2d a mile.

Gradually the use of the mort bell declined. This was partly due to the introduction of hearses which meant that large numbers of bearers were not needed any longer, and therefore a wide general notification of a death was unnecessary. It was also partly due to pressure put on people to limit lykewakes and drinking at funerals which became altogether simpler and quieter and the all-embracing invitation to attend was no longer appropriate. (Even so, into the 1930s, there was a bellman in Lauder, Berwickshire, a man who kept the house for travelling people and in addition rang the bell to announce deaths and important events. Although not the mort bell, this was a relic of it.) For the better-off, burial letters were coming into use while for others a 'bidding to the burial' was delivered verbally to specific people by local youths in return for a small payment.

One would have thought that this was an excellent thing, unless one was the bellman or beadle that is, because for them it meant a loss of income. A case in point is that of William Stivenson, beadle at Stirling in 1741. Because by then it had become fashionable there to have private burials without prior intimation by the mort bell, his perquisites were so reduced that he petitioned the Council to ask for a ruling on the matter. Knowing that till recently he had rung the mort bell at least once through the streets for each burial, as well as attending with the bell at the funeral itself, for each of which he received 1/- stg., the Council decided that he should continue to have these fees in future 'whether he beis employed to intimate the burying through the town or not'. Although this is just a local example, it was one of many restrictive practices which developed to do with funerals. In general, however, there was no compulsion to use or at least pay for the mort bell. It was necessary and therefore it was used and, unlike the mortcloth which is mentioned later, there was no temptation to use one's own or a finer one.

The mort bell is an undoubted link with Roman Catholic days and its use after the Reformation is rather interesting. It was very similar to the Roman Catholic passing bell which is carried and tinkled by the priest's server as he goes to administer the last rites and, in fact, well after the Reformation, according to Thomas Somerville, minister of Jedburgh, Roxburghshire, from 1773-1830, the mort bell was sometimes called the passing bell.

The bell which the Burgh of Glasgow bought from an unspecified source in 1577 for £10 Scots was the one which had 'yed throw the toune of auld at the burial of the deid' and it was bought so that it could continue as the common bell 'to gang for the burial of the deid', in other words, the mort bell. This can only have been an old Roman Catholic bell and, far from destroying it as happened after the Reformation to so much associated with the old faith, here was a Burgh Council buying it in order to keep it in use. It was of course a logical thing to do because deaths had to be notified somehow in order to obtain bearers and how better than by the bell? It was probably felt that this small bell so sensibly used was perfectly permissible even though tolling a church bell for funerals was not.

That use of the mort bell is understandable. It is more difficult to see how the Reformed church allowed it to lead the procession to the graveyard where it was often placed at the head of the grave to ward off evil spirits. Could it be that people who were often denied any burial service whatsoever clung to this little piece of ritual? Was it that the Reformed church took little notice of burials and saw no need to interfere, although that was not something they normally hesitated to do? Was superstition so ingrained that even Kirk Sessions hesitated to stop something which they really believed could frighten away demons? By sweeping away many familiar things in which people had put their trust, did the Reformation make them even more fearful of evil spirits and anxious to keep them at bay?

Whatever the reason, the Reformed church which tried in every way to suppress Popish practices, happily made money from the continuance of an old Roman Catholic custom. Happily too, mort bells are durable and are still comparatively easy to come across in old churches and museums.

Burial Letters

B urial letters were introduced by the mid-17th century but were more common in the 18th and especially the 19th centuries. It was considered very slighting not to attend a funeral when given this specific invitation and to avoid giving offence it was essential to send a letter giving the reason for absence, and it had to be a good one. Burial letters give the name of the person who had died and that person's relationship to the letter writer as well as the time of the funeral, along with a request for the honour or favour of the addressee's presence, as in the following letter from Jean Campbell, wife of the Laird of Newtown, Morayshire, to the Laird of Gordonstoune, in 1663:

> Right honourable, it has pleased the Lord to remove my husband, the Laird of Newtown, from this lyffe to that eternall. Therefor these are seriously intreating the favour as to honour his funeralls with your presence upone Seitterday the last of this instant, betwix twellfe and one, from Sant Julles Kirk to the Trenitie Church, to his beirall . . .

A touching plea appears in a burial letter from Robert Gibson to Mr Archibald Dunbar of Thundertoun, Morayshire, in 1701. It concerned the death of an unfortunate relative who had been confined in Elgin gaol because there was no suitable lunatic asylum. His burial was to take place the day the letter was written and though there was no request for the addressee's presence, there was this request:

> I hope you will be so Creistanlie inclined as to weip fourtie dayes weiping and wailing ffor him, because of his honestie.

Sometimes the notification was just a bald statement of a death, such as:

> Mrs. Garden Campbell of Troup died here last night.
> Carlogie Cottage, 11 July 1821.

The paper used for burial letters was usually folio – double sheets which could be folded, tucked in and addressed on the back – although sometimes single sheets were used. The favoured size of paper began as nearly foolscap and gradually diminished to about quarto down to rather less than octavo. The edging of early burial letters was sometimes slightly gilded, something found even as late as 1791. From 1770, perhaps earlier, there was a black edging but to start with it was so slight as to be barely discernible. A clearly visible narrow black edge then appeared, about one-twelfth of an inch wide, sometimes only on the back sheet so that it showed around the address, but very often on the inside sheets too. About the first decade of the 19th century wider black edging came in, about one-sixth of an inch wide and, although there were occasional late examples of narrow edging, one-sixth of an inch was the width which continued in general use so long as black-edged notepaper was fashionable which was into the 1930s. Black-edged envelopes became customary too and letters of condolence were written on the same type of notepaper.

At the beginning, burial letters were hand-written. The accounts for the funeral of Lady Mey in 1692 show that 'sex quaire of paper' were bought at a cost of £2. 8/- Scots and the charge for writing the letters came to £1. 8/- Scots. When the Laird of Balnagown, an important Highland chieftain, died in 1711, writing funeral letters, along with paper and wax, came to £35 Scots. Very soon, however, printed burial letters were introduced, hand-signed by the person arranging the funeral. This printing service was very speedy, essential in the circumstances. The wax mentioned in connection with the Laird of Balnagown's burial letters was something widely used by people of quality or affluence. It was always black and used to impress a seal with the family crest, placed above and to the left of the address. This was something not much done after the 1850s. It seems to have been superseded by little engravings – a form of imitation – such as one which appeared on a printed notice for the funeral of Janet Roberts, Inverness, in 1874. These appeared where the seal would have gone and are just over an inch long and oval in shape. In Janet Roberts's case, the illustration is of an ornate gravestone, topped with an urn and overhung by a weeping willow, denoting sorrow and tears, with below the words 'In Memory of'. Other examples show a kneeling figure praying by the gravestone, with the weeping willow again appearing and the words 'Thy will be done' written above.

Just as ready-printed invitation cards are available nowadays, so printed funeral cards became available too, only requiring to have the blanks filled in. An example from 1854, printed by H. & W. Ainslie, Fort William, is 4 inches by 2 inches with black edging and bears the wording:

> Sir, I request the favour of your Company to attend the funeral
> of............................my..............................
> to the...
> at............................on..............................
>   I am, Sir,
>   Yours respectfully,
> (Date)

Although burial letters were very formal, they might include an invitation to dine after the burial, very often at an inn. For the funeral of Sir AEneas Mackintosh of Mackintosh Bt, Moyhall, Inverness-shire, in 1820, a note was added below the signature saying, 'Breakfast will be prepared at Moyhall for the gentlemen, and others attending the Funeral', and in italics below was added, 'and dinner will be ready at Cant's Hotel at 6 o'clock in the evening.'

A more personal note appeared at the end of Jean Campbell's letter to the Laird of Gordonstoune, which has already been quoted – she asked to borrow his mortcloth, a funeral pall, which she felt would look better than the common one from Elgin.

Whether burial letters were hand-written by the bereaved person, by someone employed to do the work, or printed, once done they were hand-delivered by servants or people specially engaged for the task. Lady Mey's funeral account includes, 'Given several men that went with the burial letters £3 Scots' and about 1755, for a funeral in Ross and Cromarty there was a charge for 'four servants with burial letters 4/- stg.'. The charge of £96. 6. 6 Scots for 'disbursements for burial letters' and some other minor items for the funeral of Mr Philip Nisbet of Ladykirk, Berwickshire, in 1684 would have included writing and delivering.

In large burghs delivering such letters became a recognized occupation. In Edinburgh in 1716 a man named Colin Haig petitioned for the right to do so and was given sole power to be 'disperser of burial letters' with the following scale of charges:

> For each letter dispersed in the suburbs, viz. Canongate, Westport, Potterow and Pleasants 1/- Scots.
> For each letter dispersed in South and North Leith 1/6 Scots.
> For each undelivered letter a penalty of 2/- Scots.

To carry out this task, he was required to employ sufficient 'discreet persons', a rather different attitude to the indiscriminate and general invitation of the mort bell. Furthermore, 'for the more ready service to the lieges', he was required to let the public know his address by advertizing it in *The Courant* and putting up a suitably inscribed board outside his premises. It must have been a worthwhile appointment as just the following year a glazier burgess, upon petition, joined him.

The introduction of a proper postal service made the delivery of burial letters a slightly easier matter and in 1874 all but one of a fine collection of these letters in Inverness Library have postage stamps on them. Even so, into the 1920s, burial letters in black-edged envelopes were still being delivered by hand rather than by post in places such as Caithness, taken from door to door by senior schoolboys in return for a small sum. In the 1930s in parts of Shetland, however, to deliver a funeral notice by hand was thought to indicate a shortage of money.

But throughout all this time letters were not essential and something of the old mort bell system of verbal bidding continued well into this century, although without the mort bell itself. To take two Roxburghshire villages as an example – in Ancrum it was the grave-digger's job to 'bid the village' verbally, a service rewarded with 1/- stg. which rose to 2/6. In Lilliesleaf into the 1930s, the task was given to the lamplighter. He had to go round the village lighting up anyway and as he went he knocked on doors and announced funerals, for which he was paid 1/-.

In Comrie, Perthshire, in the 1920s is was the street cleaner who had the job of announcing funerals by going round the streets, knocking on a number of doors to get people's attention, and then making the announcement standing in the street. By the 1930s this had changed to his giving specific invitations, knocking only at selected houses, not one and all. The wording was much like that of the mort bell ringer of yore – 'You are desired to come to such and such a person's funeral tomorrow against ten hours.'

In Benbecula, in Tiree, in the Seaboard villages of Easter Ross and in Caithness funerals were notified by knocking on doors and giving the invitation until much later than the 1930s. In Sanday, Orkney, the grave-digger was doing this until the 1970s. Of course, when friends were asked to go round a village making such an intimation they considered it an honour to do so. In small, very close communities no notification of any sort was necessary. Word spread quickly and that was enough.

It is only in more recent years that press announcements have become common for all walks of life but press notices have been used for a long time by the better off. The death of Lady Margaret Stuart in 1791 was announced in *The Courant* at a cost of 5/- stg. and in *The Mercury* for 2/6, although burial letters were also sent. Although the Deaths columns of the press are the main source of such information nowadays, it can also appear on printed notices issued by undertakers – some do this and some do not. These notices may be displayed in the windows of their premises or on a board outside. One Shetland undertaker who used to put fourteen printed notices in shops around Lerwick decided several years ago to send blank notices to every country shop in Shetland – 'quite a job,' they said – and now all they have to do is to phone the shops concerned with the details of the funeral and they fill out the notices and display them in their windows. Such notices have also appeared in shop windows elsewhere.

Lykewakes

Having set the funeral wheels in motion by announcing the death and time of burial, the next stage was the lykewake. A lyke was an unburied corpse and the lykewake or late watch was the constant watch over it until burial, something which had its origins in Roman Catholic days. Originally intended to ward off evil spirits, it was meant to be a solemn, decorous occasion, with more emphasis on watching at night than during the day.

For ordinary people a lykewake was held each of the two or three nights before the corpse was buried. In the case of the poor, the funeral was held just as soon as the carpenter could make the coffin and such lykewake as they had might be nothing more than a couple of women guarding the corpse from rats and cats. For the better-off the length of time between death and burial depended on social position and financial resources and might last a week or more while a death in a family of importance attracted and required mourners to come from far afield – indeed, members of the family might have to be summoned home from abroad – so that the lykewakes in these cases might be very protracted. The larger the household, the more elaborate the arrangements for the lykewake, but for the average one the body lay, or was propped up, in bed in the best room, even in the kitchen, where all the visitors assembled. When box beds were in use, this meant that the presence of the corpse was not nearly as noticeable as it might have been. As already said, the bed and the furniture were covered and the walls draped with white sheets specially kept for funerals.

Elizabeth Grant's graphic description of the funeral of George Ross, a henwife's husband, who died in the early years of the 19th century, tells of how he was set up in bed, shaved and partly dressed, for all the countryside to come and see him because viewing the corpse was very popular. A living memory from Caithness tells how as late as 1945 a very old woman was propped up dead in bed, dressed in her white 'goonie' with the white lace-trimmed cap she wore on her head at night and everyone coming to see her in the old way. This particular instance was not a lykewake but the manner in which the corpse was presented for mourners to view smacked strongly of one.

The lykewake was an opportunity to pay respect to the corpse and every visitor was expected to touch the corpse on the forehead or the hands, with their left hand, something believed to prevent them having bad dreams of the deceased. At a Caithness funeral in 1981 not only did people touch the corpse on the forehead, but more than one of the older mourners kissed the corpse. Again, this was not a lykewake but had traces of it.

However, the great attraction of the old-style lykewakes was the hospitality shown at them, all part of 'decent burial', and no-one minded how long the interval between death and burial might be. There was sure to be a plentiful supply of tea, beer and bread, with perhaps cheese, while new pipes and tobacco as well as snuff were provided for the men. An account of Lady Mey's funeral in 1692 shows an item for 'ane gross and halfe of pypps dureing the likewake and 10½lbs. tobacco, £10 Scots.' Scottish hospitality tends to include abundant alcohol and after whisky became the national drink it was provided at lykewakes for health-drinking among the mourners. Many toasts were drunk, sometimes so many in fact that not only the memory but the health of the departed was drunk too.

Alcoholic toasts may well have originated in the idea of rejoicing in the deceased's deliverance from this earth, just as trumpets were at a point joyfully played at a burial, but very often what originated in religious practice tipped over into earthly excess. Drinking at lykewakes came in many cases to be so serious that what was meant to be a solemn occasion descended through well-meant but excessive hospitality into all sorts of unseemliness which had attendant problems, for instance the *New Statistical Account* for Croy and Dalcross, Inverness, reported that fighting at lykewakes used to be a common offence. As well as drinking, there was swearing and card-playing. Some told stories of ghosts and ghouls while the younger ones might go 'to the hot cockles and other frolics'; others were like the young people of Nigg, Ross and Cromarty, of whom the Kirk Session had occasion to complain in 1731 that 'several abuses are being committed at late watches by Several Games and Diversions in which young people exercise themselves.' These games were forbidden by the Kirk Session and church censure was promised for any future offences, but merry-making at lykewakes continued there and around the country for many years, and many a lykewake ended up like a party.

The bell-ringer's announcement of a death and his general invitation to attend the funeral was taken by many people to include the lykewake too and they flocked to them whether they knew the deceased or not because the entertainment was irresistible. The Burgh Records of Peebles referred in 1697 to great numbers of people 'who are little or nothing concerned in the defunct' going to lykewakes and misbehaving at them, as a result of which the Council forbade anyone to attend them without a specific invitation under pain of a fine of £10 Scots. In 1658, Aberdeen Burgh Council in renewing the Act anent Lykewakes also forbade any more than ten or twelve of the nearest friends or neighbours to be present at them, 'who may come to visit, comfort and bear companie with the familie where the defunct is', and also forbade the offering of 'drogues [sweetmeats] and desserts.' But such prohibitions made little difference.

The Reformers allowed neither burial service nor prayers for the dead; they also disapproved of music, thinking it superstitious; but nevertheless there was music at lykewakes is spite of official disfavour. Thus it was that in 1643 Aberdeen Burgh Council had to forbid people to ask Doctors of the Music School and Readers to sing or read at lykewakes, the effectiveness of which ban may be judged from the fact that in 1658 they had again to forbid singing at them. In spite of this, the practice of having music continued and in Captain Dunbar's *Scottish Life in Former Days* the following receipt is given, 'I, Thomas Davidsone, Master of the Music School in Aberdeen . . . received £2.18s. Scots for singing at the lyk of Sir Robert Farquhar of Mouny, 1666.' At the same funeral, John Cormack, schoolmaster in Aberdeen, received two rex dollars for reading at the lykewake 'as the custome is in this place'. Psalms and dirges at lykewakes were a common feature but it is not clear whether Thomas Davidsone's singing was sacred in nature or for the entertainment of those present. But music purely for entertainment there certainly was, something made very evident in the Kirk Session records of Inverness in 1728 which record that 'John McEdward . . . confessed that he had a fiddler in the house at a leickwake of a dead person, but said he did not think it a sin, it being so long the custom in this country.' In other words, music was part of the hospitality offered.

The same attitude was probably what lay behind an incident in Morebattle in the late 19th century when the minister heard a lot of noise coming from a house where there had been a death. On remonstrating with the householder, he was told that there were so many long faces that he had put on the gramophone to cheer them up. It seems certain that the use of music at lykewakes and funerals generally was originally intended to drive away evil spirits, just as the ringing of bells was meant to do, and that long after the reason for it was lost sight of, the practice continued.

Strange though it sounds, there was also dancing at lykewakes. Dancing, of course, was a part of early worship and was believed to be able to drive away evil and to free the living from fear, and in primitive countries music and dance are still intermingled with religion. In the Highlands particularly, the lykewake came to include a solemn dance round the corpse each night. The next of kin, whether husband, wife, son or daughter, opened what Thomas Pennant in his *Tour of Scotland* written in 1769 described as a 'melancholy ball' to the sound of a 'solemn melancholy strain called a lament.' Very often these relatives wept throughout their dancing and in spite of Sir AEneas Mackintosh's comment that 'It must have been ridiculous to see a widow begin to dance with tears in her eyes', it is easy to see how this form of funeral dancing could express grief, even although its real origins might have been forgotten. Others joined in this dancing, including women, and it carried on until morning broke. But a more cheerful type of dancing slid in and even that is understandable – there is a story of a widow calling for a merrier tune as her heart was like to break. But the fact is that Highlanders loved to dance and when opportunities for doing so were limited it is not surprising that with drink to loosen inhibitions sooner or later they danced and funeral dancing ultimately became an amusement of the living.

To the young especially, the lykewake dancing was grand. In a rather involved sentence, Thomas Pennant said that it was carried out 'with such gambols and frolics among the younger part of the company that the loss which occasioned them is often more than supplied by the consequences of the night.' The Kirk Session of Tarbat, Ross and Cromarty, put it more plainly when they dealt with a case of fornication in 1753 by a couple returning from a lykewake. Captain Burt who wrote of his Scottish travels in the 1730s said that people at lykewakes danced 'as though it were at a wedding . . . although all the time the corpse lies before them in the same room.' Elizabeth Grant's account of the funeral of the henwife's husband tells how after much refreshment the company began dancing and the jolting of the floor tumbled his corpse out of bed into the middle of the reel. The editor of the Records of Inverness and Dingwall Presbytery wrote in 1896 of much trouble at lykewakes: 'They were more boisterous than weddings, the chamber of the dead being filled night after night with jest, song and story, music of the fiddle and the pipe, and the shout and clatter of the Highland reel.'

Many accounts of Lowland lykewakes stress how decorously they were conducted, saying that though there might be drinking, the time was mainly spent reading the Bible and talking quietly. The impression is given that it was only in the Highlands that abuses occurred. Certainly the Highlands may have been worse than the Lowlands and certainly old ways lingered longer there than elsewhere but steps taken all around the country to control behaviour at lykewakes show that neither dancing nor unruly conduct was confined to the North.

All in all, what had originated in religious ritual had, as so often happened, degenerated into abuse and what were described as 'scenes of shocking licence and debauchery' continued at lykewakes in spite of many attempts to stop them. In the early 13th century the church had had to reproach people for a light-hearted attitude to funerals, forbidding singing and dancing to take place at them 'since it does not become us to laugh at the weeping of others, but in a case of this kind rather to grieve as they do'. This did no good. Other attempts at restraining dancing and similar activities were made elsewhere and at various times, as when the Presbytery of Inverness met at Moy in 1675. One of the questions put to the minister there was whether he laid any 'restraint upon pypeing, violeing and dancing at Lickwacks', to which he replied 'Not as yet.' Not surprisingly this answer was considered unsatisfactory and the Presbytery ordered him to do so and to punish the guilty with church censure. That same year the Synod of Moray considered the 'superstitious and heathenish practices' which went on at lykewakes during 'which tym sin and scandell does greatlie abound' and forbade all 'light and Lascivious exercises, sports, Lyksongs, fidling and dancing' and ordered that the ordinary 'crowding multitude' should be kept out and only the deceased's nearest relatives allowed to attend or those who might 'give Christian counsel and comfort'. They also ordered that the time should be spent in such suitable ways as reading the Scriptures.

When dancing and games at lykewakes got out of hand they were an obvious target for the authorities' attention. Over-generous hospitality was another and the Parliament of Scotland during the episcopacy made an attempt to restrain this by an Act anent Banquetting and Apparel in 1621 which, in trying to control extravagance of various kinds, also forbade all eating and drinking at lykewakes under threat of a fine of a thousand merks. This did little good and the General Assembly forbade lykewakes entirely in 1645; they were prohibited by the Scottish Parliament in the Act discharging Lykewakes in 1646 under penalty of a fine of £20 Scots to the Kirk Session and in 1650 the General Assembly ordered Presbyteries to censure all those who observed lykewakes, only to find it necessary in 1701 to revive their Act of 1645.

But public feeling was too strongly in favour of them for Kirk Sessions to attempt to stop them as had been ordered and it was often only abuses at them which were condemned, such as the games and diversions at Nigg, Ross and Cromarty, in 1731 and 'disorders and scandalous carriage' at Mauchline, Ayrshire, in 1672. So lykewakes still went on and undoubtedly had the tacit, if not active, approval of the church at local level. For instance, at the funeral of two paupers in Mauchline in 1676, the Kirk Session allowed 3/- Scots for 'tobacco and pipes that night they were waked'. This shows that the Session countenanced lykewakes and so did burghs if the following entry from Stirling Burgh Records is anything to go by: '1698, For coalls and a pund of candle to Wauch's wife's Lykwak, 8/- Scots.'

A layman's attempt to help in the matter came in 1699 when Sir John Hope, Lord Crossrig, formed a 'Society for the Reformation of Manners' in Scotland, similar to one in England, this with a view to reducing extravagance generally, including drinking at lykewakes and funerals. A Commission of the General Assembly recommended such Societies but although it was hoped to establish them throughout the country, only twenty were formed. Another lay attempt to control extravagance at funerals took place in 1729 when the Lairds of Lorn, Argyllshire, sought to achieve it by stopping the vast numbers of common people who attended lykewakes. They decided that no one should go to any lykewake or pre-funeral proceedings until the day of burial, and not even go then unless they were specifically invited. They promised to punish so far as they could anyone within their bounds who disobeyed this rule and recommended that if anyone came to a funeral uninvited they 'should sit unserved', something which would have been a nasty punishment indeed.

One of the most dramatic ways of ending rowdyism at lykewakes was found by a schoolmaster at Monifieth, Angus, about the end of the 18th century. There was so much giggling and romping at one that he decided that a good fright was needed to bring people to their senses. To achieve this he somehow persuaded everyone to leave the room for a while, then removed the corpse to the barn and induced a friend to lie down in the bed, wrapped in the shroud. The idea was that if the merriment began again the man in the bed would sit up suddenly and startle everyone and put a stop to it. Part of the plan misfired unfortunately because, far from starting up in bed, the man immediately died there but this made such an impression in the whole district that the schoolmaster's main intention was successful and impropriety at lykewakes in that area ended.

Ironically, Benefit Societies which did so much to ensure 'decent burial' for many people, indirectly encouraged abuses at lykewakes and funerals by providing funeral money which was spent on drink.

But attitudes did change and gradually abuses at lykewakes died out in line with a general reduction in funeral hospitality. They became much more sober occasions, often with only three or four people watching each night and with the minister or an elder taking a short service each night also. Tea, a dram but certainly not heavy drinking, general conversation and perhaps new clay pipes helped to pass the time until morning. In the 1820s an Ayrshire man wrote of a wake in his diary saying, 'Sat up . . . last night, 'tis an old custom but generally an unnecessary one.' But not everyone agreed about its being unnecessary – an Aberdeenshire writer in 1885 said of the dying-out of the lykewake; 'The dead are shut up in some apartment, like a bird in a cage, throughout the light of the day and the gloom of the night, deserted by family and friends, who have no wish to be near them . . .'

Lykewakes, however, are remembered well into this century, mainly until World War One, but some even later. In some places such as Skye, the body might lie in one room while the closest male friends and relatives sat in another, going through in pairs to watch. A form of lykewake still appeared in the Seaboard villages of Easter Ross until World War Two, and perhaps even into the 1950s, when an elder would take a prayer meeting in the evening while the body lay in the house. Tea was served and although no one sat up watching through the night the old name of lyke was used for these occasions. A relic of the lykewake may well appear in the custom of 'coming to see the corpse' which in some villages was usually done by the women the day before the funeral and by the men on the day itself. When women came, tea would be on the go with a lot of chit-chat in the kitchen and great discussion of the deceased's good and bad points. But whatever form the lykewake might take, it culminated on the final night in the ceremony of kisting when the corpse was laid in the coffin or kist.

Kisting

K isting – the laying of the body in the kist or coffin – was something which must have been done in some manner whenever coffins were used but its importance in Scotland arose in the late 17th century out of commercial interests.

Towards the end of that century the linen trade was in a poor state and in order to give it a boost the Act anent Burying in Scots Linen was passed in 1686 by the Scottish Parliament. This was the Act which has already been referred to as prohibiting the making of winding sheets and grave clothes from rich materials; it decreed that in future all corpses had to be buried in plain linen or cloth of hards (coarse cloth of flax or hemp) without any decoration or embellishment. The linen had to be prepared and spun in Scotland, the use of Holland or any linen cloth made in other countries being specifically forbidden. The penalties for not obeying this law were severe – £300 Scots for each offence by a nobleman and £200 for anyone else, half of which was to go to whoever informed and the other half to the poor of the parish where the burial took place.

To enforce the Act every parish minister was ordered to keep a record of all who were buried in the parish. One or more relations of anyone who died or some other 'credible persons' were required to bring the minister within eight days a written certificate, sworn by two well known people – 'tuo famous persons' – declaring that the corpse had been wrapped in Scots linen. If this was not done, it fell to the minister to seek the penalties from the deceased's estate; if he failed to take action within six months of the burial, he himself became liable for the fine.

That this was more easily said than done is clear from an entry in Edinburgh Burgh Records in 1687 when the Council recommended that the Magistrates should meet as a committee with the ministers to consider the Act and to try to find 'some method for making the same effective'. In some places, such as at Greyfriars burial ground in Edinburgh, it had been the grave-diggers' task to keep a register of all burials and taking work from one group and giving it to another was only one of the problems arising from the Act.

As with so much early Scottish legislation, enforcement was difficult and in 1695 Parliament had to ratify the 1686 Act with a further one, ordering the first Act to be strictly implemented, with some additions. Instead of relying on relatives of the deceased or 'credible persons' to produce a certificate, this new Act ordained that the nearest elder or deacon of the parish, along with a neighbour or two, should be sent for and be present at 'the putting of the dead corps in the coffin' to ensure that Scots linen was used and then to sign the certificate. The penalties were wholly assigned to the poor and any elder or deacon was empowered to pursue for them. It appears that the rich had tried to get around the 1686 Act by burying their dead in over-expensive linen because the 1695 Act put a limit on its price – not more than two hundred shillings Scots per ell, which sounds quite expensive enough.

In 1698 there was an Overture for an Act for burying in Scots green linen but only too soon it was the woollen industry which needed help, so much so that the merchants of Edinburgh petitioned against the wearing of linen as interfering with woollen manufactures. As a result an Act of Parliament was passed in 1707 rescinding the Acts of 1686 and 1695 and ordering that in future it was only plain woollen cloth or stuff that should be used for winding sheets, not linen, under threat of the same penalties as before. Whether or not there had previously been any formality at the coffining of a corpse, these Acts made sure that from thenceforth there was. No one was exempt and one result was the introduction of the compulsory use of grave clothes.

The Reformed church in Scotland forbade any burial service and another result of these Acts, albeit an indirect one, was of great importance. None of these Acts required the presence of the minister at the kisting; he was only involved in an administrative capacity. But as time went on and fear of reversion to Popery receded it became common for the minister (or an elder) to attend kistings and if he was there, then what more natural than to ask him to say grace before any refreshments were offered? This developed into prayers and ultimately into a kisting service – prayer, reading from the Bible, possibly the singing of a psalm, and perhaps a word of comfort – which might come before or after the body was placed in the coffin. Thus a consequence of the promotion of the linen and woollen trades was the opportunity of receiving religious consolation at a time of bereavement which led in time to the re-introduction of the funeral service at the house.

The presence of the minister at kistings did not win universal approval, however. Rev. Andrew Edgar, writing in 1886, said, 'The coffining of a corpse is no more a religious service than is the washing or dressing of it; and the presence of a minister or elder is not a thing that the law of the church or the nature of the operation requires. It seems to me that ceremonial coffinings, when no practical object is served by them, is an unnecessary stimulant to grief, and though they include a prayer, they might with no disadvantage be abandoned, since now whenever it is in the minister's power to be present, devotional exercise takes place in the deceased's house on the day of burial.' As to the kisting itself, it was performed by the undertaker, who was usually the local carpenter, and his helpers or by relatives, the corpse being lifted to the coffin on a variety of forms of support. It might be on 'death sheets', special white sheets kept for the purpose, or on three towels, or three bolster covers or even on a plank.

A common time for the kisting was the night before the burial, the final event of the lykewake; but sometimes it was simply when the undertaker was ready, even on the evening of the death; or it might be immediately prior to departing for the graveyard. This last time appears in a burial letter sent by Robert Grant, an Edinburgh lawyer, in 1783 in which he wrote, 'You are requested to be present at the chesting at half an hour after three on Tuesday afternoon' with the burial to follow at 4.00 p.m. Being the culmination of the lykewake, the style of behaviour and refreshments at the one was the pattern for the other, but as lykewake hospitality moderated, so did the numbers attending kistings so that latterly only relatives, close friends and neighbours attended and food and drink was limited. Those not at the kisting would be asked to come to see the corpse, of course.

Kisting was common in places such as Caithness till the 1920s and among country people in districts such as Lauder, Berwickshire, until the 1930s. It took place occasionally in Ross and Cromarty and Dumfriesshire until about 1940. It is thought to have died out during World War Two but it would not be surprising to find it still occurring in very remote places even now. It was a very deeply rooted custom, so much so that even though it had died out in Wigtown by about 1910, the minister there in the late 1940s recognised the suitability of a service at such a time and expressed his willingness to lead relatives and friends in a service on an evening prior to the burial, which became the custom there, a relic of the kisting service.

Coffins

A lthough the use of coffins goes back to Biblical days, for a very long time the common people of Scotland were buried uncoffined. But in 1563, only a few years after the Reformation, the General Assembly decided that something should be done about this and passed an Act ordaining that a bier should be made in every country parish to carry the dead poor to burial, assuming presumably that the non-poor were suitably provided for. This Act also ordered those living in the village where a poor person died, or in the adjacent houses, to carry the body to the grave and see that it was buried six feet underground. While a bier can be the frame on which a body or coffin is carried, it appears that the General Assembly's use of the word meant a common coffin, which was re-usable. It was a closed box or chest of iron or wood attached to a frame for lifting; sometimes it had four feet to stand on and in some cases it may have been painted, especially in times of epidemics when it was often blackened. Because the coffin had to be used again, part of it was hinged for easy opening. When it was the top or side which opened, the body, wrapped in a winding sheet, was lifted out at the graveside and lowered into the grave with ropes. When the base opened, the coffin was lowered half-way into the grave, a bolt was drawn, the body fell into its resting place and the coffin was hauled up for next time.

Not all parishes immediately carried out the order to provide a common coffin and in many it can never have been implemented at all although the idea quickly caught on in towns. The coffins were provided by Kirk Sessions, Burgh Councils and sometimes by craft guilds; in the latter case, they were perhaps more handsome than normal because the bier (presumably a common coffin) obtained by the Glasgow Skinners, Furriers and Glovers in 1608 was described as being 'for the honour of the craft'. The initial cost of a common coffin might be as much as four times that of an individual one. The Kirk Session of Galston, Ayrshire, paid £4 Scots for one in 1641 and nearly £6 Scots for another in 1675 but between these dates, when the common coffin appears to have been either out of repair of out of use, the sum allowed by the Kirk Session for paupers' individual coffins was 30/- Scots each. It was the fact of re-use which made the common coffin worthwhile and, in addition, it could be hired by those a little above the poverty level for about one shilling Scots each time, which brought in a little income to the church.

In some parts of the Highlands there was a different type of common coffin. In Sutherland it was a long basket of twisted rushes with a strengthened rim to keep its shape. It was called the *sgulan ruhairbh* or dead hamper. To carry it, short crowbars were put through three side handles or loops and it was lowered into the grave by ropes attached in such a way that it could be tipped over, the body deposited and the hamper recovered. Technically therefore, all bodies taken to the grave in the common coffin were buried uncoffined.

It was in times of epidemics and famine that the common coffin really came into its own. In the pestilence of 1645 the dead kist, as it was called, of Anstruther in Fife made six journeys to the pier and nine to the 'back yett' in twenty-four hours. No Kirk Session could have paid for fifteen individual coffins in one day. During the terrible Seven Years Famine at the end of the 17th century the parish of Ashkirk, Selkirkshire, found that paying up to £3 Scots for an adult's coffin and £2 Scots for a child's was too great a drain on the poors' funds when the prime need was food for the living and in July 1699 the Kirk Session records say, 'Considered the poors' box is now burdened with paying coffins for the poor, at a time when there is such difficulty to provide them with bread, by reason of the present dearth, therefore the Kirk Session thought fit to order the mending of the common coffin for burying the poor.' The repair, at £3. 14. 0¼ Scots, cost little more than the price of an adult's coffin. It was during this famine that the Kirk Session of Chirnside, Berwickshire, could not even rise to a common coffin. An entry of 1701 says 'for a dale (board) on which Alison Tait was buryed, 5/- Scots', showing that the best they could do for this poor woman was carry her to the grave on a plank.

Few common coffins survived although until fairly recently there were three examples at Abercorn and one at Linlithgow. At Abercorn the present minister says he understands that one was kept until not long ago in a sealed-off cupboard under the laird's loft but it is now no longer there. Linlithgow's wooden one was latterly kept in the triforium but sadly was thrown out some fifteen years ago when improvements were being done.

As time went on, individual coffins were provided for paupers as Kirk Session accounts show. These were simply made by the local joiner, sometimes at a contract price, but of whatever sort they were, when the second-best mortcloth was laid over them, an air of respectability was given. Even after individual coffins came into more general use, young children were often buried without them as the Burgh Records of Aberdeen make plain in an entry of 1647 when costs of burials were laid down. This shows that it was much cheaper for a child under fourteen years of age to be buried without a coffin than with one – £1 Scots as against £3. And not only children – the practice of burying adults wrapped in winding sheets but uncoffined continued in Scotland for many years after the Reformation in both town and country areas. Certainly it went on into the mid, if not late, 18th century in places as far apart as Montrose in Angus, Ness in Lewis and Buchan. Paupers were buried uncoffined in Rogart, Sutherlandshire, until the beginning of the 19th century and it is said that the practice continued in the Northern Isles till the middle of that century. It is even said that it was only the passing of the Poor Law in 1845 which ended the custom finally because under that law the Inspector of Poor was obliged to pay for a decent burial with a wooden coffin.

The Poor Law led to the imposition of rates which were as unpopular with those who had to pay them then as they are now. In an effort to reduce them, one Galloway minister suggested the re-introduction of the common coffin, putting it to the Parochial Board that a 'slip coffin' might be made for the poor, from which their bodies could be 'slipped' into the grave, just as in the old days. The Board did not agree and neither did the parish. There was a general outcry against such meanness and the minister, who had meant well, was known thenceforth as 'Slip'.

Further up the social scale things had always been different and coffins by the 17th century were of such a high standard that a Proclamation of Council in 1684 forbade coffins to be decorated with fringes or metal work and just two years later, in 1686, the Scottish Parliament in another effort to limit the expense of funerals and other ceremonies – the Act anent Burying in Scots Linen – ordered that no wooden coffin should cost more than 100 merks Scots for people of the highest quality, and so proportionately downwards for those of lesser status, under pain of a penalty of £100 Scots for every contravention. This, however, did not seem to make much of an impression.

People of importance were often laid to rest, not in graves but above ground in vaults, so it was essential that their coffins should be airtight. Thus a wooden coffin might be used to carry the body to the vault where it was placed inside the lead coffin; sometimes there was a double coffin of lead and wood, enormously heavy to carry – in 1828 the body of MacDonnell of Glengarry was carried five miles in such a coffin. Just as the common coffin might be painted black, so individual ones might be too. The Ardchattan papers, describing the funeral of John Campbell who died in 1721, list requirements for the coffin which include two barrels of 'Lamb black'. The upper classes then improved the appearance of wooden coffins by having black cloth closely nailed or glued on to give a smart appearance, especially when other embellishments were added. The dowager Countess of Traquair was buried in 1759 in a wooden coffin covered with black cloth and mounted with gilt plates and handles with gilt adornments and double burnished nails, the whole costing £16. 16/- stg. In 1791 Lady Margaret Stuart's coffin was covered with black cloth with white plates, more moderately priced at £6. 6/- stg. Between these dates, in 1773, the Dowager Duchess of Perth's coffin, described as 'neatly mounted' came to £11. 11/- stg. Coffins for the rich were splendid indeed and a press report of the Earl of Mar's funeral in 1825 tells how the public were allowed to visit Alloa Tower where his body lay in state 'to view the coffin which was of the most magnificent description, awakening a feeling of the most interesting description' – a somewhat ambiguous comment.

There was, of course, a wide range of people below the level of the quality but above that of pauper, people who could pay for a coffin but not an expensive one. For them, a simple wooden coffin was made by the local joiner but if they worked for an estate or large farm, the carpenters there might make the coffin. In a day-by-day account of the farm of Arabella in Easter Ross in 1832/3 one day's entry says, 'Remark – Finlay Munro, Millwright, killed accidentally by coming in contact with the machinery of threshing mill while at work.' The following entry shows that the two farm carpenters made a 'coffin for his corpse'. Simple such coffins might be but a standard was still expected and, in some parts of Aberdeenshire, if a coffin was found to be defective the joiner was fined £1. A living memory from Shetland tells how shocked everyone was when it was discovered that the joiner was making coffins out of scrap wood though charging for good wood – and him an elder too. This only came to light when a new and narrow gateway was made in the graveyard wall and the bearing party had to lift the coffin high to clear it so that the base was visible to all and they could see that it was made of odd-shaped pieces of wood, with wording like 'This Way Up' and 'Keep Dry'. It was, of course, the joiner's involvement with coffin-making which led ultimately to his role as undertaker, which is still common today.

A respectable coffin at life's end was a matter of concern to the living, and advance preparations were sometimes made. A Mr Harry Prentice who lived in Aberdeenshire had, nine years before his death in 1788 at the age of eighty-five, bought a coffin for two guineas stg. and kept it hanging all that time in his house. Sir James Dick of Prestonfield had a lead coffin made some years before his death but he put it to better use by filling it with bottles of wine and keeping it in his bedroom. On a very much simpler scale, old men who had no one whom they could trust to give them decent burials made their own advance preparations by collecting any suitable bits of wood which came their way and making coffins for themselves, while in the Highlands it was common for anyone going into a large town to buy a few suitable nails for a coffin.

Gradually there developed a desire for a better type of coffin for all classes, one covered with black cloth just as the gentry and nobility might have. This is mentioned in the *New Statistical Account* for Gladsmuir, East Lothian, where about 1830 a Coffin Society was formed at Penston to provide members with coffins covered with black cloth as part of their mounting so that the use of mort cloths, and the cost of hiring them, could be discontinued. This was because, however handsome or poor a coffin might be, custom for years had decreed that a mort cloth should be hired to cover it. The Society allowed non-members to buy coffins at a cheap rate, which was a great benefit to many people.

In time, and by the late 19th century, black cloth-covered coffins became common, used without the mort cloth; they are still used in some parts. While looking good, they were not over-expensive as ordinary white wood could be used and the cloth, described as looking like war-time black-out cloth, was not exorbitant either. Economy was not the only reason for using cloth-covered coffins. In some circles there was an idea well into this century that highly polished wood was unseemly and detracted from the solemnity of the occasion. However, a nameplate was always attached to the coffin, often hand-written by someone in the community, such as the schoolmaster, whose writing was of a suitable standard. Decoration slipped in and often there came to be black braiding around the edges, without which a coffin could look very sombre. An even greater elegance could be achieved with black cloth beautified with silver lace for adults and white cloth with gold lace for children.

In the 1920s khaki cloth was being used for coffins, perhaps to simulate wood, but polished wood ultimately became fashionable and widely used. The funeral expenses of a Fife man in 1929 came to £25. 8/- of which the most expensive item was £11 for a polished wooden coffin, a price which is put into perspective by the fact that the motor hearse and three cars to the cemetery and back cost only £4. 15/-. And so the style of coffins improved steadily but in 1960 the daughter of a Caithness undertaker lamented modern standards, comparing them very unfavourably with those of her father. The coffins he made, she said, were 'sacred', beautifully padded inside with a nice white fringe all round, with lovely pillows for head, elbows and feet. The outside was just as carefully prepared, with the name, age and year painted on to the plate in white and then covered with gold dust. This lady appears to have been right in her opinions because modern coffins are usually made from chipboard with a pine or oak veneer but cost is the reason for this because a solid oak coffin would cost about three times as much.

Funeral Hospitality

However many people came to the house for the lykewake, the bereaved family hoped for as great a number of mourners as possible on the day of the burial because this was to their credit and that of the departed. On top of all the hospitality already shown during the lykewake, it was of even greater importance to entertain very well those who came to the funeral itself because this was an important part of the Scottish idea of 'decent burial' even if the survivors were beggared as a result. By the 17th century, so great was extravagance at funerals that the Scottish Parliament tried to restrain it by passing the Act anent Banquetting and Apparel in 1621 which forbade, among other things, all eating and drinking at lykewakes and declared that the only refreshment to be allowed on the day of burial was bread and drink. But this made little difference in practice and permission to offer bread and drink was widely interpreted.

At both lykewake and burial there were genuine mourners but funerals were undoubtedly one of the pleasures of the people which explains the extraordinary amount of time spent at them. Ten o'clock in the morning was usually the time for which the public were bidden by the bellman (it was later when burial letters became fashionable) even although the 'lifting' – when the coffin was lifted to begin its journey to the grave – might not be until between 2.00 and 4.00 p.m. This meant that between four and six hours were spent at a house of mourning. It was a long time, but people cheerfully gave up the whole day to it, made a day of it indeed, because not only was it a grand opportunity for a news with friends and relations but the opportunity to enjoy food and drink gratis was not to be missed. According to Captain Burt, it was uncommon in the 18th century to see anyone smoking, so the tobacco which was always offered at funerals was particularly welcome.

Basically, the provisions at a funeral consisted of bread – sometimes shortbread – cheese, spirits, ale, tobacco and snuff, to which might be added cake, biscuits and wine. These were not served all at once but various combinations of these items were offered in turn in a series of 'services', a misleading term as it does not refer to religion but to food. In modern parlance, one might say that there were several courses, anything from four to seven of them. The words 'series of services' must not be overlooked because if more mourners arrived after proceedings had begun, the 'services' were started all over again.

The *New Statistical Account* for Carluke, Lanarkshire, written in 1839, gives an example of these 'services':

1. Bread and cheese, with ale or porter.
2. Glass of rum with 'burial bread'.

3. Pipes ready filled with tobacco, handed round in a riddle.
[Preparing these pipes was one of the duties of the women at the lykewake.]
4. Glass of port wine with cake.
5. Glass of sherry with cake.
6. Glass of whisky.
7. Glass of wine [variety not specified] with cake.
8. Thanks for the whole.

The details of how these 'services' were offered obviously differed with circumstances. At a cottage funeral mourners gathered at the door and went inside in turns to partake of what was offered. At some funerals the most active young man was appointed server and this was something which was considered an honour.

At a somewhat bigger country funeral, mourners would be quietly welcomed by relations outside and given whisky there by another relation or a worker, then directed either to the house for the 'services', receiving another glass of whisky as they crossed the threshold, or to the barn which was prepared for the occasion with seating improvised by laying planks over any supports that could be found such as sacks of grain. There a table was placed in the middle of the floor, covered with a cloth and piled with eatables, with jars and bottles of drink at hand, sometimes with vessels ready for brewing toddy too.

At the funeral of a more important person, the closest friends were received in a special chamber, possibly a bedroom, where food and drink were laid out for them. Substantial refreshments were set out in the parlour for the next grade of mourners and the common folk were entertained in the kitchen, if not in the barn, while at some large funerals people sat outside on the grass. In some cases, however, it was only beggars, flocking from all quarters for what they could get, who went to the barn where they had to wait until the real mourners were served before receiving what was left over. In towns, the same thing happened, within the limits of town accomodation. The company met in the street, those of highest rank, the most esteemed and strangers being invited inside.

In her *Memoirs of a Highland Lady*, Elizabeth Grant gives an impressive description of a funeral where the widow laid out her husband's body and then made all the preparations necessary for generous refreshment of the mourners but sat in total silence throughout the time they were in the house. It was natural that the domestic arrangements should fall to the womenfolk but a joiner in Ross and Cromarty who provided the coffin for a funeral in 1871 also helped with the catering as he 'set things in order, such as cutting bread and cheese and bottling whisky' while at another funeral he served the bread and cheese and whisky. Sometimes he was required to say grace too.

All was silence and melancholy nods of the head – to start with at any rate. The arrival of the mourners might stretch out over one or two hours and as they came in and settled down to await the series of 'services' they were offered pipes and tobacco (even although these might be included in the 'services') which had been made ready, with a burning candle to light them, and also snuff. An odd appearance was given to funeral processions later by these pipes stuck into the men's hat bands. Offering pipes and tobacco was common at least until the end of the 18th century and continued in some places for longer than that. In the mid-1920s long pieces of black twist and cigarettes were offered in the graveyard after a funeral in Barra which may have been an isolated case, but the person who remembers seeing it done thinks that it was customary there at that time. When the 'services' began glasses were filled by the nearest relatives or servers. There was no excuse for not drinking because if anyone refused he was told, 'You have obliged my . . . by attending, pray Sir, what have I done to be refused?' The glasses were emptied to the memory of the departed, a service of food was offered, glasses refilled and drained to the consolation of the mourners and so on. Such funeral toasts continued well into the 19th century but were dying out fast by the 1880s.

With repeated 'services' of food and drink one cannot help wondering just how long the silence with which the proceedings began, lasted. Indeed, one account tells of a servant inquiring whether more whisky should be offered, whereupon the master of the house went to the barn door and listened, saying he liked to hear a good buzz before everyone set out. When mourners sat smoking, eating and drinking for several hours, it was not surprising that some were unable to stand by the time of lifting and were incapable of accompanying the funeral procession, while of those who could walk not all could be trusted with the coffin. Drinking on the day of the burial was the continuance of the run-up to the funeral when every step had already been accompanied by 'a dram'. There was drink at the lykewake and at the kisting and even a stranger passing a house where a funeral was taking place was not exempt from its hospitality. Sir David Geikie tells of how in the mid-19th century he passed such a house in the parish of Kilchrist, Skye, and immediately two or three of the mourners made for him, carrying bottle, glasses and a plate of cake which, although he had nothing whatsoever to do with the funeral, he knew he must not refuse.

There was also drink during any long funeral procession – during the 16-mile journey for Flora Macdonald's funeral in Skye, no less than three hundred gallons are said to have been consumed. And then there was food and drink in the graveyard too. This was sometimes sent ahead in one or more carts (which could be useful for bringing home any mourners who over-indulged) or in baskets, or carried by the mourners themselves. In many cases it was the mourners who dug the grave and one excuse for graveyard refreshments was that they needed something to revive them after their exertions. Normally the grave was filled in and tidied up before any refreshment was offered but sometimes as soon as shovelling-in of the earth began, so did graveyard hospitality.

The style of service of food and drink in the graveyard varied. Sometimes it was like a picnic, with white cloths spread on the ground but at other times food was presented on trays, passed round by relatives. One or two tumblers did for everyone, used and re-used till all were satisfied.

The *New Statistical Account* for Kilmuir, Skye, referred to the practice of drinking whisky in the graveyard immediately after a funeral as a 'barbarous custom'. Barbarous it may have been to the minister who wrote this account but it was an accepted practice and when one of the Frasers of Lovat wished to show particular respect to an old family piper who had died in 1812 at the age of ninety-six, he not only ordered both his pipers to accompany the funeral procession but also sent a generous supply of whisky to the graveyard. The *New Statistical Account* for Duirinish, Skye, also speaks of drinking at funerals in earlier days, with the result that people forgot the sacredness of the churchyard and the solemnity of the occasion and renewed old quarrels and fought among the graves of their ancestors. Rev. Donald Sage in his *Memorabilia Domestica* tells of a funeral from Creich to Dornoch, Sutherlandshire, accompanied all the way by an immense crowd of gentry and common people. By the evening a 'bloody fray' broke out in the churchyard and his memories of the scene are oaths, curses and yells, blood trickling down angry faces, fists and cudgels in use and stones flying.

About the end of last century, plentiful whisky at a funeral on the mainland of Shetland is said to have led to fighting during the procession. The mourners laid the coffin down at a place called Legatrod, had a good fight and then all went home. It was only the next day when they remembered the coffin and it was buried by a small group of people but thereafter the superstitious never liked to pass that spot. There is a story of a funeral procession coming to a junction from which two roads each led to a churchyard. The mourners argued drunkenly about which graveyard they were meant to be going to, had a good fight about it and solved the whole thing by burying the corpse there and going no further. But to some a good fight at the funeral meant that it was a success, if that is the proper word to use. According to the Very Rev. Dr Norman Maclean, fights at funerals were almost expected and he tells of a woman who exclaimed, 'Johnnie is buried, and not a bloody head in the churchyard; shame is on me, for they will be saying of me that I spared the whisky at my husband's funeral.' Even without fighting, overmuch drinking could lead to forgotten coffins. A bereaved farmer and his friends indulged themselves so well at his wife's funeral in Strathbogie, Aberdeenshire, that it was only when they had gone some way to the graveyard that he exclaimed, 'Hech, sirs, we've forgotten the gudewife,' and back they had to go for her,

Excessive drinking could produce other results too. At the funeral of Archibald Fraser of Lovat in 1815, the gentry were given a great entertainment with the best of everything at Beaufort House, Inverness-shire, and whisky was provided in great quantities on the green for the tenants, so that when the procession got to the graveyard at Kirkhill, where presumably there was still more whisky available, 'several of the lower order tumbled into the vault' and were only pulled out next day when the smith went to close it. On another occasion, an Argyll funeral party set out from Inveraray to meet another group on a hill near Loch Awe who were to carry the corpse on to Oban for burial. At the meeting place there were such liberal refreshments that forty-one 'corpses' had to be carried down, only one of which was genuine.

A tragic result of funeral drinking occurred after a burial in the ancient graveyard on Isle Maree in Loch Maree, Ross and Cromarty. An inebriated mourner wandered off across the island and was left behind when everyone else sailed for home. Somehow or other he was never missed and no one thought to look for him but when the next funeral took place there, horrified mourners were greeted by the sight of his corpse. Osgood Mackenzie in his *A Hundred Years in the Highlands* describes a funeral followed by a dinner in the granary. There was a tremendous amount of drinking and as people fell out, those peeping in could see spare seats and spare bottles and joined in. When two of the genuine guests realized what had happened, they belaboured the gate-crashers with wooden chairs so much that they rushed to the stairs which had no handrail and all ended up at the bottom 'like turnips being poured out of a cart.'

There were always some people who were prepared to turn the funeral inebriation of others to good advantage and Alasdair Alpin Macgregor tells of a man in the Western Isles who had goods to sell and timed his sale for the end of a funeral. The bidding was very good. All this may seem very long ago but graveyard refreshments were still being offered this century. According to Alasdair Alpin Macgregor, it was only war-time shortages when not enough whisky could be obtained for all the mourners to have a graveyard drink, which ended the custom in Barra. At a funeral there in 1941 this was regarded as such a break with custom that the chief mourner felt it necessary to ask the officiating clergyman to explain the reason. In living memory, in the Seaboard villages of Easter Ross, whisky, bread and cheese was sometimes offered to the funeral party outside the graveyard.

After the funeral was over, a number of mourners would be asked to return to the house of mourning for a second and more leisurely meal known as the 'dredgy', an old word changed from its original Popish use to mean the entertainment after the funeral. Wealthier people held a dinner, either at home or at an inn, and once again there was drinking and as Henry Grey Graham put it, 'the house of mourning and the house of feasting were identical, often riotous and scandalous', and there might not be a sober person among them as they finished up the supplies. In a rather touching little comment, Captain Burt said, 'Some of the sweetmeats are put into your pocket or hat which enables you to make a great compliment to the women of your acquaintance.' Those who had been unfit to accompany the procession hung about the premises or carried on their drinking at the inn, as did those not invited to the dredgy. There were plenty of inns in the old days and very often there was one just across from the churchyard, handy for funeral trade. In the Highlands those not going to the dredgy are said to have gone to the hillsides and spent the time in dancing, accompanied by a piper, and drinking toasts. This can surely only have been after summer funerals as otherwise the darkness would have descended almost before such revels could have begun.

It was not just mourners who were entertained with drink. At the funeral of Lady Aldie in Ross and Cromarty in 1757, four pints of ale were given 'to the Clangers of the chapple', two pints to the baker who baked the bread, a dram to the Kirk Officer when making the grave and two pints to the Town's officers for their attendance at the chapel during the funeral. The Ross and Cromarty joiner who has already been mentioned, described a funeral in 1877 for which he made the coffin and, along with nine mourners, set off up a glen to deliver it, stopping once on the way for a rest and a dram. He dealt with the kisting, had a dram, then supper and a dram, then attended worship and had a dram, went out for a smoke and had another dram. He was put up for the night in a nearby house but before settling down had a toddy. He was up at 7.00 a.m. the next day and when a visitor or mourner was seen approaching the house, he was brought in and everyone had a dram, then breakfast and a dram, followed by another dram. They all went to the house where the body lay and had a dram, saw to things, took a walk and newsed with people coming to the funeral, then began serving out whisky, bread and cheese.

Six years before, in 1871, this joiner had made and delivered a coffin, an occasion of which he wrote, 'We had a jolly time of it by the way, for we had plenty of whisky, bread and cheese, of which we partook freely at certain intervals and rested and newsed.' At the third and last halt on the way they finished up all their supplies as they understood it would have been out of place to take any of them to the house. 'So then of necessity we had a longer sit there, for we had to drain the bottles and finish the bread and cheese, so much so that a few of our number proceeded no further.' Which shows that in addition to those incapable of accompanying the funeral procession after over-indulging in what was provided, there were also those who were incapable of arriving at the funeral at all. Little wonder that the joiner wrote, 'I made home of it quite done out. But really I have enjoyed the whole affair, for it is seldom that now the like is kept so much up to the real old state of latewakes.'

The truth was that drink was about the only vice of the common people of Scotland and was for very many years largely accepted. There was no shame in it, and at funerals to intoxicate the living was to show respect to the dead. People were used to taking alcohol even from an early age, both boys and girls from about the age of ten being given a dram at the New Year and on other occasions. Furthermore, when a coffin had to be carried a long way, possibly in bad weather and over rough ground, with much depending on the weight of the corpse, had the bearers not been fortified with food and drink they would probably have been overcome with hunger and thirst. One cannot help wondering what the effect must have been when the funeral entertainment was delayed. This was not normal, of course, but Martin Martin, writing of St. Kilda in the late 17th century indicates that this did happen. 'They kill a cow or a sheep before the burial,' he wrote, 'but if it be in the spring when they are lean, they are killed not then but as soon as they become fat.' With initial grief overcome and no coffin to carry, these must have been feasts indeed. Offering alcohol at a funeral was such an essential part of 'decent burial' that even Kirk Sessions, neither well-off nor very free with such funds as they had, would sometimes include a bottle of whisky as one of the basics for a pauper's burial, along with a coffin and the digging of the grave. It is not denigrating the Kirk Session in any way to point out that the whisky was for the living and as the Session was responsible for the funerals of the poor, they would know as well as anyone else that a dram was almost certainly a necessity if anyone was to be found to carry the pauper's coffin to the grave, when there was little at a pauper's burial to attract volunteers.

Obviously not all funerals were drunken occasions but it was considered of great importance to entertain mourners in keeping with the position of the departed and too often well above it. It is easy to believe the description of a young fisherman's funeral in Sir Walter Scott's *The Antiquary* when he says that the sorrow of the dead youth's young brothers and sisters was mingled with wonder at the preparations they saw and the unusual display of wheaten bread and wine, so that their grief was almost lost in admiration of the splendour of his funeral.

Writing of the early years of the 19th century, the *New Statistical Account* for Duirinish, Skye, says that during the wake and especially on the day of burial 'such a quantity of meat and drink was distributed as kept the nearest surviving relatives for several years in the greatest poverty in order to pay them . . .' The *New Statistical Account* for Tiree, written in 1840, says of drinking at funerals, 'It is quite melancholy to consider what sums are thrown away in this manner. There are instances of poor families parting with their last horse or cow to furnish an entertainment of this kind. They reckon it a point of honour to do so; and . . . what might have contributed to their support for a twelve-month is wasted in a day to keep up a savage and disgusting custom.' Sir Walter Scott in *The Antiquary* says, 'I have known many in the lowest stations who denied themselves not just the comforts, but almost the necessaries of life, in order to save such a sum of money as might enable their surviving friends to bury them like Christians, as they termed it, nor could their executors be prevailed upon, though equally needy, to turn to the use and maintenance of the living, the money vainly wasted on the interment of the dead.' The burden of funeral hospitality was very great, even when relatives kindly brought provisions to help out.

Not only the poor suffered from excessive hospitality; the rich did too, and it was not unknown for relatives to be bidden after a funeral to a roup, along with a dinner and, of course, drink, where they paid generously for what they bought, all to pay funeral expenses. The cost of a burial could equal a year's rent, even more, and all classes knew what it was to be pinched when it came to paying. The funeral of an adult in modest circumstances – it was less for a child – was well managed if it could be held down to £100 Scots (£8.6.8 stg.) while for the common people £2 stg. was a normal cost, a sum which many of them tried to put by against the day of their burial.

Gradually people began to realize that there was a real problem in funeral hospitality and that something must be done. As early as 1729, as has already been said, the lairds of Lorn in Argyll agreed among themselves to try to curtail funeral expenses, decreeing among other things that no one should go to any funeral unless specifically asked. In 1771, the parishes of Galston and Mauchline, Ayrshire, brought in regulations to control the length of time which people might spend at funerals, to which they tried to get heads of households to agree. Unfortunately, these regulations cannot now be found.

A Dumfriesshire minister, Dr Duncan of the parish of Ruthwell, described one of the difficulties of getting the middle and lower classes to reduce funeral entertainment: 'The minds of the relatives are apt to be unhinged on such occasions so that they are less able to act with decision.' So he and other clergymen around the country made great efforts to reduce drinking at funerals, largely by ensuring that people's minds on the subject were made up in advance. In 1800 Dr Miller, minister of the parish of Cumnock in Ayrshire, persuaded a group of local people to sign a 'Covenant of Householders regarding the Method of conducting Funerals', one clause of which said, 'That none of us shall give any general or public entertainment either immediately before or after the Burial of our friends, and that, exclusive of the members of our family and those connected with the chief mourner by blood or relationship, we will not invite any number exceeding twelve to partake of the refreshments that may be provided suitable to the occasion, which we hereby agree shall not exceed three glasses of wine, or where this cannot be purchased, one glass of spirituous liquors, and bread proportioned; Binding and obliging ourselves to pay a penalty of Five Shillings Stg. in all cases where any of us shall be found to do otherwise.' Dr Duncan of Ruthwell, writing the *New Statistical Account* entry for his parish in 1834, described how he had managed to persuade the heads of almost every family there to agree neither to give nor accept more than one glass of spirits at funerals. It had needed some attention and perseverance to prevent a revival of the old ways but people had learnt the benefits of this new system and by the 1830s it was firmly established in that parish, with neighbouring ones following suit.

In other parishes as well people were persuaded to enter into similar agreements. One Ayrshire farmer who agreed to offer no 'services' knew how hard it would be to overcome old customs and of his brother's funeral in 1824 he wrote, 'I mean to act in a kind of median between extravagance and niggardliness and wear it out by degrees when prejudices may be in some measure removed.' His solution was to offer whisky and biscuit for one round, and a choice of wine and bread for the second and last round but, even so, he put in his diary, 'After the funeral we had a nice social discourse together.' The movement to reduce funeral extravagance and its consequences kept spreading in southern Scotland and very soon it was food rather than drink which was offered at burials, for instance at the funeral in 1811 of Samuel Brown, a farm overseer and uncle of Robert Burns, all that was offered was shortbread.

1817 saw a Highland funeral where the conduct was so appalling that it can have done nothing but good to the cause of moderation in northern Scotland. This was the burial of The Chisholm at Beauly, Inverness-shire. Two hundred and forty guests were given a splendid meal by a local innkeeper while, for the common people, eight bolls of oatmeal had been baked and there was bread, plenty of cheese and twenty ankers of whisky – about a hundred and seventy gallons. Either this was too much for them or they thought it too little because they broke into the innkeeper's stores and made so free with them that one man and two women died of intoxication. There was trouble and fighting but some at any rate were not so far gone that they missed the chance of cutting off and stealing saddle flaps because this well-dressed leather was known to make good brogues.

Perhaps it was these scenes and the fact of three deaths from the effects of alcohol that spurred on the movement for restraint. Possibly also the gradual introduction of horse-drawn hearses helped by minimising the need for large numbers of people to carry the coffin, although in many places the coffin was carried by mourners for years thereafter. Certainly in 1828, only eleven years after The Chisholm's funeral, particularly careful arrangements were made for that of MacDonnell of Glengarry Inverness-shire, and although there were a hundred and fifty gentlemen and fifteen hundred others, the *Inverness Courier* was able to report that everything 'was conducted with the utmost order, decorum and solemnity suited to the mournfulness of the occasion and the better sense of propriety which begins to prevail in the Highlands.'

In Duirinish, Skye, where fighting had been common in the graveyard, an almost savage reaction took place and the writer of that parish's *New Statistical Account* said that funerals were conducted there more quietly and privately than anywhere else in Scotland. For the burial of a common man only about ten to fifteen friends would gather, with the cost only coming to between £1 and £1. 10/- stg. Although the writer felt this to be unique, it was in fact part of a general movement which various entries in the *New Statistical Account* make clear.

In Moy and Dalrossie, Inverness-shire, by the mid-19th century, drinking at funerals was limited by Justices of the Peace to two glasses of whisky in the house before starting out and one in the churchyard. In Glenshiel, Ross and Cromarty, the 'abominable practice' of drinking at funerals was nearly abolished and in Saltoun, East Lothian, the people had for some time almost all given up serving any drink at funerals, 'a resolution for which they deserve the greater commendation as its adoption originated entirely with themselves'. In Dingwall, Ross-shire, in 1846, heads of families in the town signed what was called a 'paper', which must have been an agreement, designed to curtail drinking at funerals and at the same time a similar resolution was passed at Golspie, Sutherland. There is no doubt that the Disruption and establishment of the Free Church of Scotland in 1843 did much to encourage general sobriety.

In *The Annals of the Parish* – a work of fiction but nevertheless a remarkably accurate reflection of parish life – John Galt tells how one minister began by forbidding his flock to give more than three 'services'. Wanting to go even further, he then decided to set them a clear example and at the next funeral, he accepted the first 'service' but silently refused the second and subsequent ones with a bow of the head. Thereafter he always tried to sit as near the door and as near the chief mourner as possible and just took the first 'service', nodding away the rest, and this grew into a custom for all.

One of the simplest and most effective ways of achieving moderation was to stop servers moving among the mourners carrying a bottle and glass; instead of this, whisky and perhaps port, along with cake, were set out on a table and people were quietly told to help themselves. What is surprising in all this is that in the parish of Tongue, on the north coast of Scotland, funeral moderation had become customary as early as the 1790s. No one there, even the ordinary people, went to a funeral unless invited and the mourners were seldom the worse for drink when the procession set out.

Because a funeral is a gathering of relations and friends, many of them from far away, common courtesy and consideration still requires that a meal of some sort is offered to certain of them. The old tradition of entertaining mourners at an inn is still evident in the advertisements put in the press by hotels in the vicinity of, for instance, crematoria which offer 'to respectfully cater for funeral requirements'. Perhaps affluence in some areas is bringing a slight swing to the old days, however, and a mourner at a Caithness funeral in 1981 was astonished at the amount of drink taken in an area where for years a drink had only been given as a 'warm-up' on returning from the graveyard.

As they served the mourners, few people realized that there were deeper reasons for funeral hospitality and went through the motions guided by custom and 'what people would think'. But there was always more to it than that. The fact that it was always certain kinds of food that were offered indicates a ritual and quasi-sacramental character. Equally it could be a farewell banquet for the corpse, after which the spirit was expected to go and not to return. The custom of having funeral feasts is world-wide but in Scotland, during the times when there was no religious service at burials, the 'services' may well have acquired an additional importance.

Although the male mourners have so far been stressed, women did attend some funerals. Very often, however, their presence was more obvious at the lykewake and kisting, apart from some parts of north-east Scotland where the women carried the corpse the first seventy-eighty yards, then handed over to the men to continue the journey to the graveyard, while they returned to the house for an excellent tea. Everyone usually took three cups, although later on and presumably in keeping with alcoholic moderation, it became proper to take only two cups. In the Seaboard villages of Easter Ross, a message was sent round the women living in the street, after the procession had left, asking them to come for a drink of whisky or port, but this was something which could be refused without giving offence. With all the ritual hospitality a funeral was expensive enough but when all that was done, there was yet another expense and one which had nothing to do with entertainment.

Death duties and Capital Transfer Tax are thought to be modern inventions but there used to be another form of these, in dues to the laird on the death of his tenants. When one tenant died, it was common for the laird to take the best beast from his stock. It was said in the case of a man called Alexander Ross Johnstone in Easter Ross in 1606 that the demands made on his estate were far more drastic than those of any present-day Chancellor of the Exchequer. His estate included several oxen, two cows, two steers, four horses and thirty-five sheep, as well as thirteen geese and various other items, but after payment of dues to the laird and teinds to the collector all that was left for his son was two old horses and four bolls of oats. It worked out that £340 Scots was due out of an estate of £360 Scots.

The *New Statistical Account* for Strath, Skye, describes how dramatically the custom died out. Until about 1750 it was customary there for the laird to claim the best horse when a tenant died and the ground officer or under-factor always went to demand it immediately after the burial. This went on until a man named Mackinnon died and his widow resisted strongly when the ground officer came whereupon he 'beat and bruised her to the effusion of her blood'. She told him that she hoped that her year-old son would one day avenge her and, in some seventeen years' time, when the same officer visited a nearby farm on the same errand, young Mackinnon pursued him, asked him to return the widow's horse, and reminded him of how badly he had treated the widowed Mrs Mackinnon. They fell to blows, Mackinnon got the best of it and cut off the officer's head. This he washed in a well and then rode on the disputed horse to the laird's gate, with the head on the point of his dirk. The laird was shocked to discover what had been going on in his name and immediately appointed young Mackinnon ground officer, with particular instructions that no widow on his estate should ever again be deprived of any part of her property.

9

Burial Services

T he Scottish Reformers were desperately anxious to sweep away everything Popish and that included prayers for the dead and thus it was that, although they were concerned about the decent disposal of human corpses, they forbade any form of religious service at burials. This was made clear in the *First Book of Discipline* in 1560 which stated that because of prevailing superstitions it was 'judged best' that there should be neither singing, reading nor sermons at burials but that the dead should be borne to the grave 'with some honest company of the kirk . . . and committed to the grave with such gravity and sobriety as those that be present may seeme to fear the judgment of God, and to hate sin, the cause of death.' Forbid is in fact too strong a word for the Reformers' attitude in the matter because a certain freedom of choice is apparent in the edition of the *First Book of Discipline* given in Knox's works. In this, the phrase, 'This we remit to the judgment of particular kirks, with the advice of the ministers' shows that in spite of what was 'judged best', it was still left to individual churches to use their own discretion.

John Knox himself preached at the funeral of the Regent and funeral sermons were undoubtedly popular with many people. So a loophole was left for them in the *Book of Common Order*, known as Knox's Liturgy, which was confirmed by the General Assembly in 1562. Here it was stated that if a minister was present at a burial and asked to do so, he might go to the church 'if it be not far off' and 'make some comfortable exhortation to the people touching death and resurrection'. One churchman, Wodrow, took this to mean that if the church was not at hand, then the exhortation might be given at the graveside, an interpretation with which it seems hard to agree. The implication surely is that only if the church was at hand should the minister, if requested, deliver a sermon; it was permissible for him to do so but there was no need for him to go out of his way to give one.

Although the Reformers tried to put an end to burial services, their rulings were affected by the political and religious position in Scotland which kept swinging to and fro during the 16th and 17th centuries. Following the Reformation there were many troubled years. From 1560-1572 there was a struggle between Roman Catholics and Protestants; while from 1572 until 1690 there was conflict between Episcopacy and Presbyterianism. James VI and I was succeeded in 1625 by Charles I who tried in 1637 to introduce to the Church of Scotland a new liturgy to replace that of Knox, an action which resulted in the famous riot at St Giles when it was said that Jenny Geddes threw her stool and was followed by the organization of Scottish Presbyterians to resist Episcopacy.

During the times of Episcopal influence there was a revival of burial services. Burial of

the dead was such an important part of Episcopal ritual that in 1633 the Scottish
Parliament ordered that while ordinary clergymen should wear black gowns for preaching,
surplices should be worn for celebrating the Lord's Supper, baptisms and burials – in other
words, in the matter of clerical attire, burial ranked with the Sacraments. During this time
of revived burial services, a 'Form of Burial as used in the Kirk of Montrose' about 1580
consisted of a homily on death, a prayer from King Edward's Liturgy (which was used for a
short while after the Reformation and before the introduction of Knox's Liturgy), and a
funeral hymn, all to be said or sung at the graveside. There were impressive funerals for
important people, such as that of the Earl of Dunfermline in 1622 and the Earl of
Buccleuch in 1633, with sermons and great display of earthly honours. Even so, the
carrying of 'pictures or images' at funerals was considered Popish and was forbidden by the
General Assembly in 1597.

While lychgates or lykegates are rare in Scotland, the few there are seem to date from the
Episcopal times of the early 17th century. One at Anstruther, Fife, was built at that time at
the wish, it is said, of Archbishop Spottiswoode, and an entrance gate in the west wall of the
churchyard at Chapel of Garioch, Aberdeenshire, dated 1626, is said to be a 'funeral
porch' under which the bier was laid on an iron framework during the burial service.

Strong religious feelings led to the signing in 1638 of the National Covenant. Episcopacy
was abolished by the General Assembly and once more burial services went out of favour.
In 1643 the Solemn League and Covenant was signed and in 1645 the Directory of Public
Worship of God was agreed by the Assembly of Divines at Westminster with the
assistance of Commissioners from the Church of Scotland (with an Act of the General
Assembly and Act of Parliament, both in 1645.) Concerning burial, this Directory said:

> When any person departeth this life, let the dead body, upon the day of burial, be decently
> attended from the house to the place appointed for publick burial, and there immediately
> interred, without any ceremony.
>
> And because of the custom of kneeling down, and praying, by or towards the dead corpse,
> and other such usages, in the place where it lies before it be carried to burial, are superstitious;
> and for that praying, reading and singing, both in going to and at the grave, have been grossly
> abused, are no way beneficial to the dead, and have proved many ways hurtful to the living;
> therefore let all such things be laid aside.
>
> Howbeit, we judge it very convenient, that the Christian friends, which accompany the dead
> body to the place appointed for publick burial, do apply themselves to meditations and
> conferences suitable to the occasion; and that the minister, as upon other occasions, so at this
> time, if he be present, may put them in remembrance of their duty.

Human nature being what it is, the Directory went on to say:

> That this shall not extend to deny any civil respects or deferences at the burial, suitable to the
> rank and condition of the party deceased while he was living.

Two years later, in 1647, the Westminster Confession of Faith was agreed by the
Assembly of Divines at Westminster and by the General Assembly of the Church of
Scotland. This made the Covenanters' attitude to prayers for the dead very clear: 'Prayer is
to be made for . . . all sorts of men living or that shall live hereafter; but not for the dead.' Not
only was the Scottish Kirk against all things Roman Catholic, but they could not see any
way in which prayers for the dead could be meaningful. The only possible reason for
praying for them was if such prayers could help them to increase in grace between death
and the Last Judgment and, regarding this as impossible, both prayers and services were
ruled out.

In 1649 Charles I was executed and Cromwell's rule lasted until the Restoration of 1660 when Charles II came to the throne and Episcopacy was re-established in Scotland, and burial services were too. When the young Earl of Leven died in 1664 the sermon preached at his funeral was said to be the first in Fife for twenty-four years or more, and when Bishop Sydserff, formerly of Orkney, died in Edinburgh in 1663 aged eighty-two, not one but several funeral sermons were preached while his 'corps did ly in the yle'. It is from this time too that there are various references to burials at night with torchlight and high ritual. There was a feeling that sometimes the ritual was too high and a reversion to Roman Catholicism and the authorities in Aberdeen in 1670 were much offended by the night-time burial of the Laird of Drum's daughter with what they called 'superstitious ceremonies'. There was also some sort of trouble at this funeral in which two people were injured and to prevent any recurrence the Burgh Council forbade funerals to take place during any but daylight hours, under pain of 300 merks Scots.

Edinburgh Burgh records, in enforcing a restrictive practice, show another aspect of burial ritual during these Episcopalian days: in 1682 it was declared that when any corpse was laid in any city church with torches, it was only 'the good toun's company' which might be employed to carry the torches.

Such funerals, however, were for people of importance. Writing of their visit to Scotland in the 1660s, Ray and Willoughby said, 'The people and the minister many times accompany the corpse to the grave, with the bell before them, where there is nothing said, but only the corpse laid in.' Thomas Kirke, writing in 1679, of the funeral of a man named Volli Voodcock, said, 'The bellman calls the company together and he is carried to the burying place and thrown into the grave . . . and there's an end of Volli.'

Sadly, the Reformation had snatched away from the people much that they understood and relied upon and replaced it with something which to many was bleak and intangible. Many people felt that a loved one could not be buried without some little ceremonial and so they clung to such bits of ritual as they could, including the use of the mort bell. When burial services had gone out of use after the National Covenant of 1638, people in Aberdeen were found to be laying the bier and mortcloth – a funeral pall – on the graves of the dead. The reason for doing this is not clear but it must have been a rite of some kind which was, so far as the burgh authorities were concerned, a 'superstitious practice' and denounced as such in 1643, only to re-start again within a dozen years.

Another lingering Popish custom was the use of incense at Scottish burials as late as the early part of the 18th century, its use approved by and bringing in money for the authorities. In Aberdeen in 1705 the Burgh Council ordered that 'in all time coming the Master of Works shall receive from each person who shall burn incense or perfume at the burial of their friends in church, £4 Scots, or in the churchyard, 40/- Scots.' Its use, officially at any rate, was for its fragrance and purifying properties rather than as a symbol of prayer, but who knows? People also tried to get round the ban on burial services by having singing and reading at lykewakes, as has already been said; but if it was known about it was forbidden.

For many years in Hawick, Roxburghshire, everyone who gathered around the bed as anyone lay dying, joined in an act of worship, singing suitable psalms with a low, solemn tune. When the mortal struggle was over, this was succeeded with a song of triumph and praise, very often part of Psalm 107, 'The storm is chang'd into a calm.' This was occasionally done until the 1830s and in a rather involved sentence, the writer of the *New Statistical Account* for the parish, said: 'That this practice has not originated from any species of superstitious feeling, we are not prepared to affirm, nor are we sure that the results expected to arise from it are always such as are warranted by the spirit of genuine and undefiled religion, but at the same time there is something impressive and solemn about it.' It may have been nothing more than the instinctive desire to bring religion into death. When James Boswell's wife died at Auchinleck, Ayrshire, in 1789, he read the funeral service over her coffin in the presence of his sons. While this was said to be because it was not unusual for a husband to attend his wife's funeral, it seems much more likely to be because he could not bear to see her go to the grave with no word of religion spoken.

When the burial service was re-introduced in Episcopalian times, those who had services did not necessarily have sermons. A request from several ministers to the Presbytery of Inverness and Dingwall in 1684 shows a strong pecuniary concern as they asked for the advice of the Bishop and Synod as to what they should do when they were 'importuned to preach funeral sermons when people were buried who had left no monument of their charity to the poor or other necessary works.'

Being the only non-working day in the week, Sunday was a common day for burials which could have a direct effect on Sabbath preaching. In 1640 the Synod of Moray had to forbid their ministers from leaving their congregations and going away to burials on Sundays without Presbytery approval. This was a few years after the signing of the National Covenant when burial services were again banned so their presence at funerals can only have been for social reasons. When a minister went to a burial he did little more than go to the house, shake hands, murmur a few words of consolation, share in the refreshments and perhaps walk in the funeral procession to the graveyard from where, according to Captain Burt, he was usually one of the last to leave. But his presence was valued, so much so that accounts for the funeral of Sir Hugh Campbell of Calder in 1704 show a sum paid 'for a suit of clothes for the minister'.

Nowadays burial services conducted by a clergyman are normal practice. How did this come about?

In the early days, although a minister might attend a burial, he was not *required* to be present at any part of the proceedings, not even, as is often thought, at the kisting although he had some reponsibility for this thrust upon him by the Act anent Burying in Scots Linen. In time his indirect involvement with this led to his often being asked to be present at the kisting and when food was offered, it was he who said grace. On the day of burial, refreshments were taken without any grace being said but gradually the custom came in of saying grace before and giving thanks afterwards, as in the example of 'services' already quoted from Carluke, Lanarkshire, where the final item is 'Thanks for the whole.' Funeral graces were often said by a layman with a flair for them but, as at kistings, if the minister was there, he would be asked to say them, and very long they could be too, anything from fifteen to thirty minutes. According to Sir Walter Scott, by the early decades of the 19th century, it had become the practice for most Scottish ministers to seize the opportunity of a funeral to offer prayer and a suitable exhortation, although this was still not a burial service. However, this grace over food, growing into prayer, was the thin edge of the wedge and, with Scripture reading added, ultimately became the service over the dead. In answer to a query on the matter in 1982, a spokesman from the Church of Scotland offices said that burial services 'just slid in'. Ministers were acting on their own initiative when they held a service at house or grave and doing so did not always meet with approval. When a minister held a funeral service in the churchyard in a South of Scotland parish about 1850, it caused a great to-do in the area, with all his elders leaving him because they said he was going post-haste to Rome.

Until about 1855 various Presbyteries dealt with ministers within their bounds for the same offence but slowly opposition died out and people began to ask for a burial service. Even the singing of hymns at the graveside was introduced in some cases. But all this took time and, even although by the early 1880s prayers at the house had become almost universal and were becoming common at the graveside, a burial service was still not essential. In his book, *Worship and Offices of the Church of Scotland*, written in 1882, Dr Sprott recommended suitable readings for when 'there is sometimes a service' in house or church and went on to say, 'If there be a service at the grave, it should be short and of more general character,' both phrases making it plain that at that date there was still some doubt about the necessity of holding services at all. A similar attitude came from Rev. Andrew Edgar, of the parish of Mauchline in Ayrshire, who wrote in 1886, '. . . whenever it is in the minister's power to be present, devotional exercises take place in the deceased's house on the day of burial.' Progress in the matter was certainly not uniform but as things advanced, burial services came to be regarded as essential; although interestingly enough, as late as 1911 an overture was presented to the General Assembly because such diversity existed in the practice of taking a variety of religious services, including funerals.

Since the 1950s and 1960s, it has become common to have the funeral service at church or crematorium, partly as a consequence of more deaths taking place in hospital, from where the corpse may be taken directly to these places. To these services, both men and women go, although in some places such as Wigtownshire, there was, into the 1950s, certainly also a short service for the women at the house. Women sometimes take a cord at the burial itself but there is always a preponderance of men at funerals, women not generally going to the grave.

Even so, many funeral services still take place at the home of the deceased, in the way which 'just slipped in' late last century. At these, the coffin usually lies on trestles outside the door of the house, with the minister standing in the doorway, perhaps flanked by some members of the family and the mourners, all male – any women go into the house – gathered round outside for a service of prayer, readings and perhaps a eulogy or exhortation, but not usually singing, after which the procession goes straight to the burial ground for a short committal service. There are still memories of cottage funerals where the coffin might lie in one room, perhaps on a bed, while the service was conducted in the other room; and of the coffin in the same room as the service was held, perhaps tilted up so that the corpse might be seen, seeming to show lingering traces of older ways.

The present attitude of the Church of Scotland to funerals was movingly presented by the Very Rev. Dr John Gray of Dunblane Cathedral in an article in *Life and Work* in 1982: 'Perhaps a minister's greatest privilege is to be allowed to be of help to the bereaved both by conducting a funeral service and by visits to the home.' He favours a funeral service in church, followed by a short service at the graveside or crematorium. 'Funeral parlours with canned music, plastic flowers and automatically closing curtains' he considers a poor substitute for a church where prayer is regularly offered and the Sacraments celebrated. He recommends burial for a child or young person or where the death has been sudden 'because there has been no time to accept death as a possibility or to say "Farewell" and relations find comfort in having a grave to visit. When someone dies at a great age or after a long illness the process of detachment is already far advanced and cremation is acceptable, as it is when there are no relatives to visit the grave.'

From the time of its formation in 1843, the Free Church of Scotland's attitude to burial services has been the same as that of the Church of Scotland. Free Presbyterians, however, hold a fairly long service at the house but none at the graveside, although some of their ministers may give a talk there; if the service is for any reason not held at the house, it is conducted outside the graveyards because to this denomination to have it inside would smack of Popery. Roman Catholics, Episcopalians and others bury according to their own rites.

In at least one instance in the 19th century, unofficial cremation took place. In 1824 an Edinburgh woman delivered herself of a still-born child, which she put on a blazing fire until it was reduced to ashes. According to her statement to the police 'she resorted to cremation to save the fash and expense of a burial'. Official cremation was not introduced, however, to Scotland until 1895 when a crematorium was provided by the Scottish Burial and Cremation Society. After a fairly slow start, this has become a very common method of disposing of the dead.

In some fishing communities, well within living memory, if a mother died in childbirth the baby was baptized 'over the coffin', that is, the father stood on one side of it holding the baby, the minister on the other, performing the Sacrament and then proceeding to the burial service.

Mortcloths

W hen the time for the 'lifting' came, a mortcloth was laid over the coffin. This funeral pall originated in the days when ordinary Scottish people could not afford a coffin, and the corpse, in a winding-sheet but uncoffined, was covered or wrapped in a sheet, plaid or piece of blue homespun for the journey to the burial ground. There it was unwrapped from this additional covering and lowered into the grave. Although the mortcloth originated with those who could not afford coffins, it came in time to be regarded as an indispensible feature of all funerals of whatever class. It was the done thing to use one and no one would see a loved one buried without one – with one exception. In some places, such as the parish of Coldingham, Berwickshire, a mortcloth was not used for a woman who died in childbirth; instead, she was wrapped in a sheet. While the use of the mortcloth began by the 15th century at least, a contributory factor to its universal acceptance must have been the Proclamation of Council in 1684 forbidding the decoration of coffins with fringes and metal work, at which point those who would normally have had such handsome coffins, found that a good alternative was a handsome fringed mortcloth.

Although mortcloths sometimes belonged to private people, they were usually owned by corporate bodies such as burghs, craft guilds and trade incorporations, as well as some privately-run charities. They were lent out at reduced rates, or even free, to members of these groups, and were also available for hire to other people, the income often going to the poor. Kirk Sessions also owned them and rented them out; even in rural parishes they usually had at least two, the best and the second-best, with possibly a child's size as well, so that people could choose which was within their means. The second-best was a poorer cloth altogether but it lent a touch of dignity to burials and gave some appearance to a rough poorly made coffin. It was the one which the Kirk Session allowed paupers to have free; sometimes inability to pay for a coffin, even though not on the poors' roll, was regarded as a qualification for having this cloth without charge.

Mortcloths were black. The best type was of velvet lined with a variety of materials – blink, buckram, even white satin, and bordered with fringing and perhaps lace. In 1590 the Kirk Session of Logie, Stirlingshire, bought 9 ells of finest black velvet for a mortcloth, 7 ells blink to line it, and no less than 3lbs 5½ozs of 'great and small fringe' to adorn it, costing £177. 4. 6. Scots or £14 stg. No wonder the result was described as a 'large and fine mortcloth'. In 1769 the Kirk Session of Fordyce, Banffshire, spent £11 stg. on one which was considered to be 'extremely genteel', which was just the effect being aimed at. The mortcloths of craft guilds might bear the insignia of the craft, something which was a matter of great pride, so that the cloth of Edinburgh Hammermen was described in 1497 as 'an honourabill clath to serf the haill craft'.

It was usual for the organisation wanting a mortcloth to buy the materials and have them made up by a local tailor but occasionally a ready-made one might be bought. In 1693 the Kirk Session of Fowlis Easter and Lundie, Angus, relied on the beadle's brother who was going to Edinburgh to 'do his uttermost to get one there'. A mortcloth might even be brought from abroad, as happened in the parish of Drainie and Lossiemouth, Morayshire. There, in 1670 John King, an elder of Drainie and factor to a local land-owner, left 40 merks or £26. 13. 4 Scots for the poor of the parish, money which the Kirk Session decided to use to buy a mortcloth, the income from which would go to the poor. John's son, William, a partner in the ship *Ludovick and William*, was asked to get a mortcloth from Holland. The legacy not being adequate for this purpose, William added £10 Scots and the Kirk Session made it up to £150 Scots. In spite of William's apparent generosity he did not get the cloth until 1703, thirty years on, at which point the Kirk Session were about to take him to law. When specially made, the second-best mortcloth was not of velvet but of English cloth, shag (a long coarse nap) or even of sackcloth. Sackcloth, a material which must have been connected in local minds with appearances on the stool of repentance, was used in Channelkirk, Berwickshire, in 1705 for what must have been a wretched cloth, costing only 1/- Scots or a penny sterling for making up.

When the best mortcloth was becoming worn, it was often handed down to serve as the second-best so that this could also be of rather shabby velvet. In 1694, at Coldingham in Berwickshire, there were two mortcloths, one of velvet, the other of cloth and 'worn to rags'. The velvet one was not in good condition either but the Kirk Session attempted to have it repaired, 'dying the lining and sewing of it'. However, when it needed more repair a year later it was relegated for 'the use of the poorer sort', and a new cloth was bought for other people. Another instance of hand-me-downs was when the Provost and Bailies of Dunfermline gave their old cloth to be 'redrest for the use of the poor' in 1642.

The materials used were in general expensive and not to be wasted and when a mortcloth belonging to Cromarty Kirk Session, Ross and Cromarty, was beyond use they bought a new one but transferred the fringes from the old one to it. And when a London merchant bequeathed two mortcloths to another Kirk Session in 1718, the Session decided 'that each will be two' and had them made into four. Being an investment, mortcloths were kept with great care because if they became shabby the hire charge had to be reduced, and Kirk Session records, in particular, refer frequently to the repair and relining of mortcloths. Those belonging to country parishes were kept at the church or the manse, in 'tartan wallets', leather bags or special boxes, in which they could both be stored and carried to wherever they were needed. Town Kirk Sessions had more cloths; that of St Cuthbert's, Edinburgh, by 1839 had twenty-four, of first, second and third size, graded in quality from A to F, and in addition there were special cloths for the poor. The poor ones were kept in a press, the good ones in a wardrobe, all in the mortcloth room at the church, the equipment of which included steps, a table with five labelled drawers and a clothes brush. The income for the two years from 1843-5 for the St Cuthbert's mortcloths was £36. 15. 6 stg.

Taking care of a mortcloth could present difficulties, especially when security was inadequate and insurance non-existent, hence the following item in the agreement of the Kelso trades, in Roxburghshire, about their mortcloths in 1656 – '. . . and if it shall happen as God forbid that he who is keeper of the said clothes shall loss them by any extraordinary way as by fire water or WARRES then and in that caice it shall loss generally to us all gif we be made sensible that they or any of them be lost.' Equally, when mortcloths were out on hire measures were taken to ensure that they were cared for and returned on time. In 1630 the Burgh Council of Peebles decreed that when any mortcloth of theirs was hired outside the town, those having it were required to find caution for its return unharmed within six hours if the burial was inside the parish, and within twenty-four hours if outside the parish, under penalty of £100 Scots. Likewise the officer in charge of the mortcloths belonging to the Glasgow Weavers was instructed to attend the cloths at all times when they were hired out and to be careful to bring them back again, for which he was paid 2/- Scots each time.

There were other simple ways of preventing damage to mortcloths as, for instance, when the Kirk Session of Coldingham, Berwickshire, decided in 1695 to buy 'six fathoms of small towes' – thirty-six feet of hemp or flax – to bind round the handspokes on which the corpse was carried to save the mortcloth from being needlessly torn. But velvet is a vulnerable material and there were several ways in which damage could be done to mortcloths, quite apart from that caused by handspokes and being placed in hearses.

A funeral account of 1643 from Berwick describes 'busking' or decorating a mortcloth with arms and mortheids (death's heads) and Edinburgh Burgh records in 1703 make it plain how this was done – honours and verses were nailed, stitched or pinned to the mortcloth which must have been most destructive. Surprisingly the Burgh Council did not forbid the practice; they simply ordered that if it happened then an extra £3 Scots must be paid, over and above the hire charge. This may seem strange but the habit of displaying earthly status at burials was of long standing and even when an Act of Parliament in 1681 forbade the *carrying* of all such honours at funerals, it still allowed eight branches to be put on the mortcloth or on the coffin. However, even worse than being nailed, stitched or pinned could happen to a mortcloth – one belonging to the Dunfermline Hammermen was cut up to make 'keps' or keepsakes.

When large burghs owned mortcloths, first one, then another and another were acquired until there were sizes and qualities to suit all tastes. Taking Edinburgh as an example of this: in the 1590s it was decided that the bellman should have a mortcloth to hire out for himself at half a merk for local people and one merk for strangers, with the specific condition that no one was obliged to use it. Things changed, however, and in 1603 it was decided by the Council that they should buy the cloth from the bellman for £80 Scots so that its income might go to the poor of the Trinity Hospital. This desire for income resulted in there being eight cloths by 1609, the money from which was assigned to the Town's College to augment its funds and help with the instruction of the young. In 1682 the Treasurer produced an inventory of the mortcloths showing that the number had risen to an astonishing fifty-four – twenty-four large velvet ones and one torn; nineteen 'middling'; and fifteen for children, plus a few assorted others. Such a number warranted having a keeper of the mortcloths – so in fact did far lesser numbers – a paid office and apparently an attractive one. In 1689 a merchant took the post, even with the burden of having to pay 200 merks yearly to a man who had previously received this sum from the mortcloth income, and also 100 merks yearly to the widow of the late keeper of the cloths. In 1713 it was again a merchant who was elected keeper of the mortcloths and collector of their dues at a yearly salary from the College Treasurer said to be £25 stg. but which must have been £25 Scots.

Because these cloths were a good investment, it was natural that whoever owned one wanted a monopoly of its hire and in 1614 Edinburgh Burgh Council forbade anyone 'to haif or use within this burgh' any velvet mortcloth but those belonging to the town, particularly directing this decree at the surgeons. By 1705 the income from mortcloths was regarded as such a useful source of revenue for the College that the Magistrates and Council in Edinburgh were determined more than ever that there should be no encroachments. However, they discovered that year that a Captain Henry Frazer – a herald painter, which explains how he became involved with funerals – and two other men had begun using a mortcloth of their own within the burgh, something which the authorities considered would be an 'evil example' to others unless swiftly dealt with. They forbade the three men to use any but the town mortcloths 'under the paine of forfaulter of ther freedome in ane hundred pounds Scots toties quoties to be paid by the transgressors', and ordered them to hand over their cloth when it came back from Seaton where it was at that time 'covering the corps of the decest Mr Christopher Seatone'. It appears that they either did not hand over the cloth, or else obtained another one, as five months later, in May 1705, Captain Frazer along with Captain Melville, who was another painter, and John Paterson, a coachman, admitted that they had used their own mortcloth for the body of Lord Whitlaw within the burgh of Edinburgh. Captain Frazer was imprisoned until he paid a fine of £100 Scots for the use of the College and all three men were forbidden to use their cloth ever again and, in fact, the following month the College Treasurer bought it from them for £147 Scots.

Edinburgh, however, wanted to have things both ways. Not only did everyone within the town have to use the town mortcloths but the Council tried to extend this compulsion as far as they could outside the town as well and ordered that no hearse master was to take any corpse out of the city without the town's mortcloth; if this happened then the owner or master of the hearse should pay £23 Scots for each offence although noblemen, using their own mortcloths for their own families, were exempt from this Act.

Not only noblemen but lairds, too, often had their own private mortcloths and did not always confine them to family use. In 1663 Mrs Jean Campbell, widow of the Laird of Newtown, Morayshire, wrote to the Laird of Gordonstoune telling him of her husband's death and asking for the honour of his attendance at the funeral, and added at the end of her letter,

> I doe lykweis humbely intreat your honour for the leine of your mortcloth for it is more to his credit to have it nor the commone mortcloth of Elgine, seeing we expek sinderie of his friends to be heire.

Craft guilds and trade incorporations, which had many important functions including the care of their own poor, saw the provision of mortcloths as a useful service to their members as well as a good source of revenue for unfortunate brethren. In the 17th century the mortcloths of the Skinners, Furriers and Glovers of Glasgow might bring in about £28 Scots a year while those of the Glasgow Weavers raised over £53 Scots in 1672. Money to buy and maintain these mortcloths was levied from members on admission to the guild; and in 1629 these charges for the Glasgow Skinners, Furriers and Glovers were:

Strangers	40/- Scots
Sons	10/- Scots
Sons in law	15/- Scots
Apprentices	2 merks = £1. 6. 8 Scots

This guild decreed in 1635 that freemen's sons joining them, whose fathers had already paid into the mortcloth fund, should pay 20/- Scots although in some crafts freemen's sons paid nothing. In 1650 the Glasgow Wrights required every freeman to pay 30/- on entry to the guild to help to maintain the mortcloths. If a guild required more money for this purpose, then it might come from a special levy or from the craft 'box'.

In the 17th century members of at least some craft guilds, such as the Edinburgh Hammermen, had the right to free use of the craft mortcloth, but in general they had to pay a small charge while there was a higher rate for non-members. It appears that not all the members always wanted to use the craft mortcloth but the guilds were as monopoly-minded as other mortcloth-owners and expected their members to make use of what they provided, and the Glasgow Weavers, for instance, threatened their members that failure to use the mortcloth would mean that no members of the craft would be 'warned to the burial' or notified to attend. When a new mortcloth was acquired by the guildry in Stirling in 1633, the brethren who had paid for their freedom insisted that 'gratis gildbrether' who had not made any such payments should not be allowed use of the mortcloth; it must only be used for those who had paid for their liberty. In time, various crafts joined together, town by town, to share their mortcloths, as did the Wrights, the Tailors and the Weavers of Glasgow in 1774, their shares working out at nine twenty-thirds to each of the Weavers and the Wrights and five twenty-thirds to the Tailors.

The care of the poor was a great expense. In burghs it fell on the Burgh Council or else on craft guilds who looked after their own poor, or on the Kirk Session, and although these groups might all own mortcloths there does not seem to have been any conflict among them so long as the income was used for this purpose. In country districts, the Kirk Session carried the whole burden of the poor, acting as the local authority in this and many other matters, and they too found hiring a mortcloth a useful way of bringing in money. Most country parishes had two mortcloths, as has been said, but some only one, and of course there were a few which had none, in which case people might just use plaids or hire a cloth from another parish. Kincardine O'Neill, Aberdeenshire, was one of these and there most people just used an old-fashioned plaid laid over the coffin and pinned at the corners so that it did not come off; only the wealthy used mortcloths.

Burghs and craft guilds were not alone in applying restrictive practices; parishes did it too. An example of their general attitude appears in the Kirk Session minutes of the parish of Auchterhouse, Angus, in 1724. They forbade the use of plaids on corpses so that the parish mortcloth would have to be used and they also declared that 'none without the parish bury here without our mortcloth', which meant that people living outside the parish but wishing to bury their dead in its burying ground must hire the parish cloth. This did not mean that they had to use it, they just had to hire it, which explains how accounts for funeral expenses can show the hire of two mortcloths, that of the parish in which the burial took place and the one which they actually wanted to use. When the mother of Dr Duncan Ross of Kindeace, Ross and Cromarty, was buried at Fearn, the Fearn mortcloth had to be hired but the new and finer one belonging to the burgh of Cromarty was the one used. In the same way, Mrs Jean Campbell, who asked to borrow the Laird of Gordonstoune's cloth, would still have had to hire the Elgin cloth.

To keep their monopoly of mortcloths, Kirk Sessions sometimes insisted on buying up any that were privately owned, just as the Burgh of Edinburgh did with Captain Frazer's. This happened in Nigg, Ross and Cromarty, in 1729 when the Kirk Session minutes say '... there are some private persons who keep mortcloths which are commonly made use of in the parish, and these persons apply the money which is collected for the said mortcloths to their own private use.' They forbade private people to keep mortcloths in future and ordered 'such as have these mortcloths to bring them to the next dyet of session to be purchased by the session for the benefit of the poor . . .' – in other words, a compulsory purchase order. The Kirk Session paid £12 Scots for one of these cloths and accepted another free but allowed its owner the liferent of it. In the parish of Galston, Ayrshire, a merchant at one point decided to acquire a mortcloth and hire it out but his hopes of profit were quickly dashed by the Kirk Session who realized that 'there must be money in it' and that the monopoly should be theirs alone. Surprisingly, at Castletown, Roxburghshire, even in the 1790s, the mortcloth was still in private hands. Mortcloths sometimes belonged to burial societies such as that at Penston in the parish of Gladsmuir, East Lothian, where about the 1780s Lady Ross Baillie of Lamington started a Mortcloth Society for the benefit of her colliers. She donated three mortcloths and this group were given a special right to use these cloths when burying in the parish graveyard. Private charities might also use a mortcloth to raise money: a group of farmers in the eastern part of the parish of St Andrews in Fife, had a mortcloth as one of several items which they acquired to raise money for the 'encouragement' of their schoolmaster, and one assumes that they too arranged that it might be used without hindrance in the parish graveyard. Putting a mortcloth to educational purposes as well as towards the poor was considered a good thing. It happened in this instance, and in Edinburgh for the benefit of the College, and elsewhere too, including Inverness where a mortcloth given by Provost Dunbar to the Kirk Session contributed to the schoolmaster's salary.

The organization that owned any mortcloths laid down their own charges, so there is considerable variety in these around the country, depending on date and quality. They were free for the poor but whatever the official charge, the rich were expected to pay over and above that rate; as the records of the Burgh of Peebles put it, 'forder according to thair chiritie and plesour' or 'forder according . . . to the qualitie of the persons'. The Glasgow Skinners, Furriers and Glovers phrased it thus, 'without prejudice to take more for them from any freeman who pleases to give more'. Depending on the amount of use each year, a mortcloth might bring in a return of between 1.5% and 24.5% on the original outlay. Money let out at interest could only bring in between 2.5% and 4.0% so the latter figure seems very high but it must be remembered that a mortcloth had a finite life of perhaps forty years and in the end the capital it represented was gone.

In burghs there were special keepers of mortcloths but in country parishes where there were few cloths, they fell to the care of the beadle or Kirk Officer, who usually received the fee for delivering them to the house of mourning. An idea of this comes from burial dues in the parish of Melrose, Roxburghshire, in 1763:

Best mortcloth used inside the parish 5/-	Kirk Officer received 6d.
Best mortcloth used outside the parish 10/-	Kirk Officer received 6d.
Best little mortcloth 1/-	Kirk Officer received 2d.
Second-best little mortcloth 8d.	Kirk Officer received 2d.

In Nigg, Ross and Cromarty, the Kirk Officer was allowed to charge 4d. per mile for taking the mortcloth outside the parish in 1826 while in Channelkirk in Berwickshire it was decreed in 1804 that the beadle should receive a proportion of the hire charge, thus:

Best mortcloth used inside the parish 6/-	Beadle's share 1/-
Best mortcloth used outside the parish 7/-	Beadle's share 1/-
Second-best mortcloth used in and outside the parish 3/2	Beadle got 8d.
Small mortcloth in and outside the parish 16d.	Beadle got 10d.

That same year, 1804, in Channelkirk it was decided that an additional charge should be added to mortcloths to help maintain the churchyard dykes. All those prices are sterling. Perhaps mortcloth charges sometimes seemed too high for the average person; certainly the Kirk Session records of Coldingham, Berwickshire, have a rather bald statement in 1733 that '. . . the two big mortcloths are too dear'.

Fixing charges for mortcloths was one thing, being paid was another, and irregularities in gathering in mortcloth money are apparent in the records of all types of groups who owned them. In 1717 Edinburgh Burgh Council passed an Act anent the Mortcloths, forbidding the keeper to let them out without payment to prevent what was termed any further 'rests' upon them. In Nigg, Ross and Cromarty, in 1826 the Kirk Officer had to be ordered to hand in the payment for them to the Kirk Treasurer immediately after the funeral, while in 1681 in Lauder, Berwickshire, one of the elders had to become cautioner for payment of the mortcloth money due from another man. In 1683 a mortcloth was dedicated to the Kirk of Birse, Aberdeenshire, by a man named John Turner. It was sent to them in charge of his cousin, William Turner, but sixteen years later it was still in William's hands, along with the money it brought in, but at that point he agreed to hand it over to the Kirk Session and gave the minister a list of all those who had hired it and a list of any money they were owing so that the Kirk Session could collect it. To be out of pocket for sixteen years must have borne heavily on any Kirk Session.

In Lanark in 1653 those people who had contributed to the provision of burgh mortcloths became dissatisfied with the way the mortcloth money was handled and appealed to the Bailies and Council for assistance in 'seeking in' what was owing. To this end, someone was appointed to meet the Treasurer of the mortcloths to go through his books and make 'complete sums'. The income from these particular cloths was for the good of the burgh so long as the cloths were made available to those who had originally contributed towards them, and their families and successors. This was similar to the way a number of parishioners in the parish of Tough, Aberdeenshire claimed a privileged use of church bells there for the funerals of themselves and their families because they had donated towards the cost of the bells at the outset. Perhaps the difficulties of collecting mortcloth money explains why the mortcloths bequeathed to one Kirk Session by a London merchant in 1718 were in 1733 let out to a man for seven years at a rent of £3 stg. This ensured a regular income to the Kirk Session while the man had the work of gathering in the money. In the early 18th century it was a Scottish custom to spread herbs and flowers on the mortcloth as it lay on the coffin, a custom said to be being revived in the late 19th century. In a similar way plants and flowers were strewn on the coffin itself by relatives in the 19th century in the Hebrides, a fore-runner of the modern wreath. In addition to lending dignity to funerals and raising money, the mortcloth had another useful role as an unofficial form of death register. Before the Act which introduced compulsory death registration in 1855, some parishes kept records but many did not and often details of deaths can only appear in mortcloth accounts, but even so these are incomplete because the mortcloth was not used for young children. Where such records were kept, there was a charge for doing so – in 1763 in Melrose, Roxburghshire, it was decreed that the Precentor should be paid 4d when the best mortcloth was used for someone over sixteen years and 2d for anyone younger; for the second-best cloth the charge was 2d for those over sixteen and 1d for all below that age, all sterling.

Gradually, however, the use of mortcloths died out, partly due to the availability of better coffins and of smart hearses, and partly thanks to the passing of the Poor Law in 1845 which took the burden of caring for the poor away from the burgh, the craft guild and the Kirk Session. Thereafter, the financing of the poor was achieved by assessments and there was no further need for these organizations to raise money by, among other things, the hire of mortcloths. But the dying-out was slow; such an ingrained habit could not end overnight. Channelkirk, Berwickshire, was reported in 1900 to have '*almost* wholly discarded the use of the mortcloth'; some very elderly people in Nigg, Ross and Cromarty, remember its use at a funeral about 1905, although by then the custom was to lay it over the coffin at the churchyard gate. Sadly, this mortcloth was burnt in 1948 under the impression that it was just a dirty old rag.

In his book *Architecture of Scottish Pre-Reformation Churches*, George Hay listed several mortcloths in existence at that time, 1952, but all of them have since disappeared. Midcalder's has not been seen for a number of years; those reported to have been preserved in the Perthshire church of Monzievaird and Strowan no longer exist, the church having been levelled some time in the 1960s; and that of Rosemarkie, Ross and Cromarty, has been lost some time after 1978. However, there are at least two in existence, that of Old Rayne in Aberdeenshire, which is of fine velvet but lacking almost all its lining and fringing; and that of Glasserton, Wigtownshire, which is in almost perfect condition. A former minister of Penpont, Dumfriess-shire, says that a mortcloth is still used there but in a different manner to the original. The cloth is placed over the grave before the burial and removed when the coffin is brought there but, although said to have been used in this way in the spring of 1982, the undertaker has no remembrance of this.

The pall which covers the coffin at state funerals still is, of course, really a mortcloth, and a form of mortcloth appears at cremations.

Walking Funerals

A t every funeral, even after much hospitality, the time came at last for the 'lifting'. In some places, in spite of entertaining the mourners for some five to six hours, a lookout would still be sent to make sure that no more were coming, because had any been seen the 'services' would have started all over again. A good number of mourners was a mark of respect but their presence to act as bearers was also a necessity. Both these aspects were so important that various craft guilds stated categorically that all members must attend the funeral when one of their number died; as Glasgow Weavers put it, 'it is statut and ordanit that na brether of craft absent him fra convoying of the buriall'. In that particular guild, any excuse for not attending had to be a good one and there was a penalty of 4/- Scots for absence. The nearest male relatives, with heads bared, lifted the coffin, covered, of course, with the mortcloth, and either carried it for the first part of the journey or placed it in the hearse. The closest relative lifted the head, with the next of kin on his right hand side. In some parts of the Highlands the chief male mourner walked in front of the coffin, the next closest behind it; in Tiree, and perhaps elsewhere, these two each held a long black cord attached to it.

In spite of the fact that men were expected to perform these specific functions at funerals, when a Lowlander lost his wife, it is said that etiquette required him to stay at home and not go to the burial ground, often with unfortunate results when liquor was still left over. As has already been said, in some parts of north-east Scotland women lifted the coffin and carried it the first 70-80 yards, something being done about the 1820s.

Until the latter years of the 18th century, the cortège was preceded by the beadle or Kirk Officer ringing the mort bell as he went. In Caithness a white flag was sometimes used, either along with the bell or in place of it, although this flag in no way resembled the banners carried at great funerals; the common people had no such ceremonial at their burials. The procession formed up outside the house, two by two, with everyone instinctively taking their proper place according to rank, relationship or closeness of acquaintance. There was always someone, such as an ex-soldier, who was prepared to take charge, which was important when there was a long walk and bearers had to be changed. The number of bearers varied around the country – there might be two, four, six or eight. Sometimes the coffin was carried directly on men's shoulders; sometimes shoulders were slipped under staves supporting it; and sometimes it was carried on spokes at hand-height.

The procession set off, in pairs ahead of the coffin, and every so often the leader gave the order to change over. This was often called the 'word of relief' because he simply called out

60

the one word, 'Relief', although in Mauchline and in Galston, both in Ayrshire, a handbell was rung to indicate a change of bearers. As the order was given, three or four couples from the front fell out and stood on either side of the passing line, facing inwards. When the coffin came level with them, they quickly stepped in and relieved the previous bearers who moved to a position immediately in front of the coffin, usually done without any pause although in some places they did stop for the change-over. The leader controlled the pace and saw that everything was done efficiently. Bearers changed about every forty to fifty yards but in some places, at country funerals of the ordinary people, it was considered proper for everyone to take a turn, so that bearers changed over just as often as it was necessary to fit them all in.

In higher social circles not everyone was expected to carry the coffin. In the accounts for the funeral of the Dowager Duchess of Perth in 1773 there is a charge for eight bearers at 3/- stg. each although it is not clear how far these paid bearers carried the coffin nor at what stage of the proceedings this might have been. In an Agreement made by the Lairds of Lorn in 1729, when they attempted to reduce funeral extravagance, it was stated that when the journey to the graveyard was a long one, the burial letters sent to gentlemen should tell them how many commoners to bring with them, in other words, those who were to carry the coffin. Many mourners rode on horseback in funeral processions; they were certainly not carrying anything. The habit of riding to funerals and in the procession is very clear in records of the parish of Channelkirk, Berwickshire, which show that it was customary for a troop of boys to accompany funerals in the hope of being given a penny or two for holding horses at the churchyard gate during the interment; in fact, a funeral could mean a school holiday.

A longing to be buried with one's forefathers is of very ancient standing, going back to the Book of Genesis, and it meant that many people were not buried in the parish where they died but were carried instead to the graveyard where their families were interred. This is the reason for the very long routes known as coffin roads, found in isolated areas particularly in the West Highlands, which are well described in a booklet by Rev. A.E. Robertson. When someone died a long way from his burying place, a carrying party might set out from both ends. One of these has already been mentioned – when an Inveraray man died at Oban, his corpse was carried by a party of Oban men to a point between Inveraray and Lochawe where they were met by the dead man's relatives from Inveraray. In another case, a body being carried from Inverness to Dundonnell in Wester Ross was taken as far as Garve by one party and met there by Dundonnell men.

In the latter part of the 19th century, Lady Mackenzie of Gairloch died in childbirth in Wester Ross. As there were no wheel roads nearer than Kinlochewe it was decided to carry her coffin shoulder high from Gairloch to Beauly, Inverness-shire, some seventy miles. Word was sent round the parish asking for men between twenty and thirty years of age and at least a thousand volunteered. Five hundred were chosen and divided into four companies, these companies choosing their own captains. The companies were sized by height as equally as possible, one being of men over six feet, down to about five feet nine inches. The bier was carefully made so that the bearers would be able to change over as easily as possible. These men were good walkers and did about four miles an hour, covering twenty-four miles the first day, forty the second, and about nine on the last. Death in childbirth made a profound effect on people and this was a very sad, silent funeral with the change-over of bearers indicated just by a wave of the hand of the leader, and none of these men would accept more than just a word of thanks for a week's work lost and about a hundred and thirty miles of walking.

In 1812, over two thousand people, 'many of the first rank', attended a funeral at Strathglass, Inverness-shire. The man who had died was 'the object of universal regard' and so the mourners 'affectionately bore his remains on their shoulders . . . a distance of at least twelve miles'. The astonishing thing is that the deceased was an Excise Officer – could a man in such a job really have discharged every duty as conscientiously as a press report said and still have been so affectionately regarded as to warrant such a funeral? Many funeral processions, of course, went just to the local parish graveyard but even that could involve a very long journey, especially in the Highlands where some parishes are very large, such as Kincardine and Glenshiel, both in Ross and Cromarty, the first of which is twenty-five miles wide and the second twenty-six miles.

Another problem arose when a number of new churches were considered necessary in the Highlands in the 19th century and certain of them were built at some distance from the previous ones. In several cases land-owners planted the old churchyards with trees and shrubs to improve their amenity, at the same time closing access to them, so that people trying to carry out the wishes of a dead person to be buried with their forbears had to trespass and various 'vexatious litigations' followed. Short or long as the way might be, the old style walking funerals were almost always across country for, until the early 1800s, there were few roads or bridges in some areas. There were rivers to ford – at the funeral of MacDonnell of Glengarry on a wild day in 1828 the bearers had to wade up to their knees in a swollen burn carrying the weight of a double coffin of lead and wood. There was marshy ground to contend with and as death paid no heed to the season of the year the weather often made conditions arduous. Carrying a coffin on one's shoulders or on handspokes over rough ground can have been no easy matter. It was difficult to keep one's feet, quite apart from keeping in step. A cross country walk with a young child's corpse was a much simpler affair and Rev. A.E. Robertson's booklet on coffin roads tells of a keeper taking his dead baby son home to Kintail, Ross and Cromarty, for burial, accompanied by just one man who carried the coffin tucked under his arm.

Just as there was meant to be profound silence during the pre-funeral hospitality, there was meant to be the same during the procession, from the moment of lifting until the burial was over. This is difficult to envisage in view of the lavish entertainment given beforehand and the need for a 'good buzz' before setting out for the graveyard. What cannot have helped silence either was the fact that not only did people often set out in a convivial state but if the journey to the grave was long no inn was passed unvisited and where no inns were available, the procession carried its own supplies to be eaten and drunk en route. A dram taken on the way was sometimes referred to as 'taking the breath of the deceased'. Depending on the distance and the number of mourners, these supplies were carried by the walkers themselves, or in carts, or in creels slung over horses' backs. For the funeral of Lady Mackenzie of Gairloch, food and drink for five hundred people for three days and two nights was carried in these creels. In Caithness women are said to have followed the cortège with trays of bread and drink but surely that was only when the graveyard was close, or else it was for consumption after the burial rather than on the way to it.

Old large-scale maps sometimes show 'resting cairns' which are not the same thing as memorial cairns. An early Ordnance Survey map shows some in the vicinity of Murlaggan near Roy Bridge in Inverness-shire, and it is still possible to come across groups of them in that area, in Skye and in Lewis and Harris. At one spot on Harris, there are about a dozen of them which is considered an eerie sight although they indicate nothing more than the refreshment halts of funeral processions. The coffin was not rested on these cairns – it was laid down on any handy bank or wall – they simply developed out of the custom of everyone adding a stone to mark where they rested.

Silence there was meant to be and sometimes it was achieved, but Highlanders love music and used to consider it essential at funerals, and thus the coronach and the bagpipes made their appearance at them. Men in the Highlands left the outward display of grief to the womenfolk, thinking it unmanly whatever their feelings to show sorrow, and so it was the women who 'cried the coronach' in impromptu verses and phrases which were always addressed directly to the dead person. The coronach described the genealogy or connections of the deceased, told of their exploits and skills, their love of their families and their courage. Sometimes there was a reproof, albeit a gentle one, for dying and at other times there was a vow to avenge the death, and just occasionally this display masked complicity in the death.

What the coronach sounded like seems to have been a matter of opinion or perhaps it really did vary widely. Captain Burt, writing in the 1730s, called it a 'hideous howl or Ho-bo-bo-bo-boo'. Martin Martin, describing St Kilda about 1695, said of the women, 'they bewail the deaths of their relatives exceedingly and upon those occasions make doleful songs which they call Laments.' The index to Thomas Pennant's *Tour in Scotland* written in 1769, refers to 'the coronach, or howling at funerals' while the BBC in a radio programme in December 1982 gave one beautiful example, and another tragically sad one with the voice of the grief-stricken woman nearly breaking down with desolation. I.F.Grant was told of the strangeness and sadness of the coronach by someone who had heard it and the Ochtertyre MSS gives the translation of a very beautifully worded coronach from St Kilda, the original of which was in verse and sung to a plaintive tune. While any woman might cry the coronach for a loved one, it seems that every Highland community had an expert, a local mourning woman whom the township kept in food for her beasts, summer and winter and who, in turn, bewailed their dead for them.

Well-off Highland families hired professional mourning women to cry the coronach. These were usually old women, who covered their heads with a small piece of cloth, usually green. They are described in the Ochtertyre MSS as sitting a little way off in a cluster until the corpse was brought out of the house whereupon they would gather round it, clapping their hands and raising hideous cries while many tore their hair or head-dresses and copious tears were shed. During the procession these women kept behind the men, crying the coronach at intervals in paroxysms of grief, beating their breasts, as in Irish keening. The women of any valley through which the procession might pass and even women whom it chanced to meet on the way are said to have joined in the coronach briefly although they did not know the person who had died. When the procession reached the graveyard, the mourning women cried the coronach during the digging of the grave, briefly raising it even louder when the body was placed in the grave. Then they fell silent and as soon as the burial was over they sat down to share in the refreshments that were offered.

Crying the coronach died out in the eastern Highlands by the end of the 18th century. On the west coast it was common until the mid-19th century and in some of the Western Isles, especially in South Uist, it is said to have lasted well into the second half of that century. At the end of the 19th century it occurred in a reduced form in Mull and Skye as the nearest relatives mourned their dead in impromptu verse, but this they only did inside their houses. Nevertheless, the BBC radio programme in 1982, already referred to, said the coronach had been heard in the Western Isles in 1965.

Although the coronach, which has no religious significance, is thought to be a peculiarly Highland and Irish form of grief-display, in fact the practice of wailing and chanting dirges at funerals is both ancient and world-wide. It was largely superseded by the playing of the pibroch on the bagpipes but in some areas such as Argyll, there was some overlap with one or more pipers leading the procession and the mourning women following; where there were no women, the piper might follow the coffin.

For a funeral, the bagpipes had narrow streamers of black crape or a black flag attached to them. The music played for the procession usually began with the chieftain's march, then various melancholy tunes and for the last, a peculiarly plaintive one suitable to the occasion. The bagpipes were still being played at funerals on the west coast and in the islands this century and have been heard, even in recent times, on the mainland, played as a special tribute to the deceased. Whether or not pipe music was thought to have any special virtue, Highlanders believed that without the coronach the soul would wander sadly about the earth after death and that was something which everyone wanted to avoid.

As the procession approached the graveyard, it halted in two lines and the coffin was carried between them. In some places it was believed that the spirit of the last-buried corpse had to watch in the graveyard until another one came along, when it took over. Naturally enough, when two funerals fell on the same day each group of mourners wanted to get to the graveyard first so that their corpse would not have to watch for long and unfortunately this could lead to indecent haste, and even fighting, among the rival processions. At Pettie in Inverness-shire, there was a variation on this. There it was thought that the ghost of the last person buried waited at the graveyard gate to grab the first mourner at the next funeral and so the parish custom was to run to the graveyard with the coffin as fast as possible, presumably to outwit the ghost and prevent anyone from being caught by it. Sometimes they ran so fast that those carrying the coffin fell. In neighbouring parishes, if they wished to speed-up a funeral procession they used to say, 'Let's take the Pettie step to it.' The Pettie step was common about the 1790s, then declined, but was revived about the early 1830s by some lads at the funeral of an old woman who had a reputation as a witch. Since then, according to the *New Statistical Account*, the step at Pettie has been as decorous as elsewhere.

The desire for the spirit of the dead to go and never return was strong and in some areas there was a belief that a body could be kept securely in the grave and safe from evil influences if it were carried three times sunwise round the church before burial. This superstition was condemned by the Presbytery of St Andrews in Fife, in 1642 in an Act which included the phrase, 'lykewyse that all those who superstitiously cary the dead about the kirk before buriall . . . be taken notice of.' Condemnation of this custom did not eradicate it and it continued for quite some time although with some variations such as walking round the corpse or carrying it around the grave. This superstition is not confined to Scotland – it occurs all round the world.

Funerals were notable for their appeal to the half-witted. In one Ayrshire village there was one young man of simple intellect who, when anyone was seriously ill, would go from time to time and knock on the door and inquire, hopefully, whether the patient was any worse. Dean Ramsay, writing in 1871, said that in country places, hardly a funeral took place without the village idiot – and why not, when everyone else went too?

In the 17th century there was an odd notion about transporting bodies across water – rivers, lochs or arms of the sea. Before the corpse was put on board a vessel, the value of the ship or boat had to be ascertained because it was believed that otherwise some accident would happen which would endanger the lives of those embarked on it.

When meeting a funeral cortège it was customary to stop and let it pass. Well into the 1950s this was done by cars in favour of a motor procession but modern traffic conditions have put an end to this respectful habit. Although road transport has ended the great cross country walking funerals of early times, local walking funerals are still vivid in many memories.

Great Funerals

'T he proud remembrance of outstanding funerals still survives in some clans,' wrote I.F. Grant in *Highland Folkways*. And well it might, considering what some of them were like. What a moving occasion, for instance, it was which Martin Martin described in his *Voyage to St Kilda* about 1695. When one particular laird died there the people, in a manner which was positively Biblical, abandoned their homes and for two days mourned him in the fields, in the same way that the children of Israel had wept for Moses in the plain of Moab for thirty days.

When a member of a great family died away from home, the body was usually brought back there for the funeral and even that journey, though far simpler than the burial procession which would follow, was something which made a marked impression on those people through whose communities it passed. When the Earl of Mar – he of the magnificent coffin – died in 1825 his remains were brought to Alloa Tower in a hearse drawn by six horses, accompanied by several mourning coaches. The Duchess of Sutherland died in London in 1839 and her body was taken by sea to Aberdeen and thereafter all the way by hearse to Sutherland. One can imagine the effect which such cortèges would make on the simple country folk who saw them pass by.

When the Earl of Dunfermline, Chancellor of Scotland, died in 1622 at Pinkie, near Musselburgh in Midlothian, his body was embalmed and placed in a closed oak coffin. It remained there for three days, after which his servants took it by coach to the coast and by boat over the Firth of Forth to Dalgety in Fife. There it was met and carried up to his house to be watched over for three weeks. All this sounds quite simple but would have been an impressive sight, although nothing like the splendour of the funeral which was to follow.

First in that procession went twenty-five of what were called 'poor-ons' who must have been attendants of some sort, carrying on the end of a staff the Earl's arms painted on buckram with one of them carrying the funeral banner known as a gumpheon. Then came the master stabler on horseback, dressed in armour and carrying on the point of a spear the colours of the house – yellow and white taffeta with a fringe. Two liveried servants came next, in black velvet coats with the family crest on either back or front, leading a horse 'with a Rich Footmantle for the Parliament'. Two more servants dressed in mourning led another horse which was itself clad with a footmantle and caparisoned in mourning. Next in the procession came three trumpeters followed by two pursuivants and then the Master of the Household who carried another gumpheon of state on the point of a spear. This particular gumpheon was made of black taffeta powdered with 'tears' and embellished with a death's head. Four gentlemen followed, carrying the four branches – the arms of the houses of Hamilton of Sorne, Yester, Cassilis and Seton. Behind them was borne the pinsell – a small pennon or flag – made of black taffeta with the crest and the word 'Semper' painted on it. After that came another man carrying the standard of black taffeta on which was painted the whole hatchment – the arms of the deceased shown within a black lozenge-shaped frame – followed by three more trumpeters, a pursuivant and Albany heralds in their coats of office.

The dead Earl's servant carried the mace covered with black crape, a Knight carried the Great Seal (which Dunfermline retained as Chancellor) accompanied by its Keeper and that Knight's son carried the Earl's Parliamentary robe of crimson velvet 'lyned with white tafety the ferits taill and sleives edgete with Ermine'. The sword and vest were also carried in the procession; so was the gold 'comitall (earl's) coronet' on a velvet cushion; and four ordinary macers went alongside the three 'pieces of Honours' guarding them with their maces. The coffin came next, covered with a 'fair mortcloth' of black velvet with a gold earl's coronet on a velvet cushion placed on the head of the coffin. Then came twelve chief mourners, people of importance. Six gentlemen, with servants, bore the rich black velvet pall carried above the corpse, with the four branches painted on its banners, and behind them followed close mourners.

On arrival at the church the coffin was placed before the pulpit and the Archbishop of St Andrews preached an excellent sermon. Then the coffin was borne to the little aisle which the Earl had had built earlier and where his two wives and several children already lay, and there it was placed in a specially made lead coffin. No wonder that the corpse had been watched for three weeks; all of that time would have been needed to organize this funeral. The particular account of it which has been quoted ends with a cheerful note, saying that when the coffin was finally disposed of, all the people craved God for a happy resurrection of his soul 'with sound of trumpets and great regraite of his loss. The heralds got 100lbs. the purs. 50lbs.'

This funeral fell close to the time of the Act anent Banquetting and Apparel 1621, the Act which sought to control eating and drinking at lykewakes and burials but which also concerned itself with ostentation and extravagance at great funerals, something which must have become very serious for the Parliament of Scotland to feel the need for such measures. The Earl of Dunfermline's funeral was undoubtedly an example of what they sought to limit.

This Act restricted the number of mourning clothes for the funeral of an earl or countess to twenty-four, for a Lord of Parliament or his wife to sixteen, while only twelve were allowed for what were termed 'privileged persons'. It also stated that the number of 'saullies' allowed should be in proportion to the number of mourning clothes. A saullie, a word which appears with a variety of spellings, was a hired mourner. Saullies were sometimes called mutes which is misleading to modern ears because they were not dumb. In some cases, a mute might be regarded as superior to a saullie but under either name they were simply funeral attendants. Sometimes a couple were posted on either side of the house door prior to the departure of the procession but their main role was to walk in front of the cortège, often proclaiming a simple verse in a doleful manner. This might have no more than a couple of lines as in the example given by J. Train in 'The Mountain Muse':

Alas Sir Archibald Kennedy's gone
And so good behind him he has left none.

The name, of course was varied as required. This particular role of the saullie was very similar to that of the women mourners in the Highlands hired to lament the deceased. The presence of saullies was almost always confined to upper-class funerals although in *The Antiquary* Sir Walter Scott places a couple of them at a fisher boy's funeral, an instance of the poor aping the rich in a passion for funeral ceremonial. Saullies were depressing figures, all in black, with hoods or hats from which broad bands of crape hung almost to their waists. Each of them carried a long black pole hung with black drapery looped up, sometimes known as a 'gumfler' from the word gumpheon. 'Two poles with black silk mountings for mutes' appear in the inventory of funeral equipment at St Cuthbert's Church, Edinburgh, in 1839.

In spite of the Act anent Banquetting and Apparel, extravagant and showy funerals of great people continued and during the 17th century there were several very imposing ones. One was that of a Baron of Roslin, a family whose head until 1650 was always borne to burial clad in the armour he had worn during his life. Another was the funeral in 1633 of the first Earl of Buccleuch who had died in London towards the end of the preceding year. His body was embalmed, fortunately as it turned out, as the ship on which it was being taken to Scotland was driven over to Norway by a storm and only after a long delay did it reach Leith. There it rested for almost three weeks and was then taken to his house at Branxholm, near Hawick in Roxburghshire, where it remained until the funeral could be arranged. Far from having just the prescribed twenty-four saullies at this funeral, there were forty-six, headed by one described as a conductor, who was himself attended by an old man in a mourning gown. They led the procession, all of which bore a marked similarity to that of the Earl of Dunfermline. A trumpeter in the Buccleuch livery, sounding his trumpet, followed the conductor; then came a fully armed man on horseback, carrying on the point of a lance a little banner of the dead earl's colours, azure and or. Next came a horse clad in black led by a servant in mourning, a horse in a crimson velvet footmantle and three trumpeters on foot, all dressed in mourning and 'sounding sadly'.

They were followed by the great gumpheon of black taffeta carried on a lance, after which came four members of the Scott clan who each carried one of the dead earl's earthly trappings – his spurs, his sword, his gauntlets and his coat of honour. Thereafter eight gentlemen of the clan each bore one of the coats of arms of one of the various paternal and maternal ancestors of the dead man. Other Scotts carried the great pinsell, the deceased's standard, his coronet and his 'arms in metal and cobur', with whom were three more trumpeters and three pursuivants, all wearing mourning. 'Last of all came the corpse, carried under a fair pall of black velvet, decked with armes, larmes (tears) and cipress of sattin, knopt with gold, and on the coffin the defunct's helmet and coronet, overlaid with cipress to show that he was a soldier.' Thus they all marched to the church in Hawick for a funeral sermon, after which the dead man was buried among his ancestors.

Neither this account nor that of the funeral of the Earl of Dunfermline makes any mention of the very many ordinary mourners who were present but they do make plain what impressive spectacles such funerals were, with long columns of people and horses, largely in mourning but with brilliant touches of colour, winding along to the place of burial.

In 1645 the Directory of Public Worship had stated that the prohibition of funeral services should not deny civil respects and deferences, something taken only too literally, and the continuance of such elaborate ceremonials at funerals and at other occasions too, led in 1681 to the passing of the Act restricting the exorbitant expense of Marriages,

Baptisms and Burials, which ordained that these occasions should be gone about in a 'sober and decent manner', and in regard to funerals it restricted the numbers of people who might be invited in proportion to the rank of the deceased. It forbade the use of mourning cloaks and the carrying of any flags, banners or other honours except the eight branches of the family arms on the pall, or if there were no pall on the coffin itself.

This latest legislation could still not stamp out extravagance at funerals, as proved by just two examples. In 1704, Sir William Hamilton, a Lord of Session, was buried at a cost of £5189 Scots (£432. 8.4 stg.) or two years his judge's salary. In the early years of the 18th century Lachlan Mackintosh of Mackintosh died and lay in state at Dalcross Castle, Inverness-shire, for six weeks until his heir could return from abroad. The expense of this funeral came to £700 stg., an enormous sum then, and one which embarrassed the chiefs of the clan for a century thereafter.

The desire for the outward forms of funerals was very strong and the basic principles on which such funerals as those of the Earls of Dunfermline and Buccleuch were drawn up were also used for the lesser funerals of the gentry. At the burial of Dame Katharine Campbell in 1752, the gardener went first in the procession on horseback, followed by six baton men (to clear the way but who may also have been saullies), then a led mourning horse, the butler and three other principal servants as gentlemen ushers bareheaded, the hearse with a dress pall drawn by six dressed horses, and thereafter there came about two hundred gentlemen, three by three on horseback, the grieve in deep mourning followed by the tenants, two by two, and last of all, the servants of the mourners, also two by two.

Any funeral was expensive but those of great families were that much more so. First and foremost there were compulsory dues payable on death. These arose from an Act of the Scottish Parliament in 1662 in favour of the Lyon King of Arms to enable him to register genealogies, 'considering how much the honour and credit of the Nobility and Gentry of this Kingdom consists in preserving the noble office of arms in careful registration of genealogies'. For a Duke or Duchess, the fees were £600 Scots; for a Marquis or Marchioness £480 Scots; for an Archbishop, Earl or Countess £380 Scots; a Viscount, Viscountess or Bishop £340 Scots; Lord of Parliament or their ladies £300 Scots, to be paid immediately after either the death or the funeral.

Apart from that, like lesser funerals, the expense was largely hospitality. Special mourners often arrived at the time of death and stayed until after the burial and all that time they, their servants and their horses were kept at the expense of the bereaved family. Account for funerals show how extra cooks and other staff had to be taken on – in 1692 for Lady Mey's burial in Ross and Cromarty extra servants were engaged for four weeks and for Lachlan Mackintosh's funeral cooks and servants were brought from Edinburgh to feed and look after the many mourners in the house. Vast amounts of food and alcohol were bought for these people, as well as for the lykewake and for the day of burial too, when in addition to providing for the general public there was a sit-down feast for special mourners and a dinner for them afterwards too, while yet another expense was the custom of handing out money to the poor at burials.

This was a time when landowners received a large part of their income as rents paid in kind, part of their tenants' produce. They might therefore have plenty of grain, beef, mutton, poultry, eggs, honey and butter but virtually no ready cash to pay for the alcohol and wines consumed at a funeral or the special eatables thought necessary for the occasion or the extra staff engaged.

One wonders who bore the brunt of the expenses of the following funeral – Lord Huntly wished to entertain the company attending the funeral of the second Duke of Gordon at Thunderton House in Moray and wrote to the Laird of Thunderton asking him for the use of his house, 'as none in the toun is so fitt for me as yours, I expect, from the friendship which has been between this family and you, that you will allow me use of it for some days, and that my friend, Lady Thunderton, will consent to take some trouble on this occasion.'

So the funeral procession was imposing and the entertainment of invited mourners and all-comers generous and expensive. The one thing, elaborate though it might be, which was more in keeping with the occasion than anything else was the dolorous preparation of the house and church. In *The Antiquary*, in which Sir Walter Scott described some of the manners and customs of the 1790s, there is a description, albeit fictional, of the mourning preparations of a great house. He tells of a room hung with black cloth which waved in dusky folds along its high walls while a screen covered in black baize was placed in front of the window and kept out much of the light. The trappings of woe were gloomy indeed and this happened in real life as well as in fiction. For example, when the young Countess of Sutherland died at Bath in 1766 it was planned that her body should be taken to Cyderhall, near Dornoch, Sutherland, where it would lie in state in a room hung with black, just as Sir Walter Scott described. (In fact, her husband died just sixteen days later and they were both buried in Holyrood Abbey.)

At the funerals of lesser landowning families and indeed much farther down the social scale, rooms might be whitened instead of blackened, and certainly the room where the corpse lay. This has already been referred to, but sometimes rooms were actually whitewashed for the occasion, one instance of this being at the funeral of the mother of Dr Duncan Ross of Kindeace, Ross and Cromarty, about 1755 when '3½ stone chalk and 3lb glew for whitning a Room' appears in the funeral accounts. This was perhaps a form of whited sepulchre, in the manner in which early Christians white-washed their tombs.

When someone of importance died, the doors of the house and the gates at the entrance might be painted black. In addition the doors of the church where he had worshipped, or with which he had a strong family or territorial connection, might be painted black too. This was very probably the use to which the 'quarter of glew and two barrels of Lamb black' were put which appear as funeral expenses in the Ardchattan papers in 1721. Similarly, for the Countess of Sutherland's burial in Dornoch, Sutherlandshire, in 1766, the one which in the end took place elsewhere, the doors of Dornoch Cathedral were to be painted black and the pulpit and Magistrates' pew hung with black cloth.

Such decoration, if it can be called that, could become a nuisance and a list of the beadle's duties in Edinburgh in 1702 includes taking care that the 'mourning clothes of the several fore lofts hang no further down than the lower part of the loft so that the voice and view of the minister may not be interrupted', and one of the reasons why the Bailies and Council of Aberdeen forbade burial inside churches in 1647 was because by allowing it, other abuses had crept in such as hanging flags, boards, honours and arms and 'such-like scandalous monuments'. However, it was not a nuisance to everyone; it could be an opportunity for acquisition. In the parish of Galston, Ayrshire, the black cloth which had been put on the pulpit at the death of Lady Marchmont was needed for the death of the Prince of Wales 'but the beadle had appropriated it'. Another form of domestic preparation for great funerals appears in an account of 1562 which shows that for one burial 'the halls and chambers was all perfumed with sweet odours which was very costly'.

One of the gumpheons at the Earl of Dunfermline's funeral has been described as 'powdered with tears'. These were black or white tears looking like tadpoles or fat commas, which were painted on to various objects to represent the tears of the bereaved family. They can still be seen as part of the decoration of the Bolton hearse at the Royal Scottish Museum in Edinburgh. They were often applied to doors – of the afflicted house, the laird's vault, and the church, and sometimes to the inner walls of the church too. A bill in 1742 to the Laird of Murdoston in the parish of Shotts, Lanarkshire, is for 'colouring and tearing church doors and lettering them, colouring and tearing the wall opposite to your burial place and lettering the same, 8/- Scots'. But like mourning cloths and flags, they too could become a nuisance and in 1686 a complaint was made about people who had buried their dead inside Greyfriars Church, Edinburgh, having whitened or blackened much of the walls with mourning tears.

The gloom of the church and house was somewhat enlivened by the display of heraldry which was thought necessary. A hatchment has already been mentioned at the funeral of the Earl of Dunfermline. Sir Walter Scott in *The Antiquary* describes one placed over the gateway of the house when the old Countess of Glenallen died: it was huge and by mingling the countess's hereditary coat of arms, with all its quarterings, along with symbols of mortality in the form of scythes, hour-glasses, skulls and other emblems of death, it showed a combination of earthly pride and mortality. These were common at great funerals; and they must have been costly to prepare. In 1711, for the burial of the Laird of Balnagown in Ross and Cromarty, William Kerr, a painter in Nairn, was paid £306 Scots for painting 'scuthins and brauches', in other words, escutcheons and branches. So important was this earthly display at funerals of distinction that one or more heralds might be needed to see that the arms of the dead person were properly marshalled on the various flags and banners carried in the procession and also on the hatchments which were erected at the church, as well as at the house.

The following account appears to be from the diary of one such herald who attended the funeral of Dame Katharine Campbell, wife of Campbell of Shawfield and a daughter of Lord Cardro, in 1752, which has already been mentioned. Two days before the funeral the herald ordered the escutcheon to be put up on the front of the house and to remain there. On the day of burial, he went to the Kirk of Bothwell, Lanarkshire, and put up another escutcheon over the outer door of the church, then returned to dress the hearse and horses. In the afternoon he went with the burial party to Bothwell and gave directions for taking the escutcheon there into the church, with the eight pheons (pennons) which had been on the hearse, placed round it. Like the mourning cloths hanging in churches, these banners could also be a source of trouble, as in Aberdeen in 1647.

Black candles, known as flambeaux, used to be a feature of great funerals. It had been intended that a dozen would be used for the burial of the Countess of Sutherland, the funeral which did not take place in Sutherland after all, while for a Moray funeral in 1733 forty-eight flambeaux, weighing 87½lbs, and valued at 3/- Scots per lb. were supplied. Torches were also a feature of many of the funeral processions of Highland chieftains and lairds. They were probably often a necessity as much as a luxury as it was common for processions to set out late in the afternoon and, in winter, when the cortège might be several miles long and the journey to the graveyard also several miles, natural light would have soon gone. For instance, the funeral procession of MacDonnell of Glengarry in February 1828 left the house to go to the graveyard at Kilfinnan, Inverness-shire, after 4.00pm and there were five miles to go on a very wild day so part at least of this journey must have been made in darkness.

According to the *New Statistical Account* for Moy and Dalrossie, Inverness-shire, at funeral of 'persons of respectability' those who were invited watched the body in the churchyard alternately, two by two. This account was written in 1836 while people were still very much aware of body-snatchers (although the Anatomy Act had been passed four years before which should have ended these activities) but obviously this particular form of watching was not designed to prevent bodies being stolen as the writer describes it as 'a very unnecessary trouble'. It must have been purely a mark of respect and was perhaps what lay behind the fact that watchers sat at the graveside of Sir William Scott in the churchyard at Ancrum, Roxburghshire, for two nights as late as 1902. Various unfortunate funeral occurrences have already been mentioned but bearing in mind the days or even weeks of hospitality which preceded great funerals, culminating in the feasting and drinking of the burial day itself, it is not surprising that unfortunate things sometimes happened, over and above deaths from intoxication at The Chisholm's funeral and people falling into the vault at a Lovat burial.

Towards the middle of the 19th century the change from lavish funerals to more solemn and sensible ones had affected great families as it had lesser ones. The 'judicious arrangements' at the funeral of MacDonnell of Glengarry have already been mentioned, and in 1833 the funeral of the Duke of Sutherland, although attended by an estimated ten thousand people, was notable for the absence of pomp and pageantry. His coffin was made by one of his own carpenters; women of his household and his estate sewed his shroud and although bread, meat and ale were provided on the day of burial, there was no whisky, something which set a valuable example. And so simplicity gradually came in.

Just occasionally, however, people of high position went to their graves in a less than splendid manner. One of these was the Earl of Traquair who died in 1659 and was so financially reduced that it is said that there was no mortcloth, just a black apron; no towels to move the body for kisting but leashes belonging to some gentlemen who were present; and even the grave had been dug two feet too short and there was a delay until it was enlarged.

Town Funerals

A s burghs grew in importance, so did funerals within them and especially those of civic dignitaries. Thus when Sir Archibald Muir died in 1703, having twice served as Provost of Edinburgh, the Council and Magistrates attended the burial 'in their formalities with the Mace and ane goun in mourning, as well as the Incorporation of Merchants and trades, and Ministers and faculties of the College, the Guard were drawn out with drums covered with black cloth and the City bells were tolled.'

Eight years later, in 1711, Edinburgh's Provost Adam Brown died in office and this time the Council decided that their last respects to him should be paid in a manner almost worthy of the nobility and ordered the following procession:

Eight town officers on the right and as many on the left of the magistrates, with their halberts in the funeral position.

Four batoners on the right and left of the honours.

4 Batoners to clear the way.
The Nobility and Gentry.
The citizens that are not in public office.
The constables in threes at a convenient distance among themselves, and from those that marched before, with their batons.
The ensigns and train bands by threes.
The Livtenants after the same manner.
The Captains likewise.
The Professors of the College in gowns.
The craftsmen of the Town Council in their gowns by twos.
The three Merchant Councillors in their gowns.
The old Magistrates in their robes.
The present magistrates in their robes.
The sword with the Lord Provost's mace on the right and the College mace on the left, all in black and to be carried the sword with the point to the ground and the maces hanging in the bearer's hands.
The Lord Provost's gown covered with black, carried by the Town's wardrop keeper.
The Corps.
The City Guard in a funeral pouster (posture).

A report of this funeral said that the Magistrates carried the corpse from the steps at the churchyard gate, in their robes, to the grave. 'And all the time the Citie Bells were tolled.' Not only did the Council order this imposing funeral but they spent £10. 4. 9½ on it.

When John Stivensone, Provost of Stirling, died there in 1703, the Treasurer was instructed to buy four 'mourning strings' as a symbol of grief. These were to be worn above their belts by the town officers on the day of the Provost's burial but it was particularly stated that they were to be returned to the Treasurer after the days of mourning were over and he was to be accountable for them, altogether a much more economical attitude than that of Edinburgh where, on another occasion, in 1701, the Council allowed £200 Scots, equivalent to £16. 13. 4 towards the expenses of the funeral of James Currie, their 'deceast late Provost', because of the many good services he had done for the town.

In some cases a town council might act as money lenders for a funeral, as in 1689 when Edinburgh's Burgh Treasurer was authorized to advance £10 stg. for the funeral of Mr William Annand, Dean of Edinburgh. Even Kirk Sessions, who buried the poor because they were obliged to do so, also helped on occasion with the burial of others by acting as a source of funds. In 1712 Inverness Kirk Session ordered their Treasurer 'to advance the sum of twenty shillings sterling for defraying the expenses of the deceased John Robertson, Dean of Guild officer, his funerals, and this to be repayed to the church Treasurer by the Representatives of the said Defunct when his debts are got in.' There is no mention of the interest which it was usual for a Kirk Session to charge on money out on loan.

As time went on, it became customary for burghs to be represented by their Magistrates at the burials of local notables. When bidden to such funerals it was normal for Magistrates to have a small entourage of suitable townspeople and they had the power to order a number of burgesses to accompany them. In Peebles in 1670 the Council decided that whenever such an occasion arose the Magistrates might order 'twenty persons of the ablest honest burgesses' to go with them, an order accompanied with the threat of half a crown to pay for failure to comply. In 1684 the number of 'substantial burgesses' was reduced to ten and the penalty became half a merk. This penalty was necessary because in spite of the fact that people enjoyed funerals, going to them in official attendance on the town's representatives was obviously not popular as the Burgh Records of Stirling make very plain. In 1634 the Dean of Guild there 'regretted the disobedience of the brethren that are warned to ride to burials with the Magistrates,' who failed to go even when the cost of hiring horses was paid for them and they were told that they must go whenever instructed to do so. Such attendance at these funerals was a drain on Burgh funds – Glasgow's Burgh records have an entry in August 1702 which shows that £72. 18. 4 Scots was paid to 'Thomas Sheills in Portglasgow spent at his house be the provost, baillies and dean of guild, with divers others of the inhabitants attending them, when attending Sir John Shaws burial in May last.'

When Bailies attended funerals officially, they were entitled to be accompanied by the Town Officer who attended them at courts. This was part of their job but it had its compensations – an account for the funeral of Lady Aldie in Ross and Cromarty in 1757 shows 'Two pints to the Town Officers for their attendance at the chaple when the Corps was a Burying.'

Craft guilds in towns also paid deference to local lairds and sent representatives to their burials and those of their families as well, as the Glasgow Weavers' accounts for 1672 show:

> At the laird of Balvies burriell 6/-.
> For ryding of the laird of Pollokis sones buriell £3. 6. 0. (Scots.)

While country funerals had much evidence of mourning, the inventory of funeral equipment in the Recorder's room at Edinburgh's St Cuthbert's Church in 1839 gives a good idea of the paraphernalia thought necessary for town funerals. It included a large press for holding 'Batonmen's Hates and Mutes' Mountings and Batons, 16 Batons with green baize covers, 2 Poles with black silk mountings for Mutes, 2 cloaks, 2 cocked and 2 flat hats, 12 velvet caps, a band box containing 12 white linen bands for Hats, 2 white silk rosettes, 4 white silk knots, 4 crape knots and 2 linen cravats. A box containing seven sets of black silk ribbons, 9 in each set; and 3 old sets. 5 sets of white silk ribbons, 9 in each set; and one set narrow ribbons, 9 in it, and 2 odd ones, and one set narrow ribbons, 8 in it.' some of those items were available for hire and in the two years 1843-5, ribbons brought in £3. 16/- stg. and weepers £4. 9/- stg., weepers being several things, including white linen bands round the mouth of sleeves of mourning dress or crape hat bands or anything hanging down.

Just as torches were a feature of some great funerals, so they became popular in burghs among those who could afford them. Restrictive practices appear in many funeral usages and this was one of them. In Edinburgh in 1682 the Council declared that if any corpse was laid in a town church with torches, then 'the good town's company was to be employed for carrying the said torches, this to be intimated to the beadles'. Later, in 1716, a man named Colin Haig who received from Edinburgh Burgh Council sole permission to deliver burial letters, was at the same time given the monopoly of employing people to stand with flambeaux and links (torches of pitch and tow) at the homes of the dead. What he might charge for these services was laid down by the Council: from 1st September to 1st April, for each man standing from 5-10 p.m. at night with 'flamboys' the cost was 8/-. During the rest of the year, the charge for each man standing from 8-10 p.m. was 6/-. Each man holding a link in the winter months was paid 7/-, and in the summer months 5/-, all the prices being in Scots money. The Council ordered that these people should have a black 'goun or coatt and cape' and instructed Colin Haig to notify his address in *The Courant* and also to put up a suitably worded board so that everyone should know where to find him.

The funerals of ordinary townspeople surely cannot have equalled those of people in similar circumstances in the country. Desperately cramped housing conditions cannot have been conducive to funeral hospitality and with no barn or extra space to put the mourners into, this important part of the proceedings must have been very limited but nevertheless the mort bell and mortcloth lent an air of dignity whatever the circumstances.

It was in towns rather than in rural areas that a royal death made most impact. On the death of the Duke of York in 1827, for instance, in Edinburgh, theatres and other places of amusement shut down on the day of the funeral, artillery fired minute guns between 3.00 and 4.00 p.m. on the ramparts, bells tolled and, as it was a dark January day, there was a real feeling of gloom. The Burgh Council recommended that all shops and warehouses should shut at four o'clock and stay shut for the rest of the day but thoughtfully added that those shop-keepers who really could not comply with this suggestion should just close their shutters, not their shops, 'without detriment to themselves or inconvenience to the public'. In Aberdeen, the death of George II in 1760 was marked by a mourning concert attended by many gentlemen and over one hundred ladies, all dressed in deep mourning. The concert was considered to be 'exquisitely good', and its anthems and solemn music very suitable to the occasion so that the audience were greatly satisfied. The press marked royal deaths with deep black edging to their newspapers and this too was something which made more impact in towns than in the countryside.

Handspokes and Hearses

W hether of high birth or low, some means had to be found to carry the corpse to the grave. For years, the bodies of the common people were taken there as best might be managed and just how this might be done is made plain in Edinburgh Burgh Records of 1585, an epidemic year, when it was ordered that corpses were no longer to be carried to burial on people's backs or on sledges, but on the bier. The word bier has two meanings, one of which as already said, is the common coffin. In its other meaning, it was a skeleton frame for carrying the corpse – two or three poles or a plank or two of wood on which the body was laid, coffined or uncoffined, and covered with the mortcloth. This frame was often referred to as handspokes or just spokes or spakes.

Although always basically the same, spokes had slight variations in different places. For instance, in the west where there were long distances to cover, the coffin was placed on a platform of two planks which were nailed at right angles to three spokes. The middle spoke was longer than the other two so that the bearers did not trip on those in front. The ends of the spokes were always shaped for comfortable handling; although a memory from Benbecula is of iron handles projecting from the sides, this was not usual.

An account of burials in South Uist says the coffin was kept in place on the platform by pieces of wood skilfully nailed in as wedges, but a living memory from Harris says that the spokes used there were three loose spars on which the coffin was laid, with nothing to hold it in place, which sounds not only surprising but downright risky. Could it be that there *were* wedges but so neatly placed that they were not noticed? A fairly recent account of a funeral in Fair Isle tells of a coffin simply being lashed to two long poles below it.

Until about 1830 in the parish of Bonhill, Dunbartonshire, a couple of handspokes were used like a stretcher, carried by one of two men at each end. The number carrying might vary from two to eight – two or four were sufficient when carried stretcher-style; six were needed when there was a man at each end of three poles; while two men at each end of two poles required eight in all. A coffin on spokes was normally carried at hand height. It was not usual to use spokes at all if it was carried on men's shoulders although sometimes staves were slipped in to make matters easier. Handspokes were usually available for hire from Kirk Sessions. In country areas they were often stored somewhere along with the mortcloth while in a large town parish the number and variety of sizes frequently justified storing them in a special place such as an 'under-apartment' at St Cuthbert's Church, Edinburgh, where there were no less than twenty-five sets in 1839.

Sometimes a bier was referred to as a litter, a word which appears in the records of the parish of Channelkirk, Berwickshire, where in 1706 a litter cost £1. 6/- Scots to make, and where in 1755 it was stated that the charge of 2/9 stg. for the smaller mortcloth included use of the litter, presumably a convenient all-in price. The Kirk Session records of Melrose, Roxburghshire, also show a joint charge for the mortcloth – the best one, however – and the litter of 8/4 stg. in 1757. A different type of litter was the kind carried between two horses and known in the Highlands as 'carbad', a word later often applied to the coffin. In some cases the coffin was laid on a frame across the backs of two horses which walked side by side.

Many a graveyard still has a bier somewhere about it, used for carrying the coffin from hearse to grave, but these are different to the earlier ones and look for all the world like ladders. One at the small church of Cille Choireill near Murlaggan in Inverness-shire, is about ten feet long with a notch in one of the cross spars to hold the head of the coffin and holes at the other end where pegs can be inserted to hold all in place.

Gradually, and certainly before the turn of the 18th century, horse-drawn hearses were introduced where it was practical, and profitable, to have them, although at the outset they were beyond the reach of ordinary people. In Edinburgh Burgh Records in 1691 there is a reference to children's corpses being carried to burial in coaches, perhaps because the funerals of children were seldom given as much prominence as those of adults, but possibly as a way of avoiding the hire of a hearse. In the Highlands there was a bias against hearses. Even in the first quarter of the 19th century in many rural areas, even if available they were little used except by the well-off or when a death occurred at a considerable distance from the graveyard. Sometimes provision of a hearse was part of a benevolent scheme. At the end of the 18th century, the philanthropic farmers of the parish of St Andrews, Fife, who have already been mentioned as providing a mortcloth for the 'encouragement' of their schoolmaster, also acquired a hearse to be hired out for the same worthy purpose.

A hearse could bring in money just as well as a mortcloth, something which did not escape the attention of the church and many Kirk Sessions obtained hearses for the benefit of the poor and parish hearse-houses are still to be seen attached to or within church grounds. The Kirk Session at Kirkliston, West Lothian, had a fine hearse, fairly high and with a yellow body. It was made in Edinburgh and presented to the parish by the Earl of Hopetoun but unfortunately it has not survived. The parish of Bolton, East Lothian, acquired its first hearse in 1723. Its cost is not known but a set of harness for it cost the Kirk Session £19. 10/- Scots in 1744, plus £1. 4/- Scots to the man who fetched it. The income from this hearse varied from year to year depending on how many well-to-do people died. What it brought in in 1744 was £14. 6/- Scots. It was apparently used only three times that year – for a three-mile journey £2. 4/- Scots was paid, for going to Edinburgh and back £11. 4/- Scots, the balance of the sum coming from the third trip. In that year, church income included about £60 Scots from collections and about £20 Scots from mortcloth and bells. The following year, the mortcloth and bells realized about £46 while the hearse income rose sharply to £42. The position changed in 1746 when mortcloth and bells brought in £49 Scots but the hearse only £15 Scots. The hearse may well have been hired by non-parishioners as well as, quite apart from going to Edinburgh, it went to Humbie, 'to Haddington and thence to Giffard', and elsewhere, all still within the country of East Lothian but outside the parish of Bolton.

In 1783 the heritors decided that a 'new fashionable hearse' should be bought and to pay for it called in money out on loan to an Edinburgh firm of merchants. The old hearse was sold and the cost of the new one, including some alterations to the hearse house and other expenses came 'upon the whole' to £39. 13. 2 stg. In fact, the hearse itself cost £37. 14/-stg. Even allowing for the change in the value of money, it is astonishing that this elegant vehicle, which is preserved in the Royal Scottish Museum, should have cost so little. Fashionable is certainly the word for it; indeed, it seems positively un-Scottish in its elegance while its elaborate top looks distinctly eastern. Its sides are black and painted on them in muted colours are two of the symbols of mortality – skulls and hour-glasses – with the words *Memento Mori* ('Remember you must die') and *Hora fugit* ('The hour flies'). In addition there is 'tearing' which, strangely, goes unremarked in the written description given alongside the hearse. Uprights around it sides are yellow – could this apparently surprising choice of colour, the colour also of the Kirkliston hearse, have had anything to do with the belief that yellow is obnoxious to evil spirits? Although described as new, this hearse was fitted to an undercarriage which may date from the mid-17th century which would make it the oldest surviving wheeled vehicle in Scotland. The body has been extended from about six feet to eight feet which may indicate that people were growing in stature and needed longer coffins; it might even suggest that they were using coffins instead of being buried without them. What seems particularly surprising is that something so splendid was built in 1783, a time of desperate famine in Scotland as a whole, but perhaps the reason was that, like the mortcloth, it was important to keep up standards to ensure profitable hiring.

The cost of hiring this particular hearse was 10/- stg. per mile when two horses were used and 12/- stg. per mile for four horses, money which went to the poor. In addition, each time that the hearse went out its keeper received 1/- for himself, with a further 2d. stg. a mile if he actually had to go with it. Immediately it came into use, income from it increased. In 1784 it brought in £8 stg. as against £4+ stg. for collections and £1+ for mortcloths, but at 10/- or 12/- stg. per mile that did not indicate much distance covered nor many hirings. Only the best-off could have afforded it, possibly few besides the heritors, and in December that year the charges were reduced by 2/- on the first mile, to 8/- and 10/- stg. respectively.

The horse hearse encouraged the development of businesses entirely devoted to funeral undertaking. One was established in Edinburgh in 1820 and at one point had over three hundred horses, with twenty hearses and a hundred carriages, an indication of the popularity of this easier form of transport for the deceased.

In 1883 a Dundee undertaker named David Bell made the funeral arrangements for a Mrs Brown. A hearse and two horses, a mourning coach with two more horses, and two one-horse carriages from house to graveyard cost £1. 19/- stg. This seems little enough but Rev. Andrew Edgar who wrote *Old Church Life in Scotland* in 1886 complained that in spite of the big improvements in the conduct of funerals – no drinking or smoking, no monstrous luncheons nor Bacchanalian 'dergy' afterwards, no unnecessary delays before the lifting – yet a new and undesirable feature had come in. 'Ever-changing fashion has introduced at burials, through the use of hearses, a new element of expense which many people can ill afford.' He suggested that there should be a new form of bier, set on wheels, which would save the cost of a hearse; failing this, he thought that Parochial Boards might be empowered by law to provide a hearse for their parishes at a rate which would cover the cost of the horse hire. But fashion prevailed and horse hearses continued.

In towns, where there was a demand for elegant transport, stables quickly learnt the value of keeping good black horses. Hotels and inns, which often had horses for hire and for meeting guests at the railway station, also realized the benefit of having black horses and it became by no means uncommon for them to keep a hearse as well. Fine black horses with black plumes on their heads and black pompoms on their bridles, driven by a man who in all probability wore a black frock coat and lum hat, made an impressive town turn-out for a funeral.

This 'new element of expense' which went on as long as horse-drawn hearses continued and of which Mr Edgar complained was fortunately one that could be got round by those unable to hire an expensive parish hearse such as that at Bolton, nor those provided by undertakers. There was no compulsion to use any particular hearse and so in many areas people banded together in community co-operatives to provide one of their own for their subscribers. One such was in Selkirkshire where the Caddonfoot Hearse Company was founded in 1854 to provide a hearse for members in an area of some half a dozen parishes. The hearse was housed in a wooden building near the Post Office.

There was a hearse society in Midlem, Roxburghshire, and people there still remember the book which listed the subscribers' shillings paid in so that they and their families might ultimately be entitled to a ride in the hearse. The 'pall hoose' where it was kept is still there, not at or in any churchyard, but next to the smithy. Though not as handsome as the Bolton hearse, this one was a smart black two-wheeled vehicle, with glass sides and a domed top with a black wooden ball on top of each of the four corners and black streamers hanging down at intervals all around it. A set of harness was kept in the 'pall hoose' but as people often used their own horse or borrowed a neighbour's, the official harness was seldom required. The rural hearse was smart but the same could not always be said for the horse pulling it. Not far away, at Ancrum, also in Roxburghshire, there was a two-wheeled hearse whose canopy was draped with black cloth for funerals. When not in use, it was kept in a building, part of which was a lodging house for vagrants. Still in the same county, the hearse in Lilliesleaf was just a black painted four-wheeled float, flat apart from a seat at the front; the coffin was simply placed on the flat part. Into the 1920s this hearse was driven by the man who sold milk round the village. It was pulled by his dun-coloured milk-cart pony with hooves specially blackened for the occasion and head bedecked with a black plume while the milkman himself turned out in a black coat and bowler hat. Still further west, at Keir near Thornhill, Dumfriess-shire, there was a handsome black hearse with glass sides and 'toories' on top.

These instances all come from the south of Scotland but in general, where the terrain made a hearse practical and people were prepared to organize a hearse society, there probably was a horse hearse. Even on the island of Sanday in Orkney there was a hearse-house so there must have been a horse-drawn hearse.

By the 1920s to 1930s, as motor hearses began to be used, neither horse hearses nor the houses where they were stored were any longer required. At Midlem the hearse was broken up about 1930 and the hearse-house taken over by the adjacent smithy. The Keir hearse-house which stood in a field some two hundred yards from the road suffered a singular decline – for some time it was used for keeping chinchilla rabbits. Similar fates overtook most of these non-church hearse-houses and children were thus deprived of the delicious horror of peering into them and then fleeing in terror.

Where there was no hearse, a horse and farm cart carried many a coffin to the graveyard. A Shetland memory of the 1920s tells of an ad hoc hearse, improvised by using a cart and Shetland pony. Because a pony cart was too small to take the coffin inside, spokes were laid upon its sides and the coffin placed on top of these, a very eye-catching sight. But not everyone there had access to a pony trained to the cart, nor to a cart, and very often in Shetland a boat was the hearse for part of the journey – it was far easier to row perhaps two or three hundred yards across a voe than to carry a coffin two or three miles round it.

There were places, of course, where there never was a horse hearse and funeral transport went from being man-borne to motor conveyance. In country districts, to start with, the motor hearse was often provided by a local garage; in fact, the transport might not be a hearse at all, just a lorry with no refinements or a lorry which could be adapted for this special role. At Ettrick Bridgend, Selkirkshire, for instance, about the 1930s, a special black hearse body was fitted on to an ordinary lorry for funerals, just as stock sides are put on for carrying animals. But in time, any such improvisations gave way to proper hearses nearly everywhere and towns made even greater progress. By 1960 the Edinburgh undertakers who have already been mentioned as starting operations in 1820, had five motor hearses and twelve motor cars. Another Edinburgh firm, established in 1851 with two horse hearses, eight horses and four carriages, by 1960 had six motor hearses, fourteen cars and a staff of fifteen undertakers, twelve chauffeurs and eight coffin-makers. In 1980, on the mainland of Orkney, *The Orcadian* reported the Golden Jubilee of their Rolls Royce hearse – yet on another Orkney island, Sanday, in the 1970s, the mini-bus which took the children to school could be adapted as a hearse when occasion required.

In a walking funeral the procession usually went ahead of the coffin so that the change of bearers could be easily accomplished but, when a hearse is used, the cortège follows behind. If the distance is not far, mourners follow on foot; but it used to be regarded as a mark of respect for the owners of carriages to allow them to follow the procession. If the distance was long, mourners entered their transport after walking some little way and followed in greater comfort. In Caithness, till recently and perhaps even now, it was the custom to 'walk a farmer off his ground' – in other words, to walk behind the coffin until they were off his property before entering cars. And, of course, walking funerals still continue if circumstances permit. Even in towns motor-hearses were at first followed by mourners on foot.

There are many living memories and stories of horse-hearse days. There is the story of the notorious Prince Robert, of the Yetholm gypsies, who got a lift in a horse-hearse returning from a funeral in Berwickshire. There was no room up front so he got inside the glass-sided compartment and lay down. At one point he wanted to know the time so, seeing a woman in a field, he sat up and called out to inquire, causing her immediate collapse. And there are some people, one of whom eventually became a Member of Parliament, who remember how as children they whooped and shouted as a hearse passed to make the horses bolt, with consequent consternation. They even remember that the beating they got was worth it.

Graveyards

T he development of formal graveyards as we know them today – 'God's acre' was the name sometimes given to them – seems to have originated with the division of the country into parishes by Alexander I (1107-24) and David I (1124-53). Norman and Saxon nobles who came to Scotland with grants of land from these two Scottish kings, brought with them the custom of dedicating a piece of land for religious purposes and it became common for the lord or laird to build a church or chapel on his property for himself, his household and his people, and to gift it to some religious foundation. Consecration of these buildings seems to have been accepted simply because Mass was said in them. It became customary to establish a graveyard round these various churches and chapels which explains how several old examples may be found still in many parishes. They too were consecrated although, for many years after the Reformation, the Church of Scotland would not agree that churchyards were holy ground. They are regarded as such now and when new graveyards are laid out they are always consecrated.

Where several of these churches or chapels existed in one parish, ultimately that of the most important landowner became the parish church and churchyard, whether or not this was convenient to the local people, which explains the impractical siting of a number of country churches. It was because of these early gifts of land for church purposes that landowners, under the description of heritors, were entitled to preference in the choice of burying places for themselves and their families, often inside the church. Parishioners were entitled to be buried in the churchyard but non-parishioners required the consent of the heritors for this.

Burial in churchyards seems normal to us but it met with disapproval in some quarters. In 1590 a leader of the Brownists – a group which led to the English Congregationalists – wrote, 'Where learned you to burie in hallowed churches and churchyards, as though you had no fields to burie in? Methinks the churchyards, of all other places, should not be the convenientest for burial; it was a thing never used till Popery began; and it is neither comely nor wholesome.' In spite of that, it is understandable that people should feel that the environs of a church were the most fitting place for Christian burial, but there was a practical reason as well. It was the easiest means of ensuring publicity of burial and so gave society some protection against crime.

In towns, burial grounds also developed around churches but many of these, along with monastery buildings, were destroyed either during the Reformation or by English raiders. Such destruction, however, made land available for burial purposes. In large burghs, churchyards came under the authority of the Burgh Council and, as we have seen, the

Reformers were against burial in church. The Burgh Records of Edinburgh show that in 1561 a new burial ground was needed to avoid the 'savour and inconvenience' which might follow any more burials in the St Giles' churchyard in the 'heit of somer'. Queen Mary solved this problem by granting the gardens of Greyfriars Monastery to the town as a burial place 'in all time coming', and the old graveyard at St Giles was closed and ultimately disappeared under Parliament Hall after 1632.

The same thing happened elsewhere. In Dundee, for instance, where the church of St Clement had been ruined in English raids and its burial ground was needed for some other purpose, it was again Queen Mary who dealt with the matter in the same way as she had done in Edinburgh, by giving the town the lands and orchards of the former Greyfriars Monastery in Dundee as a burial ground, a graveyard still known as the 'Howff'. Dundee's former burying-ground must have been in as unsavoury a condition as that of St Giles because the licence given by the Queen referred to pest and infectious illnesses being engendered there and encouraged to continue, to the great hurt not only of the town of Dundee but of the whole realm as well.

Many people ask why there are so few memorials in churches or churchyards prior to the 17th century. The reason is that until then heritors had the right of burial inside the church and as they were the people who could afford memorials, it was into the church that these went, only to find that many were demolished at the Reformation. Ordinary people who buried outside the churchyard could not, for a long time, afford monuments. The practical effect of this was that the graveyard, empty of tombstones, was regarded as or at any rate used as a public open space. Landowners guarded their property so zealously that open space was very valuable to ordinary folk with none of their own. In towns such space was even more valuable, so that over and above being places for burials, graveyards were put to many different uses.

One of the earliest of these uses was for the 'wappenschaw', literally a weapon show. Defence was of such importance that there were compulsory periodic gatherings of the men of each district to see that each was properly armed and ready to take the field if required; and where better to hold these, in both town and country, than in the churchyard? The Scottish Parliament in 1457 provided not only for wappenschaws to be held four times a year but for archery practice to take place every Sunday at parish churches. Another use to which the churchyard was put is implicit in an early but undated ruling by the Parliament of Scotland which said, 'Courts may not be held in churches, cemeteries or in any other consecrated place.' Yet Thomas Kirke, writing in 1679, told of courts being held in churchyards at that date.

Because in many parishes, the church was the only public building, the churchyard was also used as a place of punishment. In 1593 Parliament ordered that prisons, stocks and irons for the punishment of idle begging vagabonds should be placed not only at head burghs and principal fair towns but also at parish kirks. Jougs can still be seen hanging outside a number of churches – they were used for a variety of offences, including ecclesiastical ones. Taking churchyard punishment even further, at Greenlaw, Berwickshire, a tower was built on to the present church about 1700 to serve as a gaol; it still stands there although a new gaol was erected elsewhere in 1824. This may sound surprising but in violent times neither church nor churchyard escaped. In 1592 Parliament deplored the fact that things had come to such a pitch that violence and blood-letting in church and churchyard were common during worship and they declared that anyone who committed a murder there and at that time would be declared rebel or fugitive and the king would have the power to confiscate their goods.

Though sometimes the scene of violence, the churchyard also gave protection from it. By an early ecclesiastical decree it was ruled that every church which had the right to baptize and bury, should also have the privilege of sanctuary. This extended originally to thirty paces around the church but in many cases stretched out far round church and churchyard, as at Tain and Applecross, both in Ross and Cromarty, where the area of safety was several miles in depth. Anyone fleeing there was safe and, in the old Biblical sense, those fleeing there from vengeance were thus given an opportunity to put their case. Another kindly, but much later, use of one particular graveyard occurred during the Highland Clearances. In 1845 almost ninety people, twenty-three of them under the age of ten, were evicted from their homes in Glencalvie in Ross and Cromarty and had to take shelter in the little churchyard of Croick, but not, of course, inside the church itself. They used such materials as they had to erect a sort of tent for themselves behind the church and left a permanent reminder of their presence there and the reason for it by scratching their names on the window glass.

Going back to earlier days, the churchyard was the regular site for many fairs and markets, often held on a Sunday. When crowds gathered at churches and monasteries in Roman Catholic days for religious festivals it was inevitable for them to sell goods, food and drink, and to enjoy some entertainment, under the shadow of church protection, and this continued after the Reformation. When people worked long hours for six days a week, going to church on the seventh was more than an opportunity for worship. It was a great meeting place too and provided an opportunity for business transactions which developed into full-scale trading. This was disapproved of by Parliament who in 1503 ordered that no markets or fairs were to be held in kirks or kirkyards, but this made little difference. At the beginning of the 17th century, the Presbytery of Ellon, Aberdeenshire, tried to take steps to stop Sunday markets at churches. The *Statistical Account* for Fordyce, Banffshire, written in the 1790s, mentions particularly that people then still alive could remember churchyard markets on Sundays. Sabbath trading in that particular churchyard was ended by the Rev. Alex. Gallie who ministered to the parish from 1684 to 1715. His method was simple. When he saw a bag of snuff offered for sale, he simply tossed it out of the churchyard but was fair enough to pay the would-be seller its cost.

The habit of Sunday trading, even if not in the graveyard, was tackled in the parish of Alyth, Perthshire, in 1675 when the merchants of the town had to appear before the Kirk Session and were made to promise not to sell any wares on Sundays between or after sermons, except for necessities. These necessities were specified as being for the sick or things to do with the 'bureing of the dead or such needful thing'; they included tobacco and bread, obviously for lykewakes. As late as 1782, Rev. John Bethune, minister of Dornoch, Sutherland, drew the attention of the heritors to the shocking state of the kirkyard which was 'without the least appearance of a fence and makes a part not only of the market place but of the common high road'.

Even at the beginning of the 19th century, markets were still held in some churchyards though not, it seems, on Sundays, and Dornoch was still one of these. Rev. Donald Sage who, as a boy, went to school there from 1801 to 1803, remembered the market stance in the churchyard, the only public square in the town. The merchants' canvas tents and booths were stretched over poles inserted well into the ground, even into graves and deep enough to reach coffins. Even to this day in this graveyard there is a large stone with a plaque attached to it, explaining that it was the Plaiden Ell – a tailor's measure – for measuring cloth at markets which were held there from mediaeval times.

The principle which led people to bury their dead around a church and to hold fairs under its protection, also encouraged them to build houses as close as possible to the churchyard. This could lead to a problem when back doors opened into the churchyard. A manuscript of 1777 shows that the heritors and parishioners of Kincardine O'Neill, Aberdeenshire, wanted markets removed from the churchyard but the customs belonged to Lord Forbes who naturally opposed the idea. Another opponent was a Mr Clark who leased houses in the village from Lord Forbes and sub-let them. Many of them were built against the churchyard fence and some had back doors into the churchyard to make it easier to sell refreshments to people at markets there. Mr Clark felt that if the markets were stopped his rents might fall.

The answer which the heritors and Kirk Session gave to these objections included a good description of the effect of a market in a churchyard. Because the rainy season had usually begun before the market was held, the ground was poached by horses' hooves and chapmen and others had no compunction about digging up 'fael' (turf) and sward for their stalls. The damage was considerable and the churchyard became very dirty. Digging up churchyard turf at market time was obviously a general problem. In 1638 the Kirk Session of Galston, Ayrshire, ordered that whoever 'delves or breaks the sward of the laigh kirkyard and common mercat place' should pay £5 to the Kirk Session, with whatever extra punishment they should order.

The old Scots word 'howff' means a meeting place, anything from an inn to a churchyard. Aberdeen Burgh Records in 1643 refer to St Nicholas churchyard there being made into 'the form of ane houff, for the more decent bureing of defunct persons'. Even without markets, the churchyard on Sundays was a great place for exchanging all the local news and gossip, 'worldly unnecessary vagging converse' as it was put by the Kirk Session of Nigg, Ross and Cromarty, in 1707, forgetting the social value of such get-togethers. The importance of the churchyard as a focal point in communities is clear from the fact that it was always on the church door or churchyard gate that public notices of any importance were displayed. Verbal announcements of lay importance were made in the churchyard too. There appears to be a note of pride in the *New Statistical Account* for Edinkillie, Morayshire, when it says, 'The practice of announcing sales etc. by the crier in the churchyard, upon the congregation retiring from church, has been quite discontinued.'

The churchyard was a gathering place for other purposes, too, and in towns graveyards often came to be the recognised meeting place of craft guilds. As early as 1576 the Bakers first used the Howff graveyard in Dundee, followed by other crafts, each using a different part of it. In 1581 the Agreement uniting the Nine Trades of Dundee into one was signed in the Howff and this new Convention also held its meetings there, gathering round a gravestone referred to in their minutes as 'the stone'. The use of the graveyard in this way was officially recognised and a yearly payment of £5. 12. 0 Scots made to the Town Council. The Incorporated Trades used it as a meeting place until 1776. And it was the same elsewhere with, for instance, the Kelso Glovers' Book reporting in 1650 that 'the traid convined in the kirkyeard'.

Some crafts did more than meet in graveyards, they made practical use of them too. It was not always easy to find space for bleachfields and an Act in the middle of the 16th century ordered that 'nane water their webbs in the kirkyard and if any be found therein the bellman cast them out'. In Kelso too, the skinners and glovers, after being debarred from using the Ana, found the churchyard a very good place for drying hides.

When sanitation was non-existent, a public open space had additional advantages to offer people and between 1681-9, the gravemakers of Greyfriars, Edinburgh, were forbidden by the Burgh Council to allow, as they had been doing, women and children 'to abuse the said kirkyard by filth and excrements'. Horses and cattle were being allowed to graze there too and they also defiled the graveyard. The gravemakers were ordered to report offenders for punishment as well as fining them 6/- Scots for each offence. The pasturing of animals in the graveyard was a major problem. The grass in country churchyards was the property of the heritors but it was customary for the minister's beasts to graze it in summer which also kept it under control so that access to church was easy. But even the minister's beasts could prove a nuisance – the Magistrates and Council of Peebles complained in 1773 that they had gone to great expense to build a stone and lime dyke round the old churchyard but when the minister's horses were put in, several of the monuments were 'wronged'.

In some places in the Highlands, to cut the churchyard vegetation was thought to be disrespectful to the dead. Could this have been, in fact, a legacy of the days when grazing was not only a good form of control but, being free, was something which was looked for by others than the minister? The dykes were usually poor so in animals went, encouraged by their owners, the result being summed up by the minister of Fordyce, Banffshire, who described the constant presence of animals in the churchyard as 'offensive to the feelings of those who come to bury their dead'.

The church tried hard to protect graveyards from these abuses as the records of many Kirk Sessions show. In 1634 the Kirk Session of Galston, Ayrshire, ordained that if 'anie hors or ky beis fund in the kirkyaird in tymes cuming (the kirk dyke being at the present sufficientlie bigit and made fenceable) they sall be keipit untill the awners thereof pay 20s toties quoties (as often as the offence occurred)', and in 1638 two parishioners appeared before the Kirk Session and 'purged themselffis of the horse being in the kirk yaird the last Saturday at night.' At the church of Fordyce, Banffshire, it was reported in 1684 that 'the kirkyard dykes are compassed with middens wherethrow beasts have free entres to the kirkyard . . .' These were the middens of houses alongside the churchyard dyke which enabled animals to climb over them and get in. This also happened at Rathven, Banffshire, in 1628 and was sufficient of a problem for the Kirk Session to decide to fine the owners of offending middens 40/- Scots each. This was a problem in many places but at Rathven it is possible that the middens were not the whole trouble as only two years later, in 1630, the report of the official Presbytery Visitation said, 'kirkyard dyke ruinous . . . hors and kye enter thereby'.

Townspeople often kept animals too and also grazed them in the graveyard. Indeed some went further and had stables there as well, something which the Kirk Session of Perth in 1587 had to forbid under threat of a fine of £10 Scots. Horses, cattle and sheep are all referred to in graveyards references in various Burgh Records. Time and again, the practice of grazing them in graveyards was forbidden, fines were laid down and damaged dykes ordered to be repaired but it was a long time before the practice died out. Even as late as 1822, sheep were being fed on turnips in the churchyard of Lauder, Berwickshire, and it was only when Lord Maitland informed the heritors of his disapproval that it was forbidden.

Parish schools, which were closely associated with the church until 1872, were sometimes in the church or adjacent to it and therefore in the churchyard, and this also was something which could bring animals into the kirkyard. At Ashkirk, Selkirkshire, in the late 16th century, some at any rate of the boys came to school on donkeys, with the result that the heritors had to ask the minister, Rev. John Hamilton, to ensure that'the laddies, when they attend school, keep their cuddies out of the churchyard'. Those laddies' offence was hamless enough but, between 1557 and 1571, the great gate east of the Kirk of St Giles in Edinburgh had to be closed to prevent laddies breaking the church windows and turning the churchyard into a playground – what is referred to as a 'symmer field'. Poor laddies – with the churchyard so widely used as a place of resort they must have felt hard done by. Elsewhere, however, things might be better for them – at Kincardine O'Neill, Aberdeenshire, a vacant area behind the church and within its dykes was the football field and known as the ball green.

Many of the graveyard abuses mentioned were summed up in the Kirk Session minutes of Mauchline, Ayrshire, in 1779, which said:

> By reason of the school kept in the church, by reason of many doors opening upon the churchyard and ready access to it from all quarters, it is altogether a thoroughfare and a place of rendezvous for all sorts of idle and disorderly persons, who break the windows of the church, break the tomb and grave stones, and deface the engravings thereon, and the complainers are sorry to add the churchyard is now become a sort of dunghill and common office-house for the whole town, a receptacle of all filthiness, so that one can scarce walk to church with clean feet.

All this made the maintenance of graveyards very difficult although there was no lack of legislation on the matter. Parliament passed a number of Acts in relation to graveyards in 1503, 1563 1597 and 1640. That of 1597 ordered that dykes of kirkyards should be built by the parishioners with stone and mortar to a height of two ells – 6½feet – with sufficient stiles and entries to give access to churchgoers. The *Statistical Account* for Bedrule, Roxburghshire, describes those dykes as being 'partly for ornament, partly as a preservative to the dead bodies from being digged up and devoured by beasts'.

The Act of 1640 provided for Presbyteries to appoint stent masters to tax the parishioners for the repair of kirkyards. This system had already been used locally to a certain extent as in 1634 the ministers and elders of Fordyce, Banffshire, after the Visitation which criticized their dykes, promised to 'stent the parochin' to repair them. But as so often happened in Scotland, Acts of Parliament did not achieve their aim and in spite of the threat of penalties and further legislation, there are many accounts from all around Scotland of the problems caused by inadequate churchyard dykes. One of these is from South Ronaldsay and Burray, Orkney, and describes the churchyard dykes in 1663 as 'failled and almost fallen, so that the beasts and swyne ar abusing and digging in the burrials of the dead'. In 1770 the General Assembly found it necessary to make a representation to Parliament saying that in many places ministers had no manses and some had to preach in the fields because their churches were ruinous. That being so, it is not surprising that churchyards were no better. Various fund-raising methods were used to repair churchyard dykes. At Fordyce, Banffshire, it was decided to sell trees in the churchyard, which had been valued to fifty-two merks, to improve the dykes. At Deskford, Banffshire, the penalties of delinquents, which normally went to the poor, helped to keep church and dykes in good repair while at Channelkirk, in 1804, an additional charge of 6d was added to the hire of mortcloths to maintain the church dyke.

Heritors, who had preference in the choice of burial places, also had obligations in the parish and ultimately the burden of keeping up churches fell on them, a form of tax paid no more willingly then than taxes are nowadays. The work was often poorly done and as most of the elders were likely to be tenants of the heritors, it was very difficult for them to put pressure on their lairds. 'How averse people must be to entering into law with the very people of whom they hold their lands,' said the *Statistical Account* for Bedrule, Roxburghshire, yet a strong minister could achieve much. It took Rev. William Auld only ten years to improve the disgraceful condition of the graveyard of Mauchline, which has already been described, but where such a driving force was lacking things were slow to improve and the churchyard of Fordyce, Banffshire, where animals got in via middens in the late 17th century, was still 'open to the intrusion of cattle' in 1816.

A further maintenance problem arose when graveyards were very near the sea. In 1612 the kirk of Gullane, East Lothian, was translated to Dirleton, not only because it was outside the parish because it was so close to the sea that both church and churchyard were constantly overblown with sand. At North Berwick, East Lothian, the 'Auld Kirk' burial ground was very near the shore and, year after year, was eroded in north-easterly storms, exposing the bones of the dead, bones which ultimately had to be removed and re-buried in another churchyard. Even now, a graveyard on the mainland of Shetland still has an erosion problem on the seaward side, leaving bones exposed; and there must be a number of other instances of this happening elsewhere. It was one thing to re-bury the bones of those long dead, as happened at North Berwick, but it was quite another to be the first to bury a dead body in a new graveyard, which made the opening of new burial places difficult, however necessary they might be. It is said that when one particular graveyard was closed and another opened to replace it on the coast of Aberdeenshire, nothing would persuade the people to bury their dead in the new one. It was only when the village schoolmaster thought to tell them that there were 'yird swine' in the old graveyard, producing a water rat to prove his point, that they willingly took their dead to the new burial place. The yird swine was a source of great fear to many Aberdeenshire folk. Just exactly what it was is not clear; some said it was half rat and half mole; some maintained that it was the grey rat which replaced the black rat but it was contended that the yird swine was here before the grey rat. Whatever it was or was not, it was mysterious and a source of dread because it was believed that shortly after any burial it would gnaw its way through the coffin to feed on the corpse and that this gnawing could be heard above ground.

In the country areas parishioners were entitled to burial in the parish graveyard but townspeople wishing their own particular burial place had to petition the Burgh Council for it and received it by Act of Council and, when circumstances justified it, permission was granted with a recommendation that something should be given to the poor. For instance in 1696, when an Edinburgh man was granted a piece of ground, thirteen feet by sixteen, in Greyfriars' churchyard, he was required to pay 300 merks to the Treasurer for the use of the poor, just as another man was advised to give 'a gratification to the poor in return for his licence' for a burying place there in 1693. The *New Statistical Account* for Colinton, now part of Edinburgh, reports a variation on this theme – two damask towels for baptisms were gifted to the church there by David Pitcairn of Dreghorn in 1706 on his getting a seat in the church and a burying ground assigned to him. Before the Reformation, of course, craft guilds in towns buried their dead either in their own chapels in churches or in the portion of the churchyard adjacent to their sittings.

Although country parishioners, as already said, were entitled to a place in the churchyard, those wanting a personal family plot received these 'by act of Session'. The Kirk Session minute book of Nigg, Ross and Cromarty, for 1810 to 1849 consists mainly of information on this subject. Written into it are certificates showing grants of burial plots from the Kirk Session to individuals, or from person to person, and also sales of such plots as anyone owning burial space could, in Nigg at any rate, sell it to others. About 1824 'two coffin rooms' as they were called, six feet square, were sold for £2. 5/- stg. and one eight feet long for £1. The various certificates of ownership of these plots give details of size, exact location and markings on stones. Transactions were signed by the people involved and witnessed by the Session Clerk and sometimes the Kirk Officer as well. Burial places were also bequeathed to others. Although sale of plots was allowed in Nigg, in the St Duthus churchyard at nearby Tain, the regulations drawn up in 1874 stated clearly, 'No purchaser shall be entitled to sell, assign, or sublet any of his lairs, nor for pecuniary or onerous considerations to inter any stranger therein.'

It meant a great deal to people to own a burial place of their own in a graveyard and it is understandable that disputes arose in earlier days when few graves had tombstones and most were not clearly marked. So graveyard plans became a necessity. The *Statistical Account* for Carluke, Lanarkshire, written in the 1790s, describes how this was done. Different lairs were ascertained by public advertisement, after which a plan was made and, beginning at a certain corner of the graveyard, each man's property was marked and described, with his name and number in order, and the plan was lodged with the parish clerk where anyone might see it.

Churches are usually so placed in the churchyard as to leave plenty of space to the south, although there are exceptions such as Hutton in Berwickshire and Penpont in Dumfriesshire. The south side of the church was the desirable one for burials and it is there that the oldest and most interesting stones are usually found. The north side of the churchyard was usually reserved for unfortunates of various categories. When burial charges for St Nicholas Church, Aberdeen, were fixed in 1647 the north side was appointed for 'the poor and their children who are not able to pay for their burials the prices set down', and this was the common custom. In Edinburgh it was ordained in 1704 that those who died in the Correction House should be buried to the north of the church. In 1699 a thief, tried by a Baron Court in a Highland glen, was hanged and thereafter buried at 'the back side of the kirk yard'. Not surprisingly, with these instances from various parts of the country, there was a prejudice about burying in certain parts of graveyards.

Many graveyards had a 'Ministers' Corner' for their pastors and, after the Disruption of 1843, space was provided for Free Church ministers too, but usually some way from those of the established church. There might also be a 'Strangers' Nook' and special ground for still-born children. Regulations from Edrom Church, Berwickshire, state that, 'One or more portions of the graveyard are to be set aside for foreigners or strangers, whose parish or settlement is at a great distance or cannot be ascertained'; and they too provided for these unfortunate little infants.

Gradually the deplorable condition of graveyards improved. To start with, if they were adequately enclosed that was enough but as time went on, things got steadily better although such changes did not always meet with approval. Robert Carruthers in his *Highland Notebook* of 1843 made it plain that he did not admire the innovation of flowers, evergreens and fine walks in graveyards which he thought conflicted with the old Scottish habits and feelings. But others did approve and Dean Ramsay, writing in 1871, said, 'Within the last few years, cemeteries and churchyards are now as carefully ornamented in Scotland as in England with shrubs, flowers, turf, gravel walks, headstones, crosses etc. in freestone, marble and granite; 'everlasting' wreaths in keeping with French sentiment, are placed over graves as an emblem of immortality and in several Edinburgh cemeteries I have seen these enclosed in glass shades.'

In 1855 the Burial Grounds (Scotland) Act was passed. This regulated the management of graveyards; it enabled local authorities to provide new burial grounds where any had to be closed, acquiring land by compulsion if necessary; it empowered them to buy private cemeteries or to use them by contract with the owners; they were allowed to make arrangements for conveying bodies to burying grounds and to provide places where corpses might be kept until burial. New burial grounds were undoubtedly needed by the mid-to-late 19th century. The wording of the Public Health (Scotland) Act 1867 almost smacks of the days when Queen Mary had to provide new burying grounds in Scottish towns. Under that Act it is a nuisance if any 'churchyard, cemetery or place of sepulture is so situated or so crowded with bodies, or otherwise so conducted as to be offensive or injurious to health'. Many old graveyards in both town and country have now been closed from sheer necessity.

There were amending Acts to the Burial Grounds (Scotland) Act from 1857 onwards, with major changes in 1929 and 1947. Now, although parish churches still belong to the General Trustees of the Church of Scotland, graveyards are controlled by District Councils. Maintenance is costly and some strange things have happened. Some graveyards have had their walls removed and access paths put through them, as at Kelso, Roxburghshire, where the graveyard is the main route from car park to shopping centre, and where children often play – 'a symmer field' or 'altogether a thoroughfare'. Others have been opened up almost as parks, with some of the gravestones, broken before or during operations, made into attractive paving around which seats are pleasantly placed for people to sit and chat – 'worldly and vagging converse'. Even the bleach-fields of older days have a reminder of a sort in washing seen hanging out to dry on a clothes-line at Turriff Church, Aberdeenshire, in 1982. In some places earth has been spread over flat gravestones and sown with grass so that mowing is made easier; at least one has the consolation of knowing that the stones, although invisible, still survive. Elsewhere, graveyards are kept locked up, often unsuccessfully, to prevent vandalism.

A visit to an old graveyard is still full of interest, quite apart from the gravestones in it. There are often special features to be found such as the Cholera Stone at Nigg, Ross and Cromarty; devices to foil body-snatchers; stiles, mounting blocks, stables, hearse houses and much else besides. There are various private burying grounds to be found. These are family ones in private grounds or at least in a special place. An unusual instance of this occurred at Gogar, in Corstorphine, Edinburgh. A small part of the church there was converted into a burying ground by Sir Robert Myreton of Gogar who had managed, in 1748, to obtain a feu from the Presbytery of not only the glebe but the churchyard as well, the whole amounting to four acres. This state of affairs continued until 1825 when the minister, discovering it to be illegal, raised an action against the then proprietor, Mr Ramsay of Barnton, and recovered the glebe and the churchyard for the parish.

There are also graveyards, often around their own churches, for those of different faiths and denominations, such as Roman Catholics, Episcopalians, Quakers and Jews. The desire to be buried with one's forefathers frequently meant burial in the family grave and long continuance of this practice has resulted, in the North and West Highlands, of some very humpy graves in very humpy graveyards, a rather surprising sight.

It may seem as if burial in a consecrated burying ground was always available. Sadly this was not so. In 1645 a supplication was made to Parliament by people in the parishes of Kelly and Dalry, Ayrshire, stating that the parish church was so remote that not only were they 'defrauded of the comfort of the Word and benefit of the Sacraments' but that many poor people were often buried in the fields because there was no one to carry their corpses the twelve miles to the churchyard. In fact, if no graveyard was accessible a body might have to be buried where convenient. Equally, the body of someone dying at sea was often buried at the nearest possible piece of land, possibly in the sand. In some Highland areas, bodies washed ashore were sometimes buried at high water mark in the belief that the sea would claim them and that therefore it would be risky to bring them further inland. However, Kirk Session records show that in many cases such corpses were given a normal pauper's funeral, in the graveyard and at the Kirk Session's expense.

Church Burial

It was the common folk who particularly benefitted from the development of graveyards because, for many years, people of consequence were virtually always buried inside the church, where earthen floors made this an easy matter. The right of heritors to choose a burial place arose, as has been said, from gifts of land many years before to religious houses; it was a right which meant a great deal to them. They bore many financial responsibilities in the parish, albeit unwillingly, and probably felt that burial inside the church was the least they were entitled to. It also had the advantage of separating them from the common throng, in death as in life. Craft guilds sometimes bought burial places inside churches for a number of their members, presumably their top men. The Edinburgh Hammermen, for instance, had ten such burial places by 1553.

Continual burials inside a church, especially if it were a small one, were not satisfactory, and in some parishes, not just the gentry, but all ranks were buried there, making the problem worse still. That was the case at Boleskine, Inverness-shire, where in 1684 the minister reported that so many had been buried there that some of the coffins were barely covered. The Kirk Session records of one Highland parish tell how 'the commons did commonly bury within the church so that the floor of the church was oppressive with dead bodies, and unripe bodies had of late been raised out of their graves to give place to others for want of room, which frequently occasions an unwholesome smell in the congregation, and may have very bade effects on the people while attending divine service.' The Kirk Session must have felt that the situation was beyond them as they decided, instead of doing anything about it themselves, to petition the Presbytery to 'put a stop to such a bade practice'. Much of the problem arose because graves were so shallow that bones stuck out of the floor and got in the way of worshippers' feet or were gnawed by the dogs which came to church with their masters. Churches became revolting – 'nauseating and unhealthful', as Mr Bethune, the new minister of Dornoch Cathedral, Sutherland, said in 1778 when he arrived there and found intra-mural burial still going on. Sunday church-going could be both unpleasant and unhealthy and the smell of decomposition inside churches was thought to be as much responsible for the fevers to which the people were prone as the insanitary conditions of their houses.

Things got to this pitch even although the General Assembly had realized very early on that burials inside churches were unsuitable and had forbidden the practice in 1576 under threat of excommunication. Burial in churches had also been condemned in the 1st Book of Discipline in 1560-61. In 1588 they repeated this prohibition saying that transgressors would have to make public repentance in addition to being suspended from benefits of the church and that any minister who gave his consent to such a burial would be 'suspended fra his functioun of the ministerie'. In yet another attempt to stop burials in churches, the General Assembly decided in 1597 to send a supplication to the next Parliament asking that every nobleman should 'beg ane Sepulture for himself and his awin familie', in other words, build a special aisle or vault for his own use. There cannot have been much improvement in the situation as in 1631 the Assembly again forbade intra-mural burial, ordering those guilty of doing so to be suspended from church benefits until they repented formally.

Yet again, in 1643, the Assembly ordained that no one 'of whatevery quality' should bury anyone within the body of any church where people met 'for hearing of the Word'. In a large church, such as St Michael's, Linlithgow, West Lothian, the word was heard sometimes in the chancel and sometimes in the nave throughout the 17th and 18th centuries and so long as burials were not taking place in the part being used for the time being for services, then that was all right, even although ultimately the whole church was 'filled with bones of the dead'. It was this kind of thing which made it possible in some places for graves to be found even under the pulpit.

The need for the General Assembly's prohibitions, repeated over many years, is proof yet again that making and enforcing regulations in Scotland were two different things. However, the suggestion of 1597 that noblemen should build themselves family sepultures outwith churches bore some fruit and gradually private vaults were built, such as those of the lairds of Barr and of Galston, Ayrshire, who craved permission in 1634 from the Kirk Session of Galston 'to bigg any ylle to the body of the Kirk for their burial places'. Subject to certain conditions, these lairds were each allowed to build such an aisle – really a vault with windows – behind their church seats. About the same time, James Lindsay of Belstane pledged himself to build 'ane yle for his awin buryall' when he appeared before the Presbytery of Lanark for burying his child in the Kirk of Carluke. Various vaults, fine tombs and enclosures appear in graveyards from the mid-1600s onwards, showing that some people of importance were prepared to move their burials out of the church.

Although the General Assembly disapproved strongly of burial inside churches, there must have been wide acceptance of the practice by the general public. How otherwise could there be so many reports of its long continuance? Although officially forbidden, churches still had special charges for such burials. The records of the church of Fordyce, Banffshire, for instance, show that in 1624 the charge for burial within the church was ten merks, and in 1711 and 1726 the cost of a lair there was £4 Scots, heritors of course being excluded from this.

Burgh records show that there too intra-mural burial was accepted. When Linlithgow Burgh Council in West Lothian fixed burial fees in 1694, the charge inside the church was 24/- Scots, as against 12/- Scots 'within the six quarters of the Kirk wall' and 6/- Scots in the rest of the churchyard.

The Records of the Burgh of Stirling in 1731 show that the Council was frequently asked for permission for burials in the West Church 'without any gratification being made' and it was decided that thenceforth no such privilege would be granted without first of all 'satisfying the Council'. If Linlithgow's charges are anything to go by, burials inside churches brought in more money and that was a prime consideration, but as with the mort bell and the mortcloth there seems to have sometimes been some difficulty in extracting payment which explains why, at Fordyce, Banffshire, in 1624 the Kirk Officer was forbidden to open the ground for a grave without first of all being paid. Another indication of acceptance of church burials at local level, is how slight were the actual penalties, in spite of anything that the General Assembly might say. One must remember, of course, that the average Kirk Session and Presbytery were more aware of the power of their own lairds than they were of a distant General Assembly.

An instance of such leniency appears in the case of John Mure, laird of Ancistoun, who appeared before the Presbytery of Lanark in 1625, confessing that he had taken the key of Symington Church from the minister in order to bury his father inside. He was simply dismissed with an admonition to 'abstain from all kirk burial in time coming'. It was this same Presbytery which did no more than censure James Lindsay of Belstane, who has already been mentioned, when he buried his child in the church, although they were more severe in 1639 with the laird of Shieldhill for 'forcibly entering the structure' of the Kirk of Quothquan in order to bury his wife. His use of force probably explained why his punishment was in accordance with the General Assembly's orders in 1631: he had to confess his guilt in public before the congregation. Each of these cases had been remitted by the Kirk Session to the Presbytery which could be an indication of the seriousness of the offence or merely an attempt by the Kirk Session to pass the buck. Interestingly enough, none of the General Assembly's penalties for church burial were nearly as severe as those for ante-nuptial fornication, for instance, which would have rated three appearances before the congregation at least, as well as a fine.

But it was not only lairds who used devious means to try to bury their dead in the church – even elders were not above doing so. It would be interesting to know the outcome of yet another case which came before the Presbytery of Lanark when a ruling elder 'wyled' the church key from the Kirk Officer by pretending that he had lost something in the church, but when he got inside he quickly made a grave and 'would no ways be stopped'. There is no doubt, however, about what happened to an elder in Lochbroom, Wester Ross, in 1650 who 'presumptuously avowed his resolution to bury in church'. He had to appear before the Presbytery during their Visitation to Lochbroom, was desposed from his office as an elder and ordered to appear again before the Presbytery in Dingwall, a distance of some forty-five miles over very difficult country, a journey which must have been a punishment in itself.

Not only were the penalties none too severe but sometimes lairds received co-operation not condemnation from the Kirk Session. In 1695 the Kirk Session of Kilmarnock, Ayrshire, made special efforts to help with the burial inside the church of the families of Rowallan, Craufordland and Grange. The North aisle being by then filled with pews, the Kirk Session agreed that when any member of these families required burial, the pews would be lifted and put back again at the expense of the Kirk Session. This was during the Seven Years' Famine so such generosity on the part of the Kirk Session seems strange but, as has already been noted, burials inside the church brought in more money; in addition it was the heritors who would have to be called on for additional help should the famine get worse, so it made sense to humour them. One reason for the local church attitude to all this may be that clergymen themselves liked to be buried inside the church – before the days of the Ministers' Corner in the graveyard – and it is said that in the isles, long after the practice ceased elsewhere, they still liked it for themselves.

As we have seen, Aberdeen Burgh Council briefly stopped intra-mural burials because allowing them had encouraged people to bring a variety of articles into the church which were inappropriate there. This was only one of various disadvantages to which church burials led, quite apart from health considerations. In 1686 it was found that people who had been allowed to bury their dead inside Greyfriars Church in Edinburgh had whitened or blackened much of the nearby church walls with mourning tears, giving the impression that they owned more burial space then they did, which could result in lack of room for other burials.

Another disadvantage of church burials was found by Mr Bethune, minister of Dornoch Cathedral in Sutherland. In 1782 he reported a shortage of seats in the church, not because people refused to build or buy them but due to the custom of 'the better sort' burying in the church. This caused frequent removal of seats with the result that instead of being neatly connected, they were detached and so took up more room than they needed, and therefore reduced the space available for other people to sit in church. Flooring was put in at Dornoch shortly after this and it seems that the introduction of proper flooring in place of bare earth put an end to intra-mural burial far more effectively than any directives from the General Assembly ever did, not only in Dornoch but elsewhere too.

Burial places in churches were frequently near or under the family pew which was often associated with a particular property in the district and this was something which may have resigned people to burial in the churchyard instead because, when property changed hands or changed tenants, the new occupiers did not wish to mix up their dead with the previous burials and so they were readier to obey the rules and move outside, where the introduction of gravestones must have greatly softened the blow. Even so, Glasgow Burgh Records show that when the crypt of St David's Church was completed in 1825, the Council fixed an upset price for burial places there which were to be sold by public roup, after advertisement in the press and on church doors.

Burial in, or at least alongside, churches is still available to those with old family connections and their own vaults.

Grave-making

T he making of graves was a matter which came under church or burgh supervision and these authorities very soon became aware of the importance to the community of proper burial of the dead. The General Assembly must have felt some qualms about how the poor were buried because, as early as 1563, they ordered that when any poor person died their immediate neighbours should carry them to burial and see that they were buried six feet underground – 'eirdit sax futt under ye eird', as the Assembly more graphically put it. In 1576 the Assembly not only forbade burial inside churches but also ordained that every parish should have a grave-digger (who also helped to keep a register of deaths), before which it must be assumed that people dug graves how and where they chose in the churchyard.

Large burghs were in the best position to carry out the General Assembly's instructions about grave-diggers. The Burgh of Edinburgh in 1581 appointed a Mr William Little to be Master of the Burial Place and ordered that neither the bellman nor anyone else might 'brek na earth nor mak graiffis thairintill' except as instructed by him. Three years later he was given four assistants and ordered to engage a grave-digger to put 'ane decent order' into the burial place. The rules for the grave-digger were carefully laid down. He had to make graves so many feet deep – unfortunately the actual depth is not given – and to do so in accordance with the 'device and rule' of William Little and his assistants. He had to fill up and level graves as they settled and to collect all human bones and gather all the stones from graves into one place, as well as keeping all doors and passages clear of filth. (Interestingly enough, the funeral accounts for the Dowager Duchess of Perth's funeral in 1773 include a payment of 10/6 stg. for 'cleaning the rubbish in the Abbey'.) For this work the Edinburgh grave-digger was to receive a quarter of the payment for each grave although this was phrased in more complicated terms: he was to be paid 2/- out of every grave that cost 8/- and of all those paying less, he was to have the fourth penny. Apart from paupers' graves, the other categories appear to have been based on size and depth.

The office of 'grave-maker', as it was often termed, was apparently desirable. In Glasgow in 1639 a merchant and a cordiner (shoemaker) both petitioned the Burgh Council for the post; in 1683 Edinburgh Burgh Council appointed a merchant burgess and a brewer to the job. The fact that two Edinburgh grave-makers were deposed in 1689 because they were not burgesses implied that the post was one of some standing and one cannot help wondering whether, in large burghs, some at least of the grave-makers were really grave-making contractors, taking the fee and sub-contracting the work, just as bellmen sometimes had others to do the ringing for them. An entry of 1598 in Edinburgh Burgh Records shows that the grave-maker was granted the profitable right of the custom of the sacks in the beer market in return for payment of forty shillings. He had to provide boards (tables) and was entitled to twopence out of each load. It may be that the office of grave-maker was purely coincidental but it may also be that the office of grave-maker entitled him to this privilege which would explain the desire of merchants and others to be grave-makers.

The job had other attractions as well. Not only did the grave-maker receive a proportion of the cost of each grave, he also got a proportion of other charges which could be levied, such as for providing staves and for turf to cover new graves. When a graveyard was used for markets and fairs, decent turf could well be in short supply and providing it seems, sometimes at least, to have developed into a kind of racket. This was something which Mauchline Kirk Session, Ayrshire, tried to end in 1796 by suggesting to the heritors that when they appointed a new grave-digger he should be told, among other things, to keep any turf and replace it after graves were dug, without charging extra for doing so.

Town grave-makers might have to ring the dead bell as well as dig a grave, yet another source of income. Prior to 1603, for instance, two Glasgow grave-makers shared equally in the fees for the dead bell. Sometimes corpses were laid in the church or Session House prior to burial, and here too there was something for the Kirk Officer, who was often a grave-maker too. Inverness Kirk Session ordered, about 1703, that these officials should receive 'half a dollar out of every corpse that shall be laid in the Session House, for their attendance upon the said corpse and friends therein concerned'. The usual ideas of funeral hospitality brought a bonus to the grave-digger too – the accounts for the burial of Lady Aldie in Ross and Cromarty in 1757 include 'a dram given to the Kirk Officer when making the grave'.

Grave-digging involved Sunday work, something which probably arose from a superstition about the desirability of making graves that day. Doing so must have been very distracting during time of worship – in Alyth, Perthshire, in 1650 the minister intimated an order from the Presbytery, 'that in time coming, when people shall burie their deid upon the Lord's day, they doe it timouslie; in the winter season before sermon, and in the simmer tyme after the afternoon sermon'.

Sunday burials were forbidden by the Presbytery of St Andrews, Fife, in 1643 unless permission was given by the minister and Kirk Session in cases of special need. Nevertheless they continued all around the country and it was only in June 1840 that St Cuthbert's Kirk Session, Edinburgh, forbade them, with a proviso that they could be permitted in special cases of need, such as when someone died on a Friday or Saturday and the disease or state of the body could be dangerous to the family if burial were delayed, and also where a large family lived in one room and would have to share it with the corpse. No funerals were to be allowed on these or other grounds where death took place before Friday.

Personal preference played a part in such things, of course, and the *New Statistical Account* for Edinkillie, Morayshire, said in 1842 with apparent pride that there had not been more than two instances of Sunday burials in the past five years. This is something which still shows diversity around the country. Regulations from the Burial Grounds Department, Duns, Berwickshire, in 1966 allowed for Saturday afternoon and Sunday burials at 100% extra for the latter but only 50% for the former. Regulations from Nithsdale District Council, Dumfriesshire, at present forbid burials after 11.00 a.m. on

1. The watchtower in St Cuthbert's Church graveyard, Edinburgh.

2. The solid metal mort safe at the door of Colinton Parish Church, Edinburgh

3. Grilled metal mort safes at Logierait, Perthshire, one of them a child's size

4. The morthouse at Crail, Fife

5. The circular morthouse at Cluny,
   Aberdeenshire, known as the Round House

6. The watchtower at Eckford, Roxburghshire

7. 'A Highland Funeral' by Sir James Guthrie.
   Painted in 1882 the painting depicts the funeral
   of a small boy in a rural community in Highland
   Perthshire
   (*Courtesy Glasgow Museums & Art Galleries*)

8. 'The Funeral of Thomas Carlyle' by Robert Weir Allan (*Courtesy Glasgow Museums & Art Galleries*)

9. The church bell hanging in a tree at Ewes, Dumfriesshire

10. A memorial cairn at Cille Choreill,
    near Roy Bridge

11. The hearse house at Edrom, Berwickshire

12. The Mort Cloth at Glasserton, Wigtownsh

13. The elaborate hearse (1783) belonging to the parish of Bolton, East Lothian
(*Courtesy of the Royal Scottish Museum*)

14. The Mort Bell at Linton, Roxburghshire (*Hector Innes*)

EXCLUSIVE

THREE AT A TIME!

HOW THEY CUT THE FUNERAL COSTS

THE MAIL CAMERAS CATCH THE COFFIN SWITCH

The new look Anne
IN COLOUR PAGE 10

Bill's Triple Crown
—Centre Pages

£2500 BINGO
—Page 29

■ The Sunday Mail can today reveal how funeral firms are boosting their profits on the sly. Coffins are being shuttled three to a hearse — unknown to the grieving relatives.

■ Two coffins are carried beneath the one on view and in between funerals the hearse is driven "round the corner" where the crew switch a coffin to the top.

■ Known in the trade as the "bunch finish" it means that undertakers have to make only one trip to their mortuary for up to three funerals or cremations.

■ One firm using this practice is the Co-op — the country's biggest funeral undertaker.

A DEAD GIVEAWAY—PAGE 7

● THE SWITCH between funerals ... Out of sight, a coffin is pulled from the secret compartment of a Co-op hearse and (right) is loaded on to the platform above.

PICTURES By RONNIE ANDERSON

15. The fascination with funeral customs persists to this day. The front page of *The Sunday Mail,* February 26 1984

Saturdays or on Sundays, yet in Shetland burials are allowed on Sundays and public holidays, with one funeral director making no extra charge for this.

On this subject, in the 17th century no grave was opened in Jura on a Friday, nor was anyone buried that day unless the grave had been opened before. Throughout Scotland, if a death occurred just before the New Year, the burial took place as soon as possible because it was thought uncanny to have a corpse in the house on New Year's Day. Where a burial took place inside a church which was floored, this required the grave-digger to lift and re-lay the paving, and once again extra money was required – for the Dowager Duchess of Perth's funeral in 1773 this work cost £1. 1/- stg.

The grave-digger was the servant of burgh or church and as such might find himself doing jobs totally unrelated to his proper work, but it all meant extra income. In Stirling in 1735 Duncan McLauchlen, the grave-maker, received £6 Scots from the Treasurer 'for his pains and trouble in putting on the magistrates' carpet and taking care of their books in the church of late'. In 1814, in Denny, Stirlingshire, there was a dispute over sittings when a new church was built. For five years no one had to pay for seats but they gave generously to the collection instead but, at the end of that time, seat rents were suddenly demanded. Those involved paid their rents but witheld collection money and for a while the heritors stood at the collection plates in an effort to shame them into payment. When the novelty wore off, however, they handed the duty over to the grave-digger, paying him 1/- stg. for doing so.

A certain standard of dress was expected of town grave-diggers and in 1841 the Recorder of St Cuthbert's Church, Edinburgh, asked various suppliers for estimates for four or five 'suits of black clothes for the men belonging to the burying-ground'. The trousers had to be lined with strong cotton cloth and they, with the waistcoat and coat, had to be made of a specified material and a pair of stout gaiters had to be provided as well.

It was in country districts that the grave-digger, under the style of beadle or Kirk Officer, came into his own. The beadle was a minor church official whose main duty was to attend the minister – 'the minister's man' – but who frequently was also grave-digger, bellman and custodian of mortcloths. He was used to working alone in church and churchyard and was usually a character. Many tales are told of beadles. James Henderson, beadle in Channelkirk, Berwickshire, for thirty-eight years beginning in 1793, is reputed to have answered a query as to how he was getting on with the reply, "Hoot, no ava; I haena buried a livin' sowl this sax weeks." A lad who spent much time with the beadle in one graveyard told the following story: the beadle greatly disapproved of any fancy food such as shop bread and on one occasion paused in his digging to lift out of the grave a singularly large human thigh bone. "Oh man, *he* wasna fed on cookies," he declared. And there was Jocky Blyth in Yetholm, Roxburghshire, who loved a lie-down in among the gravestones – secure in the knowledge that he could get up again.

The beadle held a definite position in the local community, a position which is evident in the records of the parish of Dornoch, Sutherland. Donald Macleod, one of two beadles there, became 'superannuated' and another man was appointed in his place on condition that he paid Donald 'half the sett salarie and emoluments of the said station', just as in 1689 an Edinburgh merchant took the post of keeper of the mortcloths even though it entailed paying what can only be called a pension to his predecessor. That a workman should be willing to hand over half his income rings strangely in modern ears but it is an indication of how highly a beadle was rated and how valuable was the job. Donald MacLeod, in fact, only lived for another year but when he died in 1722 the Kirk Session continued their special consideration by paying 4 merks for his coffin. Donald's original colleague must have been elderly too as, in 1724, the catechist was appointed to his job and the Kirk Session gave the old man a small sum for his lifetime. When the catechist died in 1737 he was buried at the Kirk Session's expense – the Treasurer's accounts show that £6. 9/- Scots was spent on 'Coffin, Linnen and Aquavitae etc. for the Interment of John Ross, Kirk Officer'. The funds of Kirk Sessions were meagre enough so this generosity clearly shows the special role of the beadle.

Another instance of a rather special attitude to a beadle comes in the Kirk Session records of Mauchline, Ayrshire, where in 1782, the beadle was taken to task for being drunk at a funeral but was let off with nothing more than a private rebuke. But if the offence was serious enough it could not go unpunished and in Edinburgh in 1683 two grave-makers were dismissed for opening a child's grave, breaking the coffin and putting the body into another grave. But others than grave-diggers might move already-buried bodies. At Nigg, Ross and Cromarty, in the latter years of the 19th century, a man felt that his mother had been buried in the wrong place and decided to put this right. He gathered some of his friends together and, considerably fortified at the local off-licence shop, they removed her body from one grave and put it in another.

However much the grave-digger was respected, paying for graves was expensive for people and thus attempts could be made to bypass him altogether: in the 1730s it was reported to the Kirk Session of Drainie and Lossiemouth, Morayshire, that several people had gone to the graveyard and dug graves themselves for the burial of their dead so as to avoid the grave-digger's fee and had, in the process, disturbed the burial places of others. The minister announced from the pulpit that if this happened again those concerned would be brought before the Sheriff and accused of 'disorderly walking'. In spite of the General Assembly's ruling in 1576, and in spite of the fact that most districts had grave-diggers, there were always some places where there was no regular person to dig graves. The reasons for this varied – perhaps because at times there was no one to fill the post; perhaps because in some large rural parishes with a number of graveyards, the beadle could not be expected to dig graves far afield. There was only one thing to do in these circumstances. The mourners, having carried the body to the graveyard, laid it down in the coffin on the ground and dug the grave themselves. In Bute in 1660 the custom of leaving the corpse lying on the ground while the grave was dug was considered very unseemly and the Kirk Session of Rothesay ordered that 'in time coming the grave be hocked before the corpse comes to the kirkyard, under pain of 40/-, to be paid by him whose duty the Session shall think it is to look after the deceased's burial'.

What was forbidden in Bute in the 1660s, however, continued wherever it was found necessary for nearly three hundred years. It was frequently not practical to dig the grave ahead of time and there are living memories, well into the 1930s and possibly later, of burials carried out without the assistance of a grave-digger. To many people, digging the grave, as well as filling it in and re-turfing it, was a duty they gladly carried out; it was natural and expected, and it was one reason why the chief mourner often thanked everyone for attending. With the best will in the world, of course, only two mourners could dig at a time; the rest had to wait their turn and everyone was only too ready to partake of the refreshments available afterwards.

Wherever possible people tried to have the grave dug ahead of the cortège's arrival. In a parish on the mainland of Shetland, one man dug a grave at night with his son holding a lantern for him, something done from the best of motives, but all sorts of stories flew round about lights and strange nocturnal goings-on in the graveyard, until people heard the truth of it. The *New Statistical Account* for the parish of Cross and Burness, Orkney, written in the 1840s, tells of a graveyard custom peculiar to that parish and not found in other parishes in Orkney. The next of kin was expected to throw the first spadeful of earth into the grave – 'it is regarded as a sacred duty and is not declined even by the most afflicted widow'.

Among the suggestions made in 1796 by the Mauchline Kirk Session in Ayrshire, to the heritors about the appointment of a new grave-digger, was one that when digging a grave he should collect all the human bones within it into one place and as soon as the body was interred, should put them into the grave again before filling it in. This system became common elsewhere when a grave was re-used. 'When a grave was ripe,' as the phrase was – which was about twenty years – the contents could be lifted temporarily put out of sight and then put back in the grave on top of the new coffin. There is a gruesome memory of this practice at a Shetland funeral in the 1920s when some of the very distinctively-coloured hair of the last person buried was accidentally left in the grave, visible to those mourners who stood closest to it.

A lazy grave-digger or do-it-yourself grave-digging could account for some of the very shallow graves formerly found in many churchyards, so shallow that those attending funerals were constantly faced with the 'loathsome and painful spectacle' of human bones cast up in grave-digging. The problem must have been even worse in Orkney, Shetland and the Hebrides where in some places graves were only one or two feet deep. But the principal reason for exposed remains was the habit of laying all the members of the same family, generation after generation, in the same grave and whatever regulations might be made about depth, they were of no avail while this custom persisted. The result was described in the 1870s by the minister of Duthil, Inverness-shire, who declared on oath in the Court of Session that he had seen in his own parish churchyard 'piles of coffins and heaps of human bones, sometimes with flesh on them, and that he had witnessed dogs bounding over the fence with some of these flesh-covered bones in their mouths'. The outstanding exception to shallow grave-making is the grave of William Henry Miller, laird of Craigentinny, Edinburgh, who died in 1848 leaving £20,000 stg. for a 'notable monument' to be raised over his grave which was forty feet deep and required eighty men to make it. The monument itself is known as the Craigentinny Marbles.

The Burial Grounds (Scotland) Act brought the force of authority into grave-digging as well as graveyards. Resulting regulations, dating from the 1860s, may still be seen on an inside wall of the old hearse house in the churchyard at Edrom, Berwickshire. These state that no body should be buried at less than five feet, except for infants who might be buried at four feet. Twenty years had to elapse before a grave might be re-opened unless the first body had been buried at seven feet or more, in which case the time might be less. If any bones were found, they were to be put in the bottom of the grave, so much more sensible than the custom of putting them on top of the next coffin. The intended depth of the grave had to be given to the Heritor's Clerk at the time of application for burial, and the development of humps was prevented by the order: 'The grave-digger shall not make any mound over the ground above the general surface and shall be bound to fill and beat in the soil as far as can be done and to carry away any other soil'. Even so, the conditions quoted at Duthil occurred some fifteen to twenty years after the passing of the Burial Grounds Act. Ground conditions can affect grave-digging, as when the soil is very sandy and falls in, or when it is very rocky as it is in a part of the graveyard at Tyrie, Aberdeenshire. There the grave-diggers get round the problem by digging graves before they are needed and temporarily filling them with sand.

Bodies are normally buried with feet to the east, a custom understood to have arisen because people believed that the Lord's second coming would be from the east and thus the dead would be facing the right way, ready to greet him; in parts of northern Scotland, however, graves have feet to the south.

Throughout the sheep-raising areas of Scotland there has been for years a special custom at shepherds' funerals. A little sheep's wool was dropped into the grave before the coffin was lowered, said to be either a symbol of the shepherd's life, or to show St Peter that the reason why the deceased had not been able to attend church regularly was because he had to look after the flock in his charge. This was done in the Borders in 1967 and possibly later than that in other areas. Graves do not necessarily require graveyards. One solitary grave is that of James Blaikie, a wright in Earlston, Berwickshire. While other people sometimes made advance preparations for their funerals with shrouds and coffins, he went farther and twenty-five years before his death in 1749, he dug his own grave alongside his cottage at Craigsford. He prepared his tombstone with wording which included his wish that it would put him in mind of 'death and eternity and the dreadful torments which the wicked endure'. He also made himself a coffin but unfortunately sold it and was very mortified on his deathbed to be without one. His gravestone may still be seen, in good condition, close to his cottage. Other isolated graves may be found in various places, such as the impressive graves of Covenanters in south-west Scotland.

Gravestones

Although some pre-Reformation gravestones may be found, both inside churches and out of them, memorials to the dead of that time were in many places largely swept away by the Reformers who considered that stones and paintings which commemorated the departed were 'images' and therefore Popish. In their view, the dead should have no monuments in the same way that they were denied funeral prayers and burial services. For a long time too, graveyards were free of gravestones because the common people who buried in them could not afford stones and, even if they could, it would have been considered presumptuous for them to have any. Furthermore, the Reformed attitude was that memorials in the graveyard were no more acceptable than in the church, which explains why an Edinburgh bailie was ordered to see to the removal of gravestones there in 1603 because 'na staynes aucht to be infixit or sett at ony graiffis in the burial yard'.

However, as burials of the more important people moved out of churches into the graveyard, so did memorials become more acceptable, even for the common people, and from the mid-17th century, although mainly from the end of it, gravestones are found which commemorate people in all walks of life. This may partly have been due to the Presbyterian attitude that all people, in theory at any rate, were equal in the sight of God and therefore equally entitled to a tangible monument in 'God's acre'. It was certainly in keeping with the innate wish of all people to preserve the memory of their loved ones in a material and lasting way.

Even so, it is difficult to believe a statement by Thomas Kirke who wrote an account of Scotland in 1679 in which he says that even the meanest person had to have a gravestone singing his praises, with Latin mottoes, even Greek ones, 'all in such miserable Scotch orthography that 'tis hard to distinguish one language from the other'. By no means everyone had gravestones at that date and surviving stones from then and earlier do not bear out his unkind comments on inscriptions while, in the north and north-west particularly, many stones not only lack inscriptions altogether but are also miserably small and thin. In the parish of Nigg, Ross and Cromarty, for instance, two hundred and fifty-two out of some five hundred and fourteen surviving stones have nothing more than initials and dates, or just one or the other, but certainly no Latin, no Greek and no praise for the dead.

The styles of memorials which had appeared inside churches came to be used outside. The slab in the floor became the flat stone in the graveyard; the monument set against the church wall became the headstone; the large tombs which often carried an effigy on top became, in the churchyard, the box tomb, altar stone or table stone, the latter, because it was a horizontal slab on pillars, sometimes called a 'four-poster'. Although theoretically equal in the graveyard, the 'better sort' were able to show their superior position after death by enclosing their tombstones within railings or in mausoleums, or by the sheer impressiveness of the stones themselves. The material from which memorials were made depended on what was available locally: sandstone in many places, granite in Aberdeen, slate in Ballachulish, iron as the iron industry developed. Wood was also used for memorials – indeed still is as a wooden cross at Laggan, Inverness-shire, shows – but early examples did not survive apart from a 'mort brod', literally a mort board or wooden memorial plaque which is still preserved in St Magnus Cathedral, Orkney. Preferences for certain styles of stones vary around the country, so much so that in Caithness for instance some graveyards and especially that at Halkirk, give the appearance of being paved, so many and so close together are the flat stones. In other graveyards the headstones are so numerous that one's initial reaction is 'Standing room only'. In much of Kirkcudbrightshire and Wigtownshire the gravestones are of red sandstone, and mainly headstones with virtually no carving on them. Elsewhere, however, there is usually a nice mix of styles.

Permission to erect gravestones had to be obtained from the Burgh Council, Kirk Session or heritors and had to be paid for, with a higher charge made for larger and more elaborate stones. The dues for a headstone, for instance, at Kirkliston, West Lothian, in the 1830s were 5/7½ stg. each. It was probably to avoid payment that people sometimes erected tombstones without permission, something which caused Edinburgh Burgh Council in 1718 to instruct their Dean of Guild to order the removal of all gravestones erected in Greyfriars churchyard without warrants by Acts of Council, and grave-makers and others were forbidden to allow any stones to be placed there without these warrants. In Edinburgh at any rate, a warrant 'for erecting and building tombs', meant what it said. Permission for a tomb carried with it the responsibility for erecting one and when it was found in 1696 that a number of people had not erected the monuments for which they had been granted ground, the Council was very displeased. Their attitude was made plain when, that year, they granted ground to a man in Greyfriars churchyard, 'he being obliged to erect a tomb thereupon within a year'.

Unauthorized erection of stones could lead to presumption of ownership of a burial plot and this had to be guarded against. In Stirling, for example, it was reported in 1640 that people had begun putting little stones at the head and at the foot of graves 'whereby in process of time they apprehend to have a property' – just like those who blackened or whitened the church walls – and naturally enough all such unauthorized stones were ordered to be removed. About the 1860s the regulations for Edrom churchyard, Berwickshire, included the order that 'No tombstone or erection shall be put in the yard without the sanction of the Heritor's Clerk and all inscriptions to be put on stones shall be in the first instance submitted to him.' At the present day, control of burial grounds is mostly in the hands of District Councils and it is from them that permission for the erection of tombstones must be obtained, with prices charged according to size, although no check is made for suitability of inscriptions.

Once a gravestone was erected, unofficial meddling with it was not tolerated. In 1875 when it was learnt from the grave-digger at Nigg, Ross and Cromarty, that someone proposed to replace an existing stone with a new one, this was forbidden. The authorities would allow a new stone to be put up; what they would not have was the removal of one already there. Inscriptions on stones were for those who could read; carvings upon them were visual aids at a time when few could do so. By showing skulls, bones, hour-glasses, coffins, sexton's tools and weapons of death, gravestones could remind the passer-by of his mortality and silently warn him to watch his step because it might be his turn next. They also cheered him with the prospect of immortality by showing angels, crowns, trumpets, plants and evergreens, as well as the Winged Soul, so often thought to be a cherub but actually representing the human soul arising. Trade symbols on gravestones show a family pride in craft skills; and some stones have carving which falls into no special category but which is still a fount of local history information.

It seems strange that Gaelic so seldom appears on mainland inscriptions when it was the spoken language of much of the Highlands of Scotland well into the latter part of the 19th century. Gaelic speakers, of course, tended to be the poorest people and the little stones of Nigg, Ross and Cromarty, for instance, might technically have been Gaelic but the people could not afford to have them fully inscribed. The reason could also be that the use of Gaelic was politically unpopular after 1745 when so much of traditional Highland life was suppressed. And fashion being what it is, it may have been thought smarter to use English.

Many gravestones were erected at unjustifiable expense but with a feeling of pride in thus honouring the dead and giving a focal point for the graveyard visits made by the family whenever possible. Even so, the number of burials in any graveyard is in no way reflected by the number of stones now visible. In many cases, one stone represents a whole family, and several generations of it; wooden memorials have disappeared; many stones are broken or overgrown; some have been grassed over and some removed. Nor are the people buried properly accounted for in inscriptions because many stones have no, or just minimal wording or lettering, while many people had no stones at all.

Just as people sometimes made advance preparations for other aspects of their own funerals, very rarely someone might prepare his own gravestone. One such was Alexander Campbell, a leader of the secession from the Presbyterian Church in 1787, who died in 1829 aged seventy-eight and is buried in the north-west corner of the old churchyard at Kilchattan on the island of Luing. His grave is embellished with not one but several slabs which he carved himself, one of which, in the boundary wall, describes his adherance to the Covenant and condemns the sin of body-snatching. It would be interesting to know why, in 1734, the Kirk Session of Kirkliston, West Lothian, paid for a headstone to be erected in the churchyard for a man named John Hill, at a cost of £3 Scots. Gravestones were not regarded by the Kirk Session as funeral necessities – could he perhaps have been a favoured beadle or possibly a Session Clerk?

Graveyards produce stories and superstitions. One of the most intriguing is that of the 'chin of MacMarquis' as the Gaelic name translates it, described in *Netherlorn, Argyllshire, and its Neighbourhood* by Patrick Gillies. A minister was buried below the crypt of the old parish church of Kilbrandon at Easdale, Argyllshire, with a large Latin-inscribed slab to mark the family burying place. An oddly-shaped piece of basalt, looking like a human chin, rests or rested on the slab, and was believed to turn towards a newly-made grave, remaining in that position until the next burial. It was said that should the 'chin' be removed it would always return and it is understood that although it has been stolen more than once, it was always ultimately found in its old place.

Everyone interested in gravestones will have their own particular favourites but a few deserve special mention. One of the simplest possible memorials – just a child's slate stuck in a cleft stick – is no longer in the churchyard of Glencorse, Midlothian, but in private hands. At the burial ground of Trostan, Caithness, two long smooth stones lie on one grave, quite different to any normal gravestones; the woman buried there had the reputation of a witch and these stones were put there to keep her down. At Farr in Sutherland there is this moving inscription: 'In memory of the unwearied kindness received by the Manse family from the neighbours during the last illness of Margaret Alice Mitchell, wife of J.M. Macgregor, minister of Farr', which is dated 1891. Laggan, Inverness-shire, has a modern stone with a Gaelic inscription with the English translation given below, a wonderful example of lyrically expressed emotion: 'Graceful, skilful, was your music on the pipe chanter, Sore is the pain of missing you.'

A large table-stone at Legerwood, Berwickshire, has surprising drinking scenes on the uprights supporting it. One shows a man astride a barrel with a jug in one hand and a bottle in the other; another shows a man with his head in his hands; while on the frieze above an angel sounds a trumpet. It is inconceivable that the family would have commissioned these carvings, nor the Kirk Session allowed them, were the man commemorated a drunkard, so it seems that they were placed there as a visual aid to temperance, a cautionary tale. The stone is right outside the church door, which makes this seem even more likely. At Cromarty, Ross and Cromarty, there is the gravestone of Sandy Wood, who just wanted a little justice. He felt that the outcome of a quarrel with his neighbour was unfair and instructed that he be buried outside the gate of St Regulus Chapel so that on Judgment Day he would have a headstart and be able to put the true facts to the Lord first of anyone. These details are not given on the stone, just the fact that he is buried outside the graveyard at his own request. In south-west Scotland the Covenanters' stones which are found in various places are a vivid reminder of people hunted like wild animals and done to death for their religious beliefs, a sad and sorry time.

There are some memorials which are not grave-stones but cairns – heaps of stones which are memorial cairns, not the 'resting cairns' which simply marked the refreshment stops of burial parties. There are some fine examples of memorial cairns at Murlaggan, Inverness-shire, one with a cross on top. However, cairns of a less well-made type were often erected to mark the spot where a death took place out of doors and everyone passing by was expected to add a stone. In Nigg, Ross and Cromarty, a childish memory of the early 1900s is of how a grandmother always made youngsters, when they passed a cairn, place a stone on it, and an earlier generation were told to spit on the stones first – a form of self-protection. A similar type of cairn lies by a track from Glen Clova in Angus to Spittal of Glenmuick in Aberdeenshire, a cairn which commemorates a man named Rorie and the fact of his dying, although nothing more is known about him.

Mourning Apparel & Keepsakes

I mportant occasions – and funerals *were* important to those concerned with them – were regarded as times for special dress, not to say dressing up. The greater the funeral, the more elaborate and expensive the clothing worn at it. As such, funerals gave opportunities for profiteering by those who provided fabrics. This did not escape the notice of James V; when his queen, Madelaine, died in 1537 public mourning was worn for the first time in Scotland, and the king wisely forbade the raising of prices of black velvet, satin, damask and all sorts of black cloth, as well as French, Flanders and Scottish cloth. However, the extravagance of dress, as well as entertainment, at great occasions was such that in 1621 the Scottish Parliament had to take steps to restrain such lavish expenditure by passing the Act anent Banquetting and Apparel, which has already been mentioned. This limited the number of mourning clothes for great funerals in proportion to the rank of the departed, while a further Act of 1681 ordered that mourning cloaks should not be worn at burials, nor at any other time.

Parliament obviously directed this Act at the highest in the land but there must have been similar feelings at a more local level against the wearing of mourning. In 1672 a Laird of Brodie, Moray, wrote in his diary that although he had not attended a particular funeral, he had heard that 'several honest men' had worn mourning for it. The laird's comment was that his 'heart did rise at it' and that for his own part he meant to lay aside all outward show of mourning at burials because he saw it 'prostituted' or hackneyed and debased by commonness. His comments obviously referred to mourners who were not members of the bereaved family because within the family circle, the wearing of mourning by all families who could afford it, came to be considered obligatory. For the funeral of the Laird of Balnagown, Ross and Cromarty, in 1·711, 'murnings' were fetched all the way from Edinburgh, for the family one supposes, while one of the servants was authorized to give out £291 Scots for more 'murnings', presumably for her fellow servants.

At the funeral in the mid-18th century of the widow of a minor landowner, mother of Dr Duncan Ross of Kindeace, Ross and Cromarty, the following materials for mourning wear were bought from James Rose, an Inverness merchant:

    5 yards of black cloth.
    6 yards tammy, a thin woollen fabric.
    10 yards mankie, a kind of cloth.
    15 yards Norwich crape, a stiffish thin silk fabric, usually dyed black.
    6 yards shalloon, a light woollen stuff for linings for coats.

2½ yards fustian, a coarse twilled fabric.
2 yards bukrum, for stiffening.
2 yards wedd (wadding.)
5 large chamois skins for lining breeches and pockets.

In addition, mourning buckles were supplied, an item which also appears in an account sent to the Laird of Newmore, Ross and Cromarty, in 1724.

When the Laird of Piltown, Ross and Cromarty, died in 1755 his widow ordered the following 'necessaries' for herself and, it seems, for other members of the family: there was black cloth 'weed', (widow's mourning wear) and a black flannel gown, two petticoats, two flannel aprons, a black velvet cape and hood, two short-gowns with six and a half yards 'cheque' lining, two black napkins, six shirts, six pairs of long riffled sleeves, six lawn hoods and six weepers which, as already said, could be several things – a widow's crape veil, white linen bands round the mouth of sleeves, crape hat bands, or anything which hung down. Her list included a scarlet cloth plaid which may seem a surprising garment for a funeral but, in fact, until the end of the 18th century, many women in country districts went to funerals wearing red plaids or cloaks. In the early 18th century, in the Lowlands, gentlewomen wore their brightest dresses and ornaments for these occasions.

Among items bought for the funeral of Lady Mey, also in Ross and Cromarty, in 1692, there were twelve ells of black ribbon which cost £6 Scots, and five ells of muslin. The ribbon may well have been used to make borders for handkerchiefs while the muslin could be used in the manner described by Mr William Brown in an account of Edinburgh life in the 18th century. So long as a bereaved family was wearing black, the nearest relatives not only put on weepers but fixed a long piece of muslin to their shirt collars which hung down in front. 'They continue this all the time they wear their first mourning,' he said, 'and sometimes the excess of their grief is in proportion to these pieces of muslin.'

An element of snobbery might creep into the wearing of mourning because if the deceased was someone of consequence, however remotely connected to the mourner, it gave pleasure to answer the question, "For whom do you mourn?" with the words, "My cousin, the laird of . . ." The etiquette of mourning wear was nowhere more closely observed than in populated areas and in towns particularly, where facilities for obtaining and displaying it were greater. The list of funeral equipment belonging to St Cuthbert's Church, Edinburgh, in 1839 which has already been described, shows a surprising amount of burial attire – cloaks, cocked and flat hats, velvet caps, white linen hat bands, white silk rosettes, knots of white silk and of crape, linen cravats and sets of black ribbons – some of which was available for hire.

At the time of bereavement, a widow wore a veil of black crape, nearly to her waist, which was gradually reduced in length until it was given up altogether, but otherwise she wore mourning for the rest of her life, unless she remarried. Even the headgear appropriate for widowhood was prescribed – for out of doors, a white cap under her bonnet, with white bonnet strings, and for indoors a cap with long streamers. Even young children wore mourning, sometimes relieving the sombreness of black with touches of white.

So far as men were concerned, right to the end of the 19th century, they wore weepers and a crape bow at the back of the hat for the funeral, tall hats and frock coats having come to be regarded as essentials. By around 1900, crape and weepers at funerals had largely died out, although black was worn. Once the funeral solemnities were over, black hatbands, black ties and black bands round the upper part of the left sleeve were all that was considered necessary to show to the world both grief and respect for the dead. The width of the arm band was anything from one to four inches, the wider the band the closer the relationship to the deceased. By the 1920s, these bands were a more uniform width and as time went on, they were replaced by a diamond-shaped piece of black material, about two inches long, sewn to the upper left sleeve.

Etiquette decreed what mourning should be worn and for how long after the deaths of various categories of relatives. Death of a parent required the wearing of mourning for two years, the second of which was without crape but still wearing black – known as half-mourning. When a brother or sister died, mourning was worn for one year. In time, half-mourning permitted women the use of discreet colours such as grey or mauve, but even so, with mortality very high, many people were never out of black.

Within limits, jewellery was allowed with mourning wear. The custom of having a memento by which to remember a dead relative goes back several hundred years and was widespread throughout Europe. It first became fashionable in Britain at the court of Charles I, when it was customary to wear a miniature portrait of the deceased in the form of a ring, brooch or pendant. A ring 'sett with ane littel diamond stone and inamblit (enamelled) within ane mortheid' which appeared in an Edinburgh testament in 1646 must have been an example of mourning jewellery. Some designs were not unlike the engravings put on top of burial letters with, for instance, weeping willows. The Victorian era saw the flowering of jewellery of sentiment, most of which was to do with mourning and, of course, Queen Victoria's mourning after the death of Prince Albert in 1861 made a great impact on national custom. Widows spent a long time wearing full or half-mourning and the only jewellery permitted during that time was made of black stones such as jet or onyx. The styles, however, were as diverse as they were abundant.

Sometimes some of the dead person's hair was kept so that when the need to wear mourning was over, the memory of the deceased could still be recalled by having this hair, intricately woven, sealed under the glass of a ring, brooch or pendant, or made into a hair picture. The practice of giving mourning jewellery to the widow or widower has become unfashionable in this country although it still persists in central and eastern parts of Europe. Not all keepsakes were as elegant as this nor, to modern ideas, so acceptable. In some places, the island of Mull for one, it was common for part of the shroud to be torn off at the funeral by one of the oldest women present and given to the chief mourner as a memento. Elsewhere, such as in Shetland, into this century, as the coffin was lowered into the grave, each pall bearer took out his knife and cut off the black tassel of the cord and kept it as a reminder of the dead person. Although these tassels were kept with respect, they were never out on display in a house but, even so, a childhood memory from Shetland is of being frightened to go into the room where such a tassel was known to be kept in a drawer, even although it could not be seen.

Etiquette also laid down the rules for visits of condolence in polite circles after a bereavement. By the 18th century, in large towns, anyone making their first visit to a house in mourning, wore mourning too. The instructions of Mrs Beeton, of *Household Management* fame, about such visits were that they should be paid within a week of the event which occasioned them or, if the acquaintance was only slight, immediately after the family first appeared at church. Mrs Beeton decreed that women visitors should be dressed in black silk or plain-coloured apparel, and a lady should send in her card, a mourning card of course. Black-edged cards and notepaper were part of the outward ritual of mourning and rather like men's black arm-bands, the width of the black border depended on nearness of relationship to the deceased.

All this, of course, was for those who could afford such things but there were plenty who could not. Taking Bathgate, West Lothian, as an example, a parish in the centre of Scotland, until about 1750 men there wore the same clothes for burials as they did for church, markets and weddings, and those were homespun suits of a freezed cloth called kelt, plaid stockings and blue or brown bonnets. By the 1790s, their best had become better with the availability of manufactured materials and plain black suits for the men became common. So far as the women were concerned, they also wore their best.

Until 1745, Highlanders did not lay aside their weapons for funerals and crape alone was used for male mourning. This re-started when Highland dress was once more allowed and at the funeral of MacDonell of Glengarry in 1828 the young chieftain who was chief mourner, wore full Highland dress with an eagle's feather in his bonnet, covered with crape. Daytime wear with nothing more than a black tie to denote mourning, is still proper dress for a Highland funeral, but for the simpler Highlander, who never reverted to the kilt, funeral garb was just his 'best' for much longer than in the Lowlands.

Things have now largely swung back to the wearing by everyone of their best for funerals, and formal mourning is hardly worn except by the undertaker and the minister; the wearing of mourning after a bereavement has now died out too.

Death Registration

U ntil the Registration of Births, Deaths and Marriages (Scotland) Act of 1855, death registration in Scotland was a haphazard affair. This was in spite of the fact that from the earliest days of the Reformation the General Assembly was aware that it was something desirable and necessary, something which they sought to accomplish at various times and by various agencies such as ministers and readers, grave-diggers, Kirk Sessions and Presbyteries; it was even a by-product of the Parliamentary Act anent Burying in Scots Linen.

In 1565 the 'commissars' of Edinburgh requested the General Assembly to order that every minister or reader should keep a register of all who died in their parishes and to send the information to the Procurator Fiscal. An excellent idea, but the reason behind the request was not what one might expect. It was so that 'pupills and creditors might not be defrauded,' pupils in this case meaning boys under fourteen years of age and girls under twelve. The Assembly replied that just at that moment, so soon after the Reformation, they could hardly expect this to be done by ministers who were barely settled in their work so nothing much came of this move.

It was in 1574 that two Senators of the College of Justice asked the General Assembly, in the name of the College, to request every parish reader to give in to their Superintendents annual lists of those dying in their parishes, these lists to be passed on to the General Assembly. This was agreed but two years later, in 1576, it was brought to the Assembly's notice that the Act was not being put into effect 'becaus manie understood not of it' and it was decided, in order that the Act might 'be universallie keeped and observed,' that every parish should have a grave-digger – described as a person 'to break the earth and to make sepultures' – part of whose work it would be to notify deaths to parish readers who would inform the Commissioners to the Assembly who would in turn report to the General Assembly. How effective this was may be judged from the fact that in the quarter century from 1575-1600 a total of only six parishes had begun keeping burial registers.

It was put to the General Assembly on the king's behalf in 1616 that every parish should be obliged to keep a register of baptisms – not births – marriages and deaths, to be given in to each Synod, in return for doing which ministers, their wives and their executors would be freed from payment of the normal charge for confirmation of their wills. Complying with this, the Assembly ordered all ministers to keep a 'perfyte and formall Register,' failing which they were threatened with suspension from the ministry. As a result of this, the total number of parishes with burial registers in the relevant quarter-century – 1600-25 – rose to only eighteen. Another attempt to enforce registrations of deaths came with the passing of the Act anent Burying in Scots Linen in 1686. Although this Act was designed for a commercial purpose, a side effect was to require all ministers to keep a register of burials, even if this was really 'for the better discovery of contraveners'. But even this was not effective and in the relevant 25-year period – 1675-1700 – the total number of parishes with death registers was one hundred and forty-nine. The following quarter-century –1700-25 – saw this figure increase to two hundred and thirty-nine. Things gradually improved and between 1725 and 1750 the number of burial registers went up to three hundred and thirty-six, something which may have been because of an increase in parish schools and the availability of schoolmasters to be Session Clerks. Even so, people were not keen to register deaths because it meant paying a fee and in 1746 the General Assembly found it necessary yet again to push the matter.

Although a few large burghs managed to keep good records, the Statistical Accounts of the 1790s frequently refer to the problem of burial and death registers. Very often the only way of counting the dead was by counting burials and this was difficult where parishes had more than one burying ground and furthermore it was inaccurate because people dying in one parish might be buried in another. Accounts for the hire of the mortcloth provided a form of death registration although it could cause duplication in cases where one cloth was hired, because it had to be, but another one was actually used; they were also inadequate because they omitted mention of young children for whom the mortcloth was not used and also left out dissenters and people of other denominations. Because of what was called 'inconveniency and loss' resulting from either no registers being kept or those that were kept being faulty, the General Assembly in 1816 enjoined Presbyteries to see that every parish kept three separate registers, one each for births – not baptisms this time – marriages and deaths. In this twenty-five year period, from 1800 to 1825, five hundred and seventy-five parishes had begun keeping burial registers but the General Assembly felt that this progess was not adequate and that year formed a committee to discuss the possibility of obtaining Government legislation on the matter.

Even so, nearly forty years passed before this was achieved and it is very probable that the introduction of the Poor Laws of 1845 made the lack of proper registers even more obvious and so contributed to the passing of an effective Act of Parliament to deal with this problem. This was the Registration of Births, Deaths and Marriages (Scotland) Act, which came into effect on 1st January 1855 and made it obligatory for all these events to be properly registered. A national system was introduced, centred on the General Registry Office in Register House, Edinburgh, under a Registrar General, with all expenses both of staff and equipment met by the Treasury.

At county level, administration of the Act was placed in the hands of the Sheriff, while at local level a Registrar was appointed for each parish or district. Where church records were already being kept, this was being done by the Session Clerk and a wise provision of the Act was that any Session Clerk in office at the date of the passing of the Act should become Registrar of the parish unless he was unfit or where his other duties were incompatible with the office. Where there was a vacancy for the post, it was to be filled by election by the Parochial Board and in the event of there being no such Board, by appointment of the heritors. It was to this local Registrar that all deaths, as well as births and marriages, had to be notified and to whom medical certificates of deaths and certificates of interments had to be produced. The Act also provided for the registration of the deaths of any Scots dying at sea.

Under this Act too, all existing parish registers, minutes and documents relating to registration of births, deaths and marriages prior to 1820 had to be sent to the Registrar General for preservation in the General Registry Office, and those between that date and January 1855 were to be handed over to the local Registrar. Where such registers were intermixed with other Kirk Session matters, as they often were, copies of the pertinent entries were to be made for the Registrar and the original left in its present custody, or vice versa. Similarly, registers of burials in private burial grounds might be retained by the owners up to the end of 1854, provided that correct copies were provided for the Registrar, but thereafter proprietors of private burial grounds had to register deaths in the Parochial Registers in the same way as everyone else. Various non-established churches continued to keep their own registers of baptisms, marriages and deaths.

Before the Act came into force, steps were taken to see that no one could claim ignorance about who the Registrar was. In November 1854, each Sheriff had to display on the doors of every known place of worship in the county for two successive Sundays a printed list of the names and addresses of every Registrar and Assistant Registrar of the county and burghs. The parish Registrars had either to live in or have a known place of work in the parish they served and have their names, with the words 'Registrar for the parish or District of . . .' exhibited conspicuously outside, on or near their door. When not in use, the Register Books and forms had to be kept locked in the Register Box – a strong 'Iron Box' supplied to each parish Registrar by the Registrar General, with two keys – no more than two – one for the Registrar and one for the Sheriff. Should the number of Register Books be too much for the boxes, then they had to be placed in a fireproof place, approved by the Sheriff, which had to be kept locked, just as the boxes were. All registrations are now efficiently handled but possibly there is a lack of local flavour – the *New Statistical Account* for Hawick, Roxburghshire, described how nicknames were passed down so much from father to son for many generations that even in the register of deaths, there was a faithful regard to soubriquets.

Executions

J udicial death was an ever-present part of the way of life in former times. The heritable right of 'pit and gallows' was held by nobles and lairds in rural areas until 1747, giving them till then absolute authority over their people, with the right to drown women wrong-doers and to hang male felons. In burghs, it was magistrates who exercised authority and it was there too that more formality and ceremonial was attached to executions.

Just as funerals were one of the people's pleasures, so were executions. The death penalty was in frequent use and with entertainments few and far between, attendance at an official killing was a great occasion. It was sure to bring everyone out and, in the case of a hanging, the more the victim struggled, the greater the watchers' delight. To be fair to them, their enjoyment was probably not so different to the horrified fascination which brings people to the scene of any major accident nowadays. The executioner's duty was to carry out all sentences passed. He was responsible for punishments such as lugging (cutting off an ear), scourging, branding and putting prisoners in the stocks; and of course for the death penalty. This meant drowning women in some cases, burning for witches, as well as beheading or hanging. He also applied torture until it was abolished by Parliament in 1689 because, without other evidence and for ordinary crimes, it was thought to be against the law.

Offenders of rank were given the privilege of beheading which was quick and merciful. It was for this purpose that the Magistrates of Edinburgh in 1564 paid £5 Scots for a 'tua-handit sword, to be usit for ane heiding sword' because their own beheading sword was worn out. An innovation was the Maiden, a beheading machine like the guillotine, which was introduced in 1565 and which executed at least one hundred and twenty people in Scotland before it ceased to be used in 1710. It is still to be seen in the Museum of Antiquities in Edinburgh.

Most criminals from the common ranks were hanged, explaining the executioner's nickname of 'Hangie', as opposed to the Devil who was 'Auld Hangie'. In early forms of hanging there was little drop so that the victim strangled slowly, sometimes with his relatives pulling on his legs to try to hasten death and put him out of his misery. Even so, it was possible for victims to be cut down unconscious and people were terrified of the prospect of reviving only to find themselves on the dissection table. As early as 1505 the Burgh Council of Edinburgh had agreed that once a year the surgeons and barbers of the town might have the body of a condemned man for dissection and for many years the executioner provided the anatomist with specimens, and press reports of a murderer's execution usually included the statement that the body was to go for dissection. The public, in spite of enjoying a public execution, did not like to think of bodies being humiliated in this way and would help relatives in attempts to protect them.

An extreme case of defending the body of a hanged man occurred after the execution at Perth of Charlie Graham, son of the leader of a band of gypsies from Lochgelly, Fife. His body was returned to the tribe who held a lykewake over it but when they heard a rumour that the body was to be removed from the grave for dissection, his wife quickly had it buried in hot lime and sat on the grave in a state of intoxication until his corpse was unfit for such use. Dissection of murderers' bodies was ended by the Anatomy Act of 1832 which ordered that henceforth they should be buried within the precincts of the prison where the penalty was carried out.

Each burgh or local jurisdiction had a regular place of execution, often at a junction of streets or at a cross-roads, or on an eminent site, but on occasions the deed was carried out elsewhere. There was a real determination on the part of the authorities to see that an execution made as deep an impression as possible so that it might act as a deterrent to any other would-be malefactors. In the 16th century, an Edinburgh man who not only failed to report a case of pestilence in his own home, as he should have done, but also went about among other people himself, was condemned to be hanged 'before his own door where he dwells'. In fact, the rope broke and he was banished instead. In another case, the execution in Berwickshire of the gypsy, Rob Scott, a double murderer, was carried out on a scaffold erected as near as possible to where the killing had been done.

It was considered desirable to wear suitable dress for going to the scaffold. In the case of Rob Scott, the gypsy, it was thought that his crime would be emphasized by sending him to his death in the clothes he had worn when he committed the murders. Although not strictly within the terms of this chapter, when a soldier was sentenced to be shot for desertion at Forres, Morayshire, about 1745, he was led out from the gaol to the gallow hill dressed in his grave clothes, to impress on others the enormity of his sin. He was reprieved, but tragically, too late to save his life.

A combination of black and white was in many cases regarded as the right colour scheme in which to meet one's end. A description by a Major Topham of an execution in 1774 at Edinburgh's Grassmarket, says that the criminal wore the 'usual outfit' for these occasions of a white waistcoat and breeches, bound with black ribbons, and a night cap tied with the same. A press report of 1827 describes how a Glasgow carter, hanged for strangling his illegitimate child, was dressed at his own request in a white cotton jacket and trousers, trimmed with black, but it seems as if convention had changed by that time because he had to insist on this style of dress in the face of repeated persuasion to wear a suit of black clothes. Margaret Wishart, executed in 1827 in Forfar, Angus, for the murder of her sister – although she insisted to the last that she was innocent – wore black relieved only by a white apron. Dr Pritchard, the Glasgow poisoner, who was the last person to be publicly executed in Scotland, in 1865, is said to have gone to his death in a very smart style – frock coat, top hat and patent leather shoes.

The imposing procession which accompanied a condemned person to the place of execution cannot have been necessary for security and can only have been ceremonial designed to serve as an example to the public. There was always a company of soldiers as a guard; the town officers in their uniforms and carrying halberds were on parade; then came the Magistrates and Council, followed by the criminal, with a bare neck round which the noose of the rope might already be hanging loosely, its end carried by the executioner who walked behind him, followed by 'respectable citizens'. Having reached the appointed spot, what can only be called a platform party of Magistrates, clergy, culprit and hangman, mounted the scaffold, which probably stood some twelve feet high. A psalm was sung and prayers were offered by the clergymen in attendance – if the victim were a woman, she would be allowed to sit during this part of the proceedings – and then it was not unusual for the condemned person to address the crowd.

A nineteen-year old, convicted of breaking into a tailor's shop, made an impressive speech to the spectators, beseeching them to beware of Sabbath-breaking, drinking and bad company, and thanked the Almighty that he and his companion had been allowed time for repentance. At an Aberdeen execution in 1824 the condemned man was on the scaffold for a good half-hour by the time the psalm had been sung, fervent prayer offered and he himself had addressed the people watching. When the victim was placed on the fatal drop all the crowd uncovered their heads. When the condemned person felt ready for the moment of truth it was customary for him or her to indicate this by dropping a handkerchief. Press reports usually mention the degree of death struggle shown and also comment on the behaviour of the crowd with phrases such as 'they behaved in the most becoming manner'.

Early burgh records show how the anxiety to make executions a deterrent made the aftermath even messier than the deed itself because, in order to exhibit heads, arms and legs of criminals on gibbets in the town, there was dismembering to be done. One result of this butchery appears in the Burgh records of Edinburgh in 1566 when it was decided to make a door for the gallows and to mend and heighten its dykes so that dogs could no longer get in to carry off carrion. Twenty years later, Edinburgh's Burgh Treasurer was required to see that 'bones dead corpses and all' were cleaned up at the old gallows, additional work for which the lokman (another name for the executioner) and his helpers were paid £4.10/- Scots. Little wonder, then, that the sight of a gallows with all its implications made a profound impact on everyday life and so one might be set up elsewhere than the usual place as a warning against specific malpractices. In Edinburgh, in 1583/4, a gibbet was erected at the straw-market outside the Nether Bow for 'staying of the bikkereris' (prevention of bickering), while in 1591 a gallows was put up at one end of the leper hospital there on which to hang anyone who violated the very severe rules of that institution, a dire threat indeed.

The pay of the executioner varied over the years. With additional perquisites it was 10 merks per annum in Edinburgh in 1536/7; £40 Scots there in 1593; 100 merks in 1605 and £100 Scots after 1608. In 1699 in Peebles the price of meal must have been high as the executioner was paid a peck of meal weekly until the price should fall below a merk when he would receive a merk weekly. In Inverness, he was paid £16 stg. per annum, plus £5 stg. for every execution, in 1812; and in Glasgow in 1843 the executioner's assistant received £50 stg. a year and one guinea for each execution. A bonus might come the executioner's way for specially good work such as 10/- Scots given to the Edinburgh executioner 'for his guid service' at the execution in the 1580s of a baker 'quha was brunt qwick', that is, burnt alive. At the execution in Edinburgh in 1591 of a woman who had murdered her own child, the executioner received 6/8 Scots to pay not only for ropes but for 'drynksylver for himself'. The same amount went to the executioner 'and his man' at a witchcraft execution about the same date. In 1797, £1. 14. 3 stg. was spent on entertainment of the executioner and his assistants after an execution at Paisley. Sometimes he was required to give his services elsewhere and this brought its own remuneration. Edinburgh Burgh records show that their man went several times to hangings at Dunfermline and there are entries which refer to his taking the 'buitts' – boots, an instrument of torture – to places such as Falkland.

When not occupied in carrying out sentences, however, the executioner was expected to do some other work. In Dunfermline in 1649 the Kirk Session ordered that the burgh executioner should keep 'beggaris from entering the kirkyard on Sundays' lest this might reduce the amount put into the collection plates. In 1843, the Glasgow executioner was required to work as a labourer under the Superintendent of works, although his services were confined to the public offices and gaol, such as carrying coal, putting on fires and cleaning the pavements in the vicinity. The Dundee executioner was provided with a barrow in 1591 and required to see that the streets and kirkyard were kept clean, but he benefitted by receiving the right to the 'fulzie' (dung and street sweepings), a valuable commodity in any town. He was also authorized to kill and appropriate any pigs he found within the burgh, all this in addition to the 2/8 Scots which he received weekly. In Edinburgh in 1593, the executioner was expected to keep the High Street clear of middens and keep out pigs. Very understandably, it was decreed that though he might carry his staff, his insignia, when doing this sort of work, he should not wear his official cloak. Later, in 1605, it was decreed that he might carry his sword as well, which makes it seem as if the job was administrative rather than practical and one can imagine the haste with which people would clean up around their houses and remove or conceal their pigs when ordered to do so by an armed executioner.

Every year an executioner received a uniform of town livery to be worn at executions and, in some towns, on Sundays too. The amount of clothing given varied from place to place but often it consisted of a coat, a doublet, a pair each of stockings and shoes, and a bonnet, all of which came in the 16th and 17th centuries to about £11 or £12 Scots. The standard of the executioner's dress was a matter of civic pride – for the execution of the Earl of Morton in Edinburgh in 1581, the Provost, Bailies and Council ordered that 'for the honour of the town' the executioner should have a new outfit of livery. When an assistant executioner was engaged in Glasgow in 1843, he was required to live quietly, soberly and regularly and not be absent from duty; he was also expected to serve the city 'all the days of his natural life'. Engagement of an executioner for life was formerly normal practice and probably explains the generous treatment shown to at least some lokmen when they were no longer able to carry out their duties. In 1593, when the Burgh of Edinburgh had to engage a new man, they allowed the old one his ordinary fee provided that he gave assistance to the new one whenever needed. The following year, over and above his fee, the old executioner was given a set of clothing of grey cloth, a shirt, and a pair each of stockings and shoes. It was a generous pension.

The term 'lokman' was often used for an executioner but not because he locked people up. It was because one of his perquisites was a 'lock' or handful of grain from every sack that came into the market place. Similarly, he was sometimes called a ladleman from having an iron ladle for the same purpose. These perquisites were very valuable, how valuable is obvious from Edinburgh burgh records which show that when dues from the meal market were taken from the executioner about the beginning of the 17th century, he was allowed 20 merks yearly in compensation. But in many places, additions to executioners' salaries continued and developed and it was astonishing just how much these could come to.

For instance, in Inverness, an executioner was appointed in 1812 with a salary of £16 stg. per annum, plus the following allowances: a house, bed and bedding; thirty-six peats weekly from the tacksman of Petty Customs; a bushel of coal out of every cargo of English coal imported to the town; a piece of coal, as large as he could carry, out of every cargo of Scotch coal; a peck of oatmeal out of every hundred bolls landed at the shore; a fish from every creel or basket of fish brought to the market; a penny for every sack of oatmeal sold at the market; a peck of salt out of every cargo; and every year he was provided with a suit, two shirts, two pairs of stockings, a hat and two pairs of shoes. As if this were not enough, he also levied blackmail in the shape of Christmas boxes.

He was paid in addition £5 stg. for every execution at which he presided but that was the one thing that cannot have brought him much of an income as his services were seldom required – by 1833, there had been just three executions during the twenty-one years since he took office. His pay and perquisites must have come to £50 to £60 a year, which worked out at between £350 and £420 for each execution. Admittedly, unsocial jobs tend to be well paid but this became too much for Inverness Town Council who decided in 1833 to dispense with the office altogether. The following year, a man was hanged for murder at Elgin, Moray, by the hangman from Dundee, at a charge of £12 stg. plus travelling expenses and the records of the burgh of Inverness, from where the hangman would otherwise have come, say: 'This plan of engaging executioners only when required and not for life, according to the ancient use and wont, will soon become general. It will be a great saving to the burgh and two or three hangmen will do for all Scotland,' which indicates that by that date the death penalty cannot have been as common as tends to be thought.

All this helps to explain the executioner's unpopularity. At a time of general poverty, he was well paid; when ordinary people had nothing for their old age, at the end of his working days he might well have a good pension. His perquisites must have been greatly resented, as must have been 9 merks of public money given to an Edinburgh lokman in 1593 'to bye ane goun to his wife'. He was a professional killer who also administered other brutal forms of punishment, like public scourgings through the streets, and one can imagine the manner in which he took his dues from the market place and removed or appropriated people's precious pigs. This part of his work was open to abuse and an invitation to bullying, something which must have become very bad in Edinburgh in 1576 for the lokman to be discharged because of 'his many offences in oppressing the people'.

For all that crowds flocked to see him do his professional work, it was often necessary after an execution for the executioner to wait behind in a safe place until an opportune moment came for him to leave. It took an exceptional execution, such as that of William Burke, the infamous Edinburgh murderer of body-snatching days, to alter this. Burke's crimes caused so much public abhorrence that as soon as his hanging was over, the hangman was able to go openly into an inn in Libberton's Wynd and receive congratulations on the way in which he had performed his task. So exceptional was this particular execution, which fell in 1829, that even the joiners whose workshop was engaged to erect the scaffold, asked to be allowed to do the work, whereas under normal circumstances they were so unwilling to do it that they had to cast lots to decide on whom the unpleasant task would fall.

In spite of being well paid the role of executioner was so unpopular and unsocial that it was not unknown for people to take the job only to save their own lives. In 1605 a thief who had been banished from Glasgow under pain of hanging if he returned, did return. He should have been put to death but as the burgh was without an executioner, he was given the job on condition that he stayed in it for life; if he gave it up, he would be hanged after all. After an Inverness executioner had been attacked by a mob who considered that he had kept a prisoner waiting overlong on the scaffold, his replacement was a man pardoned for the capital offence of sheep-stealing on condition that he agreed to be hangman. And when gypsies could be executed simply for being gypsies, they could avoid death by taking up work which no one else would do and thus a number of them became hangmen which resulted, sadly, in the hangman of Linlithgow, West Lothian, who was a gypsy, having to hang two men of his own race in 1770. The same thing might happen under the 'pit and gallows' regime – in 1688 Sir George Gordon of Edinglassie rounded up eighteen Highlanders and had seventeen of them hanged by the eighteenth who was let off on condition that he did the hanging.

For all that the Burgh of Glasgow in 1843 had laid down a standard of behaviour for an assistant executioner, the calibre of hangmen was not high and it was not all one-way traffic for them. One who oppressed the people has already been mentioned; an Edinburgh lokman was executed for 'slaughter' in 1608; in 1585 the executioner of the 'fowle folk', as infected people were called, who were on the Edinburgh moor in quarantine, committed offences which caused him to be put in irons and bound to the gibbet 'till further order be taken with him.' In the reign of Charles II, Alexander Cockburn, hangman in Edinburgh, was hanged for murder; and in 1825 a former Edinburgh hangman was charged with severely assaulting his wife. In 1827 the old hangman of Jedburgh was sentenced to sixty days in Bridewell for stealing mason's tools, old iron and other articles. 'The laws are far ow'r severe,' he complained, a thought that presumably occurred to him for the first time. Quite apart from the obvious effects of having a murderer in the family, there was the loss of his or her goods which had to be confiscated – 'fallin in the tounis hands throw her being convict', as it was put in one case. There are a number of cases, fortunately, where compassion was shown and the town returned such goods to the nearest relative.

For Magistrates, the practical result of an execution in former days was some enjoyable self-indulgence. Until the beginning of the 19th century, Edinburgh's Magistrates indulged in what they called 'splicing the rope', when they met at Paxton's Tavern in the Exchange to make the execution arrangements with the help of alcoholic refreshments. Over and above this, it was normal for them to have a dinner after a public execution, such as the civic feast held in Paisley, Renfrewshire, after the execution of Thomas Potts in 1797. This cost £13. 8. 10, out of a total for the whole occasion of £33. 5. 3½.

Epidemics

I n former times, the majority of the people lived their lives only with difficulty. They suffered from cold, hunger and dirt; poverty and lack of sanitation, clothing and medical care; as well as poor, damp and crowded housing. Add to these major national epidemics, or even local ones, and the result was devastating. Bubonic plague – the Black Death – broke out at intervals from the 14th century onwards, finally disappearing by the 18th century. Typhus is thought to have been the disease which was the cause of many deaths in the 1640s and also during the Seven Years Famine of 1694-1701, a time known as 'the ill years', or 'King William's ill years'. Smallpox first occurred in Scotland at Aberdeen in 1610 and produced serious epidemics off and on during the 17th century, as well as being a steady though lesser cause of death until vaccination virtually ended it in the 18th century. Serious cholera epidemics broke out in 1832 and again in 1849.

But however short and miserable people's lives were, they were lived in the hope and expectation of 'full and decent burial' at the end. This meant, when such things were in fashion, the mort bell and the mortcloth; it meant lykewakes and kistings; even the poorest person hoped that at least the nearest neighbours would attend their funerals, that some little show of hospitality would be given, and that they would be borne by friends to their final resting place in the churchyard and buried in a proper grave. These were regarded as essentials. In the event of epidemics – often in earlier years called pestilence or just pest – everything changed and what was normally considered indispensable was thrown aside in the desperate anxiety to check the spread of disease and deal with the corpses of the dead.

When death was due to pestilence, the authorities moved in, in what must have been a traumatic experience for the families concerned. Cleaners arrived, with right of entry and considerable powers. To ensure that they were recognised for what they were they were dressed in special garb or carried a mark of office – in an epidemic in 1499/1500 in Edinburgh, this was a white wand with an iron hoop at the end. Later in the 16th century, again in Edinburgh, not only the cleaners and buriers of the dead, but the bailies who had to supervise proceedings, all wore a grey gown with a white St Andrews cross on front and back and carried a staff with a white cloth on the end. The cleaners worked at night, dealing with infected houses and taking infected people to wherever had been designated as a quarantine and hospital area. Very often this was the burgh moor. Ill though these people might be, control of infection was all-important and discipline had to be maintained and in the great pestilence of 1568 Edinburgh Burgh Council appointed an executioner for the burgh moor, a task for which he was paid £10 monthly (Scots). Not only did cleaners take people compulsorily to hospital areas, they were empowered to remove their household goods for disinfection – to be purged with fire and water, as it is put. After immersion in cauldrons of boiling water, these goods were dried for up to ten days, after which the people were allowed to return home provided their houses had also been disinfected – a mild term for being 'singit and fyrit with hather (heather)'.

Unfortunately, pestilence might mean that people lost their goods entirely. In an early outbreak in Edinburgh, a cleaner was instructed that if he found clothing or other items, he might lawfully take them as his right, or burn them, something which must have been wide open to abuse. During the cholera outbreak of 1832, Health Boards were authorized to confiscate and burn the clothing and bedding of victims, and this happened in other epidemics too. While this was necessary, it was also a desperate loss to people, particularly those who had little enough anyway. Cleaners were accompanied by buriers of the dead, although sometimes they were one and the same. In the various 16th century epidemics, in Edinburgh at any rate, not only cleaning but also burying took place at night. Although members of some great families had, even into the 17th century, been buried at night, with torchlight and some splendour, the night burial of pest victims was a hurried, almost disgraceful, disposal of human bodies, smacking of the way in which unbaptized children were buried at night in some parts of the country. Another unpleasant aspect was that due to the danger of infection, the bailies could not adequately oversee the buriers' activities, which possibly explains why there were rumours in Edinburgh in 1588 of regular 'misbehaviour towards the dead' by these people.

When an epidemic was expected to break out in Edinburgh in 1584, it was decided that should this happen and there were deaths in the burgh, the bellman would summon the appropriate bailie who would inspect the corpse and decide the cause of death. Only when he had made his decision – presumably that death was *not* due to pest – could the bell 'gang through the town' and the corpse be buried. If the death *was* due to pest, then the type of burial to be given did not require the ringing of the mort bell and non-use of it was one of the changes which pestilence brought to funerals.

It was during epidemics that the common coffin came into its own, not so much to give a decent burial as to enclose bodies which might spread infection on the way to the grave. Although all parishes were meant to have a common coffin for the poor, there were those that did not, and in some areas it took a severe epidemic to introduce its use. The common coffin of Anstruther, Fife, is reputed to have been specially made for the pestilence of 1645 when, as already said, in one day it made no less than fifteen trips to the churchyard. Elsewhere use of a common coffin might have been given up but was re-started if an epidemic were sufficiently severe. For use in pestilence, the common coffin might be made to look especially forbidding, like the two 'closed biers' made in Edinburgh in 1568, which were black with a white cross upon them and a bell hanging at the head to give warning, in order to keep people away and reduce the chance of infection. The mortcloth, so essential to funerals in normal times, was not used in time of pestilence. With hurried burial and virtually no-one present to appreciate the air of respectability it gave, there was no need for it and there was always a risk that it might carry disease. At Shandwick, Ross and Cromarty, a mortcloth was inadvertently used in 1832 for a cholera victim, either because the disease had not been diagnosed in time or because the danger of using the cloth had not been appreciated. Awareness came quickly, however, and the Kirk Session forbade its use for anyone dying of cholera and in the meantime ordered it to be quarantined for a fortnight to kill any lingering infection before it could be used again for ordinary burials.

During the 1690s, it is said of some places, such as Fordyce, Banffshire, that the people had no coffins, only winding sheets. They were lucky. Elsewhere, a great many people did not even have these. With people dying daily, shrouds could not be provided for those who had not laid them up already. The dead were just bundled into the common coffin as they were; and in 1832 at Inver, Ross and Cromarty, eleven cholera victims were buried in one day with neither coffin nor winding sheet.

Epidemics also meant that victims might not be buried in the normal manner. In many cases they were tipped into common graves as in Edinburgh when those who died in a 16th century outbreak were buried at Greyfriars churchyard in a common grave described as 'large and wide, of deipness seven feet'. The *New Statistical Account* for the town of Dumfries describes the common graves made there for the 1832 cholera epidemic. There were two rows of large pits dug in an unoccupied part of the churchyard, into which the bodies were piled, one on top of the other. At least they were in coffins and each coffin was surrounded with a layer of quicklime. When the coffins came to within about two feet of the surface, each pit was filled with lime and earth, and after closing them, a final layer of earth, about a foot thick was laid over all. There were, of course, always those who could afford individual coffins but when space in a common grave was limited, this could prove a problem and for this reason, in Edinburgh in 1597, the order was given that no pest victims might be buried in a coffin.

Many parish graveyards accepted the bodies of people who died in epidemics; many still have bare areas with no memorials which are the 'cholera ground' where the dead were tipped into 'cholera holes' in the manner just described. There may have been further differentiation in some churchyards because it is said that pest victims were on occasion laid north and south, rather than the usual east and west. But pestilence could mean that its victims might not be buried in the churchyard at all. Burial there was sometimes forbidden in order to avoid carrying infected corpses any farther than necessary and to prevent any risk to those coming to worship on Sundays. In 1645, plague victims in Falkirk, Stirlingshire, were buried outside the town at Graham's Muir, each grave – they seem to have been individual ones – covered with a flat stone and the whole area enclosed with a stone wall, since removed. At Nigg, Ross and Cromarty, burial of cholera victims in 1832 was forbidden in the churchyard because of the risk of infection yet, strangely enough, that was where the Kirk Officer chose to bury the cholera after he saw it floating about the parish as a yellow cloud and courageously caught it in a linen bag. The stone with which he covered it is there still and no one would think of removing it lest the disease escapes and starts all over again.

When churchyard burial was forbidden, the authorities, whether Burgh Councils, Kirk Sessions or temporary Health Boards, had to appoint special burial places for those dying of pest, but in fact many were buried near to where they died or in fields. At Inver, Ross and Cromarty, where in 1832 almost all of the population of a little over a hundred caught cholera and fifty-three died, many were buried near the village, close to the sea, and so strongly is this epidemic burned into local folk memory that, certainly into the 1970s, the local County Councillor was annually asked to check this burying area lest erosion by the sea should expose it and cholera re-start.

One reason why people were buried in fields or near where they died is made clear in the *New Statistical Account* for Kirkmichael and Cullicudden, Ross and Cromarty. Telling of the famine and pest of the 1690s which raged there it says, 'Whole villages were depopulated and the living were so much wearied with burying the dead that they ceased at last to do so.' It goes on to say that people who found themselves attacked by the disease 'aware that they would not be buried if they did not themselves take some previous measures, so long as they had any strength remaining, dug their own graves and laid themselves down in them until they died.'

Many sad tales are told of lack of help for pest victims. In a 17th century outbreak, a beggar woman at Kinghorn, Fife, had to scoop out a grave with her bare hands for one of her children. In the 1690s two sisters had to carry their brother's body themselves to the graveyard on bearing ropes as no one would help them. In the 1832 cholera outbreak it was said that a boy and girl in Nigg, Ross and Cromarty, had to take their father's body to the churchyard and dig the grave themselves, although this seems surprising because burial in that churchyard was forbidden for cholera victims. At nearby Nigg Ferry, when a man died of cholera at that time, all the neighbours promptly fled, leaving his wife alone to cope as best she might.

The *New Statistical Account* for Beith, Ayrshire, says of that cholera outbreak, 'It was only with difficulty that people could be persuaded to attend funerals', although by the time of another lesser outbreak in 1834 they were more composed and in spite of there being a hundred and five deaths, funerals were conducted with the usual decorum. In the town of Dumfries, however, when cholera was at its height in 1832 it was only the closest relatives who followed the corpse to the grave and more often the victims were conveyed there with no one but the driver of the hearse. However, if there were any sort of funeral procession, the mourners avoided going to the house and gathered in the middle of the street instead, then walked in front of the hearse or on the weather side of it. While elders, such as those at Drumoak, Aberdeenshire, complained about the lack of neighbourliness at such times, at least one minister had similar human frailties. The incumbent at Nigg, Ross and Cromarty, was so terrified of catching cholera in the 1832 epidemic that he refused to go out of the manse grounds at all. Knowing that it was his duty to offer some refreshment to the doctor, who came all the way from Cromarty by ferry boat and then rode round Nigg, the minister had whisky and oatcakes put out on the garden wall so that he could stop and help himself as he passed, but that was as far as he would go in offering hospitality.

Among the obvious social consequences of pest, there were others too: trade came to a standstill; the only vehicles to be seen were hearses and those of doctors; and partly because of the lack of people to do the sewing, many who had lost relatives had to dispense with the wearing of mourning. Even if bodies did not need to be piled into a common grave, they might have to be piled into a hearse. This happened at Balmullo, Fife, in an outbreak of diphtheria about 1863 when the demand for the hearse was such that one coffin had to be put on top of another.

Pestilence meant that the dead usually had neither gravestone nor epitaph because, naturally enough, it was not normal for common graves to have monuments. A large communal grave at St Michael's Church, Dumfries, has a memorial to some four hundred and twenty cholera victims buried there in 1832, but this was erected at a later date and paid for by collections made in several churches in the town. It commemorates an event, not the individuals, and that is not the same thing as having one's own personal gravestone. Gravestones which say that the person buried below died of cholera are few and far between. At Dumfries, Robert Stevenson Templeton, a doctor in the town, died of it in

1848 and is remembered by an imposing stone in St Mary's churchyard, erected by public subscription. The inscription states that he was 'without a relative to lay his head in the grave', which may have been due either to the fact of his not being a local man or to the nature of his last illness. In the Howff graveyard at Dundee, Angus, there is a stone erected to the memory of William Forrest who died of cholera in 1832 and a stone at Ashkirk, Selkirkshire, commemorates a man who died of it but was buried at Stow, Midlothian. The wording on an isolated gravestone of a man who was refused burial in the churchyard of Dornoch, Sutherlandshire, says: 'It was supposed he died of cholera but afterwards contradicted (sic) by most eminent doctors.' This was surely meant to tell the passer-by why he was refused burial in the proper place, at the same time refuting the reason for this refusal. As to the Seven Years' Famine, it was so severe that there are few gravestones at all, to anyone, pest victims or not, between the years 1695-1703, as a look around any graveyard will show.

So death by pestilence could mean a shameful type of burial, with no bell, mortcloth or mourners, uncoffined and perhaps unshrouded, in a communal grave and possibly not even in the churchyard. It could mean loss of property by official destruction but, worse of all, especially with cholera when the moment of death was difficult to ascertain exactly, it could mean premature burial. The result was obvious – during epidemics many people concealed the fact that one of their family was ill or had died.

Evidence of this concealment appears in efforts to counteract it by Edinburgh Burgh Council in 1587. An order was given to the bellman to notify the authorities before announcing a death and forbidding any burial to take place without their permission. So serious could the results of concealment be that anyone discovered to have done this was hanged. As said earlier, in order to impress on people the enormity of this crime, one man was ordered to 'be hanged before his own door where he dwells'. This was in the 16th century, in Edinburgh, and the man, David Daly, had gone to mass at St Giles while his wife was sick and told no one about her illness until she was dead. For the same offence, about the same time, a Leith woman known as Lang Meg was sentenced to hanging and a woman who brought infection from Leith to Edinburgh, and was guilty of theft, was ordered to be drowned in the Quarry Holes. Concealment happened elsewhere and in other epidemics and it is believed that the true figures of those dying of cholera in 1832 should be much higher than those given.

The striking thing about early epidemics is the impressive attempts made to control them when knowledge of public health matters was not high; and like many things, good came out of evil in the end, and the cholera outbreaks of 1832 and 1849, particularly, made people aware of the need for sanitary reform which greatly contributed to improved health.

The Poor

T he aim of everyone was a 'decent funeral' where all the men of the parish or village would be present and where the usual entertainment would be given but, for the very poor, this was impossible. To be a pauper meant a degree of poverty unimaginable today and when one of these unfortunates died, it fell to others – craft guilds, burgh councils or Kirk Sessions – to give them burial.

Craft guilds were basically designed to defend a group of craftsmen against infringement of their trading or working rights by others but they were also deeply concerned for members in need. In fact, responsibility for these people was thrust upon them in the 1400s when Parliament ordered that poor members of craft guilds should be buried at the expense of the guild and that the rest of the brethren should attend their funerals, under threat of a fine. In fact, attendance of guild members at the funeral of a fellow member was regarded not only as a duty to the deceased but to the craft as well. In 1611 the Glasgow Weavers ordered that all members must attend burials when they were 'warned' (notified) and that they must appear at the proper time at the house where the corpse lay and 'convoy the same to the kirkyeird', adding that whoever joined in along the way would be regarded as being absent and would have to pay 8/- Scots to the 'weill of the craft'.

Extracts of the Glasgow Weavers' accounts, for what seems to be the year 1672, show how practical was the help they gave to distressed members at times of bereavement:

> To help bury John Murris's man £1. 16/-.
> Robert Dalrumples relictis mortchist £2. 8/-.
> To help bury John Allansomes bairn 18/-.
> To Robert Kirklands wife when she lay on deathbed 18/-.
> Robert Kirklands wife's deid-kist £2. 8/-.   (Scots money.)

One of the main benefits of the craft guild was what it could do for its poor. Money was collected for them, almshouses were sometimes provided and, at the end, financial help was given for deathbed and burial expenses and the craft mortcloth was there to give an air of seemliness to the coffin. Burghs also had the duty of burying any dead not associated with craft guilds, for instance the accounts of the Burgh of Peebles in 1631 show:

> Item, to the wyfe quha deid in Brockes-holl to by hir ane winding-scheit 24/-.
> To thes quha wand hir (put on her winding sheet) 4/-.
> To fowr men to tak hir to the kirk 6/8.
> To Michael Young for making . . . graif, 2/8.   (Scots money.)

The church was closely involved with the welfare of the poor. At the time of the

123

Reformation the church offered to take care of them but their offer was thwarted by the seizure of church property by the Crown and landed interests. In addition, it could be that revenue fell because of reduced church collections and because of the abolition of private absolutions. Presbyteries tried to do what they could by ordering special collections for poor relief and church courts appointed deacons to manage this money. This lasted until Episcopacy was re-established in 1661. Some efforts for the poor were made under this new regime but they were not particularly effective and by the time of the Revolution (1688/9) about a fifth of the people were on the brink of starving. In August 1692 a Proclamation of Privy Council ordered that every parish in the kingdom should support its own poor, with wandering beggars returned to the parishes where they were born. This turned out to be impossible and by an Act of 1693 the Privy Council allowed burghs to tax the inhabitants for the maintenance of their poor. In rural areas, however, the care of the poor fell on the church and this, of course, included burial of paupers. Kirk Session records are full of such references:

> Nigg, Ross and Cromarty, 1822 – Christy Greasach's funeral expense 16/6.
> Edderton, Ross and Cromarty, 1835 – Funeral expense of Widow Munro 8/6.
> and – Ross, 12/-.

Obviously there could be no conviviality at the burial of a pauper, but Kirk Sessions often contributed towards a small amount of hospitality at such funerals. In 1696 the Kirk Session of Galston, Ayrshire, paid not only 27/- Scots for a winding sheet – no word of a coffin – for a poor woman but also 2/4 for a pint of ale for those who buried her. This was a Scots pint, equal to nearly three English pints or very nearly four and a half of the common pint bottles. When two paupers died in Mauchline, Ayrshire, in 1676, the Session paid £3. 10/- Scots for their winding sheets and in addition 3/- for 'tobacco and pipes that night they were waked'. This could have been pipes being primed by women during the night, ready for the funeral, rather than pipes smoked at the lykewake itself, but either way it was still provision of hospitality by the Session.

An account for £3. 10. 0½ Scots paid in 1775 by the Kirk Session of Ashkirk, Selkirkshire, to a Selkirk merchant shows that some refreshment was being allowed for the mourners as the sum paid covered the cost of not only four yards of linen for a winding sheet but also a bottle of whisky. Even so, this did not allow for any jollity and there can surely have been only one parish in the country – Borgue in Kirkcudbrightshire – where the Kirk Session had to take steps to stop drinking at pauper funerals. There, knowing that the Kirk Session was responsible for the burial costs of the poor, mourners turned them into 'occasions of bibulous mirth' which they coolly charged to the Session. This made such inroads on the poors' funds that the surviving paupers were endangered and that particular Kirk Session had to put a limit of 12/- stg. on the expense of any pauper's funeral, to include everything – coffin, grave and grave-digger's fee – as well as ale but, even so, the ale continued to account for more than half the expense.

Kirk Sessions were always very pressed for money and it seems surprising that they had anything to spare for entertainment of mourners. However, paupers' friends were unlikely to have been either sufficiently numerous or physically fit enough to carry a coffin any distance and without this little inducement and fortification, how were they to carry it to the grave? And without them to do it, what would the Kirk Session, who were responsible for seeing that the body was buried, have done? So the small amount allowed for a drink or two made good practical sense quite apart from the fact that to offer nothing at a burial would have been a disgrace to the departed.

Although the Burgh records of Peebles, already quoted, show that men were paid to carry the corpse of a drowned woman to the church, Kirk Sessions did not expect to pay money to those who carried the poor to the graveyard although, once roads improved and it became practical to use transport of some sort, they might pay for this, perhaps 1/- or so for 'carriage to the grave'. Occasionally a Kirk Session might help out even when someone was not a registered pauper. In Melrose, Roxburghshire, in 1745, the Session paid a woman's funeral costs when her very needy husband begged them for assistance because the people to whom the money was due were daily demanding it. There too, in 1712, they had given £4 Scots to a man, not a pauper but nevertheless poor, to pay for his mother's burial.

As already said, in the early days in Scotland ordinary people were buried uncoffined and although the use of coffins gradually came in, for the poor for some time thereafter there was no coffin other than the common, re-usable one in which they were carried to the grave and from which they were tipped into it. But the many references in Kirk Sessions to paying for individual coffins for paupers show that provision of these had begun by the end of the 17th century anyway. These coffins were made by the local wright, sometimes at a contract price as happened at St John's Clachan Dalry, Kirkcudbrightshire, in 1781 when the Kirk Session agreed with a wright 'that he should have 7/- for each of the coffins made for such as are on the Poors' roll'. Sometimes Sessions bought wood to be made up, something which appears in an entry of St Ternan's Church, Arbuthnott, Kincardineshire, in 1695: '. . . for twentie dales (boards) that were bought to be coffins for the poor, £6 Scots'. The decision to provide a pauper with a coffin was a matter for the Kirk Session as a whole although it seems that sometimes individual elders or others must have authorized such provision off their own bat. Because of this, in 1775 the Kirk Session of Kilmarnock, Ayrshire, made a clear statement about it and at Mauchline, Ayrshire, in 1675 the Kirk Session ordered 'none to take upon themselves to buy a coffin for any poor without consent of the Kirk Session'. Robert Carruther's *Highland Notebook* tells of how individuals could help the poor. There was a maiden lady in Garmouth, Moray, who provided both shrouds and coffins for any poor people, who knowing of her kindness, came from far and near to her door to die, sure that she would see that they had these basic essentials at the end of life.

Kirk Sessions, and in earlier days Burgh Councils, were not just responsible for the burial of their own poor but also for that of 'stranger poor'. The countryside used to be full of wandering beggars and vagrants whose numbers increased with every famine or disaster, local or national, and wherever one of them was found lying dead or, in the case of drowning, washed up on the shore or river bank, then that parish had to pay for their burial. There are many references in Kirk Session records to this, a severe additional drain on parish funds:

Alloa, Clackmannanshire, 1645, 'ane windinsheit to a stranger 30/- Scots'.
Ashkirk, Selkirkshire, 1699 'a coffin for a stranger's child'.
Ashkirk, Selkirkshire, 1699, 'a coffin for a poor stranger.'
Arbuthnott, Kincardineshire, 1721, 'A stranger woman who happened to lodge at . . . surprisingly dieing there and immediately after her decease being brought to the kirk on a cart was by the Session provided of a chest and a hood £2 Scots.'
Tarbat, Ross and Cromarty, 1770 – '4/- stg. for a coffin made by order of the Moderator for a dead body thrown in upon the shore.'
Edderton, Ross and Cromarty, 1830 – '10/- stg. for a coffin for a body found at Daan.'

Similar instances appear in the records of Drainie and Lossiemouth, Morayshire, such as a stranger woman beggar, a stranger cast on the shore, two children found at sea and three drowned seamen. But from where was the money for all this to be found? In towns, it came from taxing the inhabitants and in the country it came from church door collections and sometimes from voluntary assessments on the heritors. It came too from the fines imposed on delinquents in addition to their punishment of standing publicly before the congregation; and it also derived from the larger fines imposed on the well-to-do in lieu of making such public appearances. This undoubtedly seems like preferential treatment but it was practical and in one such instance the Kirk Session of Galston, Ayrshire, minuted that it would give them 'money in hand' which would 'pey for a sheet for a puir deid body'.

When it was other people who died, local paupers might attend the funeral as mourners and partake of the hospitality offered and that in itself was of help in nourishing them. In general, however, they went not as mourners but in company with all the beggars from miles around who, whenever they heard of a funeral, went to get what was going, as well as any vagrants who just happened to be passing through the parish at the time. In that case they shared the left-overs, which often included the shoulder blades of mutton and these, because they were given to beggars, came to be known as 'poor men'. In addition, at funerals of landowners, meal was often handed out to the poor and in time it frequently came to be money which was given, probably a commutation of the distribution of food. This was a great attraction and drew beggars to all funerals of importance where they would crowd round the house or church to receive a share of the 'dead dole'. Somewhere between nine hundred and a thousand beggars, many of whom originated from Ireland, appeared at the funeral of the Earl of Eglinton in 1723 because £30 Scots was known to have been left for alms. Excessive numbers of the poor, of course, could be a great nuisance and at the burial in 1723 of George Watson, founder of the Edinburgh college which still bears his name, the funeral accounts included an entry of £1. 4/- paid to soldiers 'for keeping off the beggars from the house'. But such extreme measures were not usual. The accounts for Lady Margaret Stuart's burial in 1791 include, 'The poor of Traquair at the funeral, £1. 1/-', and at the funeral of the Dowager Duchess of Perth in 1773, £5½ 11. 1½ was given to the poor of the Canongate, both sums being sterling.

The 'dole' was distributed by the person in charge of arrangements who went outside with a plateful of coppers and handed each beggar a halfpenny. This custom of handing out coins seems to have died out around the early 19th century; certainly the last time it took place in Aberdeen was at the funeral of Bishop John Skinner in 1816. Because the donor did not always want this money to be handed out in this rather indiscriminate manner, it was sometimes given instead to the parish poors' funds. Within a ten year span at Fordyce, Banffshire, about £30 accrued to these funds on the deaths of three heritors, either from their own bequests or, as often happened, gifted by their families. The intention that this money should go to the local poor and not to a vagrant rabble, was made very clear at Ashkirk, Selkirkshire, in 1700 when the Laird of Woll gave £66. 13/- Scots in to the poors' box on the death of his wife. He meant this to be distributed at her burial but because there were so many stranger poor present 'and every paroch being obliged to maintain their own poor', it was not handed out that day. Instead, the Kirk Session met the following day to distribute half of it and met the following Monday to share out the other half.

Kirk Sessions found it very hard to make ends meet, especially in times of famine when income fell as demands upon it rose and their main concern had to be for the living rather than the dead. Thus, not all at once, but, over many years, in many if not all parishes, a custom slipped in on which the law is silent so it may not have been legal. This required anyone applying for admission to the Poors' Roll, whereby they became registered paupers, to sign a bond bequeathing all they possessed, little enough though it was, to the Kirk Session to be sold at their deaths to pay for their burial expenses, any balance going for the general behoof of the poor. The *Statistical Account* for Melrose, Roxburghshire, said, 'As they generally wish to retain these effects as long as possible, few make application till forced to by dire necessity.' This was not as brutal as it sounds. The Kirk Session records of St John's Clachan Dalry, Kirkcudbrightshire, make the real position clear. In 1764 they decided for the future to introduce this condition for would-be paupers because their funds were so low that they could scarcely support those already on the roll and because 'others apply who cannot be reckoned among the number of real poor'. They believed that the requirement to make over their goods to the Kirk Session in this manner was the best way of ensuring that 'none but real objects of charity partake of the funds appropriate for that use'. In other words, it was essential to discourage unnecessary applications in order to ensure that such funds as were available were kept for those who really needed them. (In 1982, an English local authority expressed the wish that people going into their old people's homes should make over their estate or house, the modern equivalent of this custom.) In parishes where paupers were required to bequeath their goods to the Kirk Session, these belongings were rouped at their deaths to pay their funeral costs, explaining this cross-entry in the Kirk Session records of Nigg, Ross and Cromarty, about 1836:

> Paid for Widow Munro's funeral and grave 19/- stg.
> Received from the effects of Widow Munro 19/-.

If the pauper's goods did not bring in quite enough for the burial, the Kirk Session made up the difference, but any surplus went to the poors' funds. During the years 1833-7 inclusive, the sale of paupers' effects in the parish of Kirkliston, West Lothian, brought in £11. 14. 1 stg. The expenses connected with these sales was £4. 16. 3½, leaving £6. 17. 9½ for the poor. Should a poor person's goods be enough for a normal funeral – worth about £2 or so – then the Kirk Session might give this sum to the relatives so that the pauper could have a proper funeral. In some places, such as Johnstone, Dumfriesshire, the goods were not sold but given instead to relatives and neighbours who by regular support and care prevented the problem of the indigent from getting worse than it was.

The wandering poor, of course, could not be expected to assign their effects to any particular parish. It must have been of them that the Kirk Session of Kilmarnock, Ayrshire, was thinking when it was decided in 1775 that no coffin would be provided if there were clothes or other effects which could be rouped to pay for one and it became customary to sell anything of value found on such strangers to pay for their burials. An example of this appears in the burial records of Ancrum, Roxburghshire. A strange woman arrived there one evening, totally exhausted, and although she was given shelter, she died that night. No one ever discovered who she was but 11/- stg. was found in a purse in her pocket and 11/- was just the cost of her burial. It is noticeable that the value of the effects and the cost of the burial often tally. When a poor sick woman arrived at the manse of Rathven, Banffshire, and died there two days later, the minister advanced the sum of 7/2 stg. for her dead linen, coffin and burial. Her few goods, which included a dress and a Book of Common Prayer, were rouped, with the minister as judge of the roup and the Session Clerk as clerk to it. What a sad little affair a pauper's roup must have been, yet how seriously it was dealt with.

Even in those parishes where a pauper's effects paid for his funeral (unless they came to enough for a normal one), it was still a pauper's burial that he was given and that meant a grave in the part of the churchyard set aside for the poor. This was often the north side of the churchyard. When St Nicholas Church in Aberdeen was repaired in 1647, the north side of the churchyard was appointed for burials of the poor and their children; the south side was for those who could pay. So unfavoured is the north side of a churchyard, that there is very often little space there as the church frequently lies nearly at the north wall. But so long as there was space in this dismal sunless area, there the poor were buried in free ground; if there was not enough space, then a plot for local paupers and stranger poor was provided in some other part. If the parish of origin of any stranger paupers could be discovered, then that parish was charged with the cost of burial in the parish where they died. A letter to the *Dundee Courier* in 1973 described an Aberdeenshire churchyard where there was a Paupers' Plot. There were neither monuments nor flowers and amidst all the other graves it lay barren and bare and the letter-writer remembered being in tears fifty years before when not allowed to put flowers on the grave of a tinker's baby.

In some places, stranger poor were buried in a 'Strangers' Nook', separate from the local poor, often near the churchyard gate and also distinguished by a total lack of gravestones. The mid-19th century regulations for Edrom Churchyard, Berwickshire, include provision for one or more portions of the graveyard to be set aside for 'foreigners or strangers, whose parish of settlement is at a great distance or cannot be discovered'. Peter Livingstone, the Dundee poet, described just such a plot:

> Here's the nook wi' nae memorial
> Whar the village strangers sleep,
> At whose dying hour no bosom friend
> Was heard to wail or weep.

Into the mid-19th century, it was a kindly custom in many parts of the Highlands to drop a coin into a stranger's grave so that, by this purchase, he might have a right to his resting place. In some places, stranger poor were buried along with unbaptized children and not in graveyards at all.

Even in death, the poor were open to what can only be regarded as abuse. Burghs had Correction Houses where minor wrong-doers were put to such work as carding, spinning and making stockings; there too the begging poor and any children found begging in the streets were sent. But there was little compassion for them: in Edinburgh in 1694 it was decided that the bodies of anyone who died in the Correction House, as well as foundlings, might be used for dissection.

A pauper's lykewake might be little more than a couple of women staying awake to keep rats and cats off the corpse or it might be a very mild version of the real thing. Inadequate lykewakes could have unfortunate results when body-snatchers realized that it was easier to steal a body before burial rather than after and, obviously, an unwatched pauper's body was easy game. In 1825 the *Kelso Mail* reported that a poor woman who lived alone in Jamaica Street, Edinburgh, was put into her coffin and left alone overnight in her home. It was only when people returned next day to take her corpse for burial that they discovered that the body-snatchers had got there first. Three years later, also in Edinburgh, a very poor seventy-five year old widow died. Her body was placed in a coffin obtained from the workhouse and her friends, thinking it unnecessary to wake with the corpse, left about midnight. The result was the same. When watching societies were formed to protect graves from the attentions of the Resurrectionists, as body-snatchers were called because they literally raised the dead, the poor were rarely members and because their graves were seldom watched they were particularly vulnerable. Furthermore, although the General Assembly had decreed in 1563 that the graves of the poor should be six feet deep, often they were only four feet or so, and this too made a pauper's grave a more attractive proposition for body-snatchers than an ordinary one.

In times of pestilence, infected furnishings and goods were officially destroyed and this was a far greater blow to the poor than to the better off. At such times too, it was the bodies of the poor rather than those of the rich which were liable to be buried in communal graves and in the enthusiasm to dispose of infected bodies as quickly as possible, one or two may have been hustled to the grave rather sooner than was right. This prospect terrified the people but the poor, relying on the parish to bury them, were those most frightened of being buried before they were truly dead. There was one group of people who were not paupers, yet were treated worse. These were the serfs who worked as colliers, particularly in Fife, whose status was considered to be so low that people would not allow them to be buried beside people in consecrated ground.

When all is said and done, there is no denying that Kirk Sessions tried their best to give as decent a burial as possible to the poor, with a winding sheet, a coffin and the second best mortcloth, with a drink and perhaps a loaf of white bread for the mourners. This system continued until the passing of the Poor Law in 1845 when responsibility for the poor, in life and in death, came under the management of Parochial Boards, with Inspectors of the Poor in every parish under the control of the Central Board of Supervision.

Even after the introduction of the Poor Law, the stigma of pauperism continued and indeed still continues. In 1982 *The Scotsman* reported a mix-up which led to a woman being mistakenly buried in a pauper's grave, whereupon her friends demanded that her body be exhumed from 'her shallow unmarked grave on common ground' and given 'decent burial'.

Sadly, there are still poor people and they still require burial out of public funds. A check round the country shows minor differences in what happens in this context. In Dumfries and in Lerwick, Shetland, for instance, there is free ground in cemeteries for those who have no relatives to pay for their burials, while in Berwickshire they are given a free lair anywhere in the cemetery, as is convenient. In Dumfries these graves are no shallower than usual whereas in Lerwick they are usually only one lair deep instead of three lairs. District Councils, with some involvement from Social Work Departments, pay for these burials, usually allowing for the least expensive coffin and for one car, and normally getting quotations from three undertakers. Even so, a report from a Lerwick undertaker states clearly that although one type of coffin is made for these funerals, the same amount of work is put into it as any other one 'and a welfare funeral is given the same respect as any other funeral'.

A Spirit of Co-operation

A spirit of co-operation was the basis of the Benefit and Friendly Societies which grew up mainly in the 18th and 19th centuries to give allowances to members in times of need and financial help towards their burials. A good example of the workings of such a society comes from Saltoun, East Lothian. There, there were two societies, one of them established about the beginning of the 19th century, which by the 1830s had about two hundred members and funds of £1,000. Of this, £700 was lent out on private security at 4% interest and the rest was on deposit in a bank at 2½%. With subscriptions, the income came to just over £100 and in 1835, for instance, £74. 18. 3 was paid out, with an average of twenty-three people receiving relief. The Society paid out 5/- per week for the first three months of sickness, 4/- per week for the next three months, 3/- a week for the following three months, and for the remaining three 2/- a week and, where illness lasted longer than a year, 1/6 per week. All these figures are, of course, in sterling.

On the death of a member, £2. 10/- was given for funeral expenses and 10/- for the death of a child, with a further provision of which some writers of the New Statistical Accounts would have approved, that 15/- per annum should be given to members' widows while they remained unmarried. Methods of subscription varied from Society to Society but, in general, there was an entrance fee with a further weekly payment.

Some Societies combined the principle of a Savings Bank with that of a Friendly Society. North Berwick, East Lothian, had such a Society, with the double purpose of helping at times of sickness and death and of accumulating savings. Every member paid 1/2 weekly, the twopences of which were used as sick and funeral money. They also each paid 1/- per annum to the Treasurer for his work. Sick money was 5/- per week for the first thirteen weeks, 3/- for the second thirteen and 1/6 weekly for the rest of the year. On the death of a member, his heirs received £2. 10/- to pay for his burial, while a member was given £1. 10/- on the death of his wife and 15/- for the death of a child under twelve years of age. At the end of each year – the reason that this type of society was called a yearly one – the savings were paid out to members with interest, along with any balance of the sick and funeral money. Of this particular society, the writer of the *New Statistical Account* for North Berwick said, 'This has gone on for many years and promoted the industry, comfort and independence of the people.'

In some cases things were done differently. For instance, members of an Alloa (Clackmannanshire) Friendly Society for funerals were only required to pay anything when a member actually died – 1/- each – while the Dunbar (East Lothian) Sailors' Society was founded on a duty of 8d. in the £ Scots levied on all wages paid to shipmasters' mates and seamen using the port. Sometimes members of these societies were drawn from one particular trade or occupation, sometimes from a general group of working people. The *New Statistical Account* for Aberlady, East Lothian, reported that, 'Friendly Societies may be considered as perhaps the best contrivances which have yet been fallen upon for supporting the independence and promoting the comfort of the working classes, and they seem to be deserving of more countenance and support from the higher and middle ranks than, on the whole, they have hitherto received.' In some places, however, they did receive such support and the *Statistical Account* for Hawick, Roxburghshire, written in the 1790s, particularly mentioned that there were 'many respectable people in the Society in addition to those benefitting from it'.

But there could be problems. 'When prudently and honestly managed these societies have certainly done good', reported the *New Statistical Account* for Inverness, but unfortunately in some cases, societies were founded without sufficient financial knowledge and the writer of the *New Statistical Account* for Tranent, East Lothian, said '. . . of late years, many of those useful Societies have been broken up due to their resources failing, having been founded on erroneous calculation'. A somewhat similar opinion was expressed in the *New Statistical Account* for Prestonpans, East Lothian: 'At one period, this parish had more than enough of such institutions. The only survivors now are the Carters, Gardeners, several yearly societies, and the Sailors Incorporation . . . It is much to be feared that, except for the yearly Societies and the Sailors, the others are not based on principles which can ensure their continuance or prosperity.'

Unfortunately, lavish hospitality was so much a part of a decent funeral that money paid out by these societies for burials was often unwisely used by the recipients. The writer of the *New Statistical Account* for Ardersier, Inverness-shire, for instance, wrote that the real advantage of such societies was 'questionable as it encourages drinking at lykewakes and funerals and certainly does not promote desire for independence'.

The writer of the *Statistical Account* for Duddingston, Midlothian, was critical of a Colliers' and Carters' fund there, saying that if the scheme were altered and its chief expenditure went to widows and orphans instead of being used for expensive funerals and the 'selfish sustenance of the members themselves', then it might be a truly useful establishment. Although such criticisms were often justified, nevertheless these societies did perform a valuable service and lifted from their members the terrible fear of not having a decent funeral, just as they lifted the burden of paupers' funerals from Kirk Sessions and other authorities. These societies only developed, of course, in communities where there was a sufficient population to justify them and thus there were many areas which never benefitted from their good work. Some societies included other benefits which were of great value, such as Cow Funds to replace any member's cow which died; Alloa, Clackmannan-shire, Colliers allowed for payment of schoolmasters and two societies at Ardersier, Inverness-shire, bought coal and meal wholesale for distribution at cost to members, which must have done much to alleviate hardship and prevent death.

Body-snatchers

B ody-snatching is a classic example of the end justifying the means. Until 1832, as there was no legal provision for an adequate supply of fresh human corpses for medical schools, there was no way in which medical students could study anatomy, an essential part of their training. The result was an epidemic of stealing newly-buried bodies.

In Edinburgh some exceptions were made; in 1505 the Burgh Council decreed that once a year the surgeons and barbers of the town might have the body of a condemned man for dissection but it was only in 1694, when the College of Surgeons there received a charter, that regular teaching of anatomy began. For this, more than one body a year was needed and the first man to try to get them was an Edinburgh surgeon burgess, Alexander Monteith, who petitioned the Council in October 1694 for the gift of the bodies of foundlings and those who died in the Correction House. The Council, wishing to encourage the study of anatomy, agreed on condition that he cared for all the town's poor free of charge and admitted surgeons' apprentices to his dissections at half what would be charged to others. Ten days later, the Incorporation of Surgeons made a similar request which was granted, subject to their building an anatomical theatre by Michaelmas 1697 where, once a year, they should have a public anatomical dissection.

Such a source of corpses was acceptable, anything else was not, and when a grave was found opened in Greyfriars Churchyard, Edinburgh, in 1711, the Incorporation of Surgeons denied that they had had anything to do with it, declaring that they would expel any of their members guilty of doing such a thing, 'considering that the Magistrates of Edinburgh have always been ready and willing to allow what dead bodies fall under their gift and thereby plentifully supplied their Theatre for many years past'.

Nevertheless, when medical training in Scotland began to expand even faster, it was essential to have a better supply of bodies for students to dissect, and body-snatching began in earnest. Resurrectionists was the name often given to body-snatchers because they literally raised the dead and their heyday came in the first thirty years of the 19th century when the numbers of medical students throughout Scotland had increased enormously, with nearly a thousand in Edinburgh alone. Body-snatching appealed to medical students, naturally enough, and they were not discouraged from supplying their own medical schools with specimens in return for money to help them through their training. Unfortunately, being an unappetizing occupation, it also attracted very unpleasant people whose only concern was money.

Body-snatchers tried to learn about any forthcoming funerals and often one of them attended in the role of a mourner to learn as much about the grave as possible. Such information, of course, could be obtained from the grave-digger and there is no doubt that grave-diggers were often implicated in the dirty work. The most vulnerable graveyards were those within easy reach of medical schools and those in sufficiently well populated places for strangers with transport to pass unnoticed, but wherever a deformed body was buried, there the Resurrectionists were sure to follow because such a corpse was a real prize.

Body-snatching was a job for the night-time; very seldom was a graveyard robbed during the day. Because there was no time to waste lest they were discovered, body-snatchers only dug the part of the grave over the head and broke open just enough of the coffin to enable them to drag the body out. It was put in a sack and away they went, but not before they tidied up. A wise body-snatcher made every effort to leave the grave as if nothing had happened as an apparently untroubled graveyard was likely to remain an unguarded one and, so far as they were concerned, that was all to the good because there was no point going any farther afield than they had to. Perhaps they were disturbed at Crichton, Midlothian, in 1823, where two days after a young man had been buried in a grave thirteen feet deep, it was found open, the body gone and torn linen strewn about and a cloud of maggot flies above it. This was not normal practice for skilful body-snatchers.

It was very seldom that body-snatching was carried out in a speculative, haphazard way but in one night in 1825 at Ormiston, East Lothian, three graves were opened, obviously on the off-chance that their contents would be of use. One was a child buried for some months; the second an old man buried for four and a half months, the upper part of whose coffin was broken, the dead clothes cleared off his face and left like that; and the last was that of an old woman, dead for two months, whose coffin was broken in pieces and her body taken out, uncovered and left huddled in the grave along with the dead clothes. This was a senseless attempt at grave-robbing because after a month to six weeks bodies were useless for dissection and so the distress inflicted on this community was all for nothing.

Leaving grave-clothes behind in the grave was normal because Resurrectionists did not want to risk being accused of their theft. When bodies were lifted, each was put in a sack and carried off or else hidden somewhere, to be picked up later, perhaps after another graveyard was robbed, but this did not always work out. In 1825 a workman at a quarry about three and a half miles north of Jedburgh, Roxburghshire, noticed among some loose earth a string with a little red sealing wax on it. He found that it was attached to a sack which turned out to contain the body of a young woman. Her corpse was taken to the nearby church of Ancrum and a message sent to a man from Bedrule, not far away, whose daughter's grave had recently been violated. He identified her and she was reburied. It was thought that her body had been lifted and then hidden near the quarry until the Resurrectionists made another raid but they were spotted entering the graveyard at Jedburgh and sent to the castle gaol for a fortnight, leaving the poor girl's body to putrefy. A press report of this case mentioned into how small a parcel a corpse could be reduced. This young woman's arms were tightly corded to the body with the hands resting on the shoulders; her legs were bent backwards to the thighs and both firmly tied round the body; another cord was put through behind the knee joints and tied round the neck, and in this state she had been neatly sewn into a small bag, looking like a bundle which anyone might carry by hand without suspicion.

The custom of hiding lifted bodies for later collection led to some unpleasant finds in unlikely places, as when a boat, passing up Hawkhead-bridge on the Paisley canal in 1824 turned up a body which had been pinned under the bridge, beneath the surface of the water, with hands and feet bound. In another case, the bodies of two children lifted from Channelkirk churchyard, Berwickshire, were concealed in a sack inside a conduit under the road on the south side of Soutra Hill. Their graves had been put to rights so no one noticed anything amiss there but someone did notice the sack and discovered what it contained. The alarm was raised and armed men turned out to await the return of the body-snatchers. In the darkening, a horse and trap with two men in it passed down the road but they must have suspected an ambush and carried straight on to Carfraemill Inn, nearly two miles down the road, and on their return drove furiously past the conduit and those hoping to catch them. They got clean away, the children were reburied, and the incident led to the spot being called the Bairnies' Conduit.

Country people became mistrustful of strangers with gigs and similar forms of transport. In 1825 suspicions were aroused by two men in a gig on the road between Hardens and Longformacus in Berwickshire, and they were stopped. Immediately they fled across the moor, leaving not only horse and gig but also the body of an old man who had been buried at Edrom, Berwickshire, earlier in the month. The gig was taken to Duns and the body placed in the church where it was claimed the next day. A day or two later, someone came from Edinburgh to fetch the horse and gig but as soon as this became generally known in the town, several hundred people gathered, got a hold of the gig, pulled it through the streets to the Market Place and there broke it up and burnt it.

In towns, people began to keep a sharp lookout for unusual activities at strange hours. In 1825 in Edinburgh two men were seen with a sack about 5.00 a.m. behind St Cuthbert's churchyard and suspicions were aroused. They fled, leaving the sack which contained the body of an old woman and, although pursued, they got away. When two people were seen alighting from a gig in Queen Street, Edinburgh, in 1827 at a very untimely hour, a watchman followed them, then informed the Police Office and when a patrol went to the house where they had gone, sure enough, there in the cellar was the body of a recently-buried young man.

In 1825 the *Edinburgh Courant* recommended that facilities should be given for importing bodies from abroad, rather than forcing medical men to connive at body-snatching, which they were certainly doing. This suggestion followed a report that a policeman had seized a barrel which had been delivered at the Canal Basin, which was found to contain a human corpse. The *Courant* considered that the constable's zealousness could harm the Medical School of Edinburgh. 'Everyone knows,' said the paper, 'that if such a school is to exist at all, subjects must be procured.' This paper went further: in its opinion, the hundreds of criminals prowling about in cities had a much more useful part to play after death than they had in life. There was in fact a considerable trade in imported bodies, especially from Ireland where bodies cost a few shillings instead of the £7 or £8 stg. which they cost in this country. The true nature of these imports was concealed, of course, sometimes with unfortunate results. In 1825 it was only the smell from four casks which aroused suspicions and when opened, they were found to contain a dozen bodies. 'It was a horrid spectacle,' reported the press. These corpses were thought to have come from Ireland en route to Edinburgh, but their journey ended in the graveyard of the High Church in Glasgow.

Scottish body-snatchers did not confine themselves to their own country; they were prepared to cross the Border if necessary. Two Scots, one from Dundee, Angus, and the other from Renfrew (or so they said) ended up in Durham Gaol as a result of their activities in the Sunderland area. Suspicion fell on them after two children's bodies were lifted because, although strangers, their presence had been noticed at several funerals. One was arrested and only admitted where he was lodging when threatened with being handed over to the mob. There his accomplice was apprehended and there too one of the children's bodies was found, ready packed with an Edinburgh address. Evidence showed that they had been in the area for about a month and with some success too, as they had spent a considerable sum on cartage.

Whatever certain sections of the press though about supplying dead bodies for medical science, the general public abhorred it and in addition Scots believed that the body as well as the soul would be resurrected and therefore the body must be as whole as possible. So strong was this feeling that a limb amputated during life would be buried in the family lair to await the arrival of the body it came from so that all could go to heaven together; and therefore public reaction to real or suspected body-snatching was near lynch-law. In addition to various instances already cited, back in 1742, when several bodies were taken from St Cuthbert's churchyard in Edinburgh, one of the beadles was suspected and an angry mob burnt down his house. In 1823 when a coach was seen leaving a doctor's house in the New Town of Edinburgh at 10.00 p.m. in the evening with a coffin, it was not unnaturally assumed that it was going to fetch a corpse somewhere in the country. A number of people began to follow the coach, telling everyone of their suspicions as they went until a large crowd gathered. Finally, the coach was stopped in Nicholson Street, the horses taken out, and the coach dragged to the Mound down which it was pitched, smashed to pieces, and set on fire. The police could do nothing but arrest three young people who seemed most active in the mob.

Even a totally innocent person could be at risk if his actions were such as to make people think he was a Resurrectionist. An Edinburgh street porter was discovered one day in 1826 entering a medical building with what appeared to be a body. It *was* a body – but only that of a llama which had died in Wombell's menagerie and been sold to Professor Jameson for the College museum. A crowd gathered and refused to listen to his explanations. He was taken to the Police Office, followed by a mob who could hardly be stopped from tearing him to pieces, such was the feeling about the trade of body-snatching.

From the anatomist's point of view, the fresher the corpses the better. Emptying graves was risky and soon Resurrectionists did the most obvious thing. As the *Kelso Mail* reported in 1825, 'Those who follow the infamous employment of stealing bodies are now contriving, instead of taking them out of graves, to steal them before they are buried.' A bribe to whoever had charge of the body could mean that the corpse went straight to the dissecting table while a suitably weighted coffin was buried and no one was any the wiser. Press reports tell of old people's bodies, left unwaked, being gone in the morning, and various other methods of abstracting bodies before burial occurred. In 1829 an Edinburgh baker who was out early one morning noticed a large bundle being lowered from an attic tenement. What particularly struck him, however, was how studiously three men in the street were avoiding taking any notice of the descending bundle. He called the watchman and of course what was in the bundle was a body, that of a drummer known as 'Nosy', who was living alone as his wife was in prison.

A particularly tragic sidelight on the anatomist's need for bodies was reported in the press in 1826. An Irish woman who had lived in Scotland for some years, called on an Edinburgh surgeon offering to sell her healthy two-month old child for £7 for dissection. She also offered him her thirteen-year old son as well, 'whom he could kill or boil or do what he liked with'. He reported her and, when arrested, she admitted that she had already offered the baby to another surgeon but he would only offer £5. One press editor suggested that the poor woman must have been drunk or mentally deranged; it seems much more likely that she had reached terrible depths of poverty and despair to do such a thing, especially as her eyes filled with tears as she began undressing the baby, saying she could not let its clothing go too. She at least was offering the genuine article. The fact that many medical men were perfectly prepared to take bodies offered to them led to one ingenious swindle in Edinburgh in 1828. Four people composed a letter, addressed to a woman in their group, which said that she would shortly be receiving a 'very valuable box from the country'. She took this letter to a medical lecturer and the nature of their conversation may be imagined. A bargain was struck for £2. 10/- for what was assumed to be in the box, which was to be delivered in exchange for the money at an inn. In fact, the box was found to be full of stones packed in straw. The swindlers were sent to Bridewell (the Correction House) for sixty days, yet nothing appears to have happened to the lecturer who thought he was buying a corpse, nor to the surgeon who had offered £5 for a living baby.

Gradually people began to take precautions against body-snatchers. At St Cuthbert's churchyard, Edinburgh, as early as 1738, the churchyard wall was raised to eight feet after bodies were lifted. Tough material, such as heather, was sometimes put among the earth as a grave was filled in to make digging difficult. In some places, gunpowder was put on top of a grave to blow up anyone who interfered with it. Sometimes a loaded gun with trip wires was placed on a grave but as it could not be aimed accurately this was no more use than gunpowder. Shells or stones were sometimes carefully arranged on top of a grave so that any disturbance was likely to be noticed, although this was locking the door after the body had bolted. Resurrectionists always tried to re-place any such arrangement exactly as it had been, so that no one might know they had been there. A very deep grave was also thought to be a deterrent, although the one of thirteen feet at Crichton, Midlothian, was successfully robbed.

In 1827, *The Scotsman* reported yet another method of foiling body-snatchers – a new method of embalming was discovered by Sir George Stewart Mackenzie which, among other things, would render bodies unfit for dissection. 'Knowledge of the process,' said that paper, 'might make the fortune of an apothecary or undertaker for the expense is not so great as to exclude people of very moderate income.' The method does not seem to have caught on however.

Offering a reward was also tried. When it was discovered in 1818 that two bodies had been lifted at Kirkliston, West Lothian, the minister first of all wrote to the Lord Advocate who replied that he had given orders to the Sheriff-Substitute to make the necessary inquiries but, in addition, the Kirk Session formed a committee to discover the perpetrator themselves and in three newspapers they advertized a reward of £20 stg. for information leading to an arrest. Although the offer of a reward does not seem to have borne fruit, there was an immediate local response of £14 towards it, while a subscription paper was sent round the parish to raise the balance needed, although no one was required to hand over any money unless the body-snatchers were discovered. In any event, a decision was also made to watch the graveyard at night after funerals.

A churchyard guard was a good form of protection and in many parishes relatives began watching graves from sunset to sunrise for a month to six weeks after burial and from this developed communal watching societies in many areas – vigilantes, as they would be called nowadays – with the members taking turns of guard duty. One of these was the North Quarter Friendly Churchyard Guard Association formed in 1823 to protect the High Churchyard in Glasgow. In towns, these watching societies required the permission of Magistrates and Council and, in the case of the North Quarter Association, it took from May 1823 to September that year to have their proposed regulations approved. This Association had two thousand members. Its nightly volunteer rota consisted of nine men and a captain, with a sentinel posted in front of the guard house. Four of the men were on duty at a time, relieved every hour, and as different men were on duty each night, the opportunity for bribery was prevented. Regular watchmen, though employed in some places, were a risk as it was all too easy for them to succumb to the blandishments of body-snatchers.

The North Quarter Association used neither firearms nor swords, relying on batons, cudgels and numbers to overcome any Resurrectionists but in many places there were no such inhibitions. One of these was St Cuthbert's church, Edinburgh, where the inventory of equipment in 1839 listed '1 gun, 1 blunderbuss, 2 powder flasks', and what is more, they were used. In 1827, to name only one instance, three body-snatchers attacked the churchyard but were driven off by the watchers' gunfire and fled over the wall, leaving behind them tools and traces of blood, although that did not deter them from trying again the next night, also without success. Watching associations were voluntary and kept up by the subscriptions of members. At Paisley, Renfrewshire, for instance, where there were seven thousand members, people paid 6d. on joining and 1d. per quarter thereafter. The North Quarter Association's funding system was the same but at one point they sought additional publicity and revenue and asked permission from the Council to put up a notice on the main gate of the churchyard explaining the financial position and also asked that one of their officers might take up a collection at funerals. But valuable though the Association's service was, their request was turned down.

In the country parish of Traquair, Peebles, the watching society had just seventy-three members at the outset, all men between the ages of sixteen and sixty. Sixteen year olds paid 1/6 stg. entry money; older men paid 2/6 which seems to be entry money although this is not clear from the records. There were three categories of members – Honorary, all of whom were landowners who contributed between £1 1/- and 3/- each at the outset; Extraordinary, who each paid £1 but were not required to watch in person so long as they provided a suitable substitute or paid 2/- for each failure to do so; and Ordinary members who paid less but were required to take their turn of watching, two at a time, according to their place on the roll of names, or else to provide a suitable substitute, failing which they had to pay 5/- for each failure, although this sum could be reduced by the Society should they see fit. To assist the watchers, two guns were bought for £1. 10/- stg. Watching was provided only for members of at least three months' standing and their families although, later, it was given to any poor woman who had lived for some time in the parish, 'no man residing with her'. Each Society made up its own rules, of course, and so there was considerable variation around the country. The records of St Cuthbert's church, Edinburgh, whose firearms have already been mentioned, show an income from watching of £28 stg. for the two years 1843-5 which shows that in some cases it was the church which provided this service, not volunteers, and that it was available for a fee, just as other forms of graveyard protection came to be provided for non-subscribers, in return for payment to the societies providing them.

The shallow graves of the poor were not usually guarded. In 1829 in Inverness the body of a poor old woman was left without a guard and lifted the night she was buried. Very soon another woman with no one to look after her was buried and a few people in the town decided to watch her grave. Unfortunately, they were too late in applying to do so and could not get admission to the churchyard but spent the night patrolling in the street outside. They managed to put four would-be snatchers to flight, but when there was no one to watch the next night, the consequence was inevitable.

Most people were very superstitious about passing a graveyard at night, let alone spending the night in one and the nervous tension of the watchers must have been enormous. When watching was going on, it meant that lights flickered among the graves as the guard patrolled and that must have been an eerie sight; it meant that they had to investigate every strange noise, and in the dark there are a lot of strange noises; and the guard knew that they might come face to face with Resurrectionists and have to deal with them at any moment. And although it was a job for the men, one can imagine the anxiety of womenfolk as they saw husbands, brothers or sons off for their turn of duty.

Shelter for the guard, especially in winter, was of prime importance. To start with, some watchers used tents in the graveyards but most erected wooden huts. The North Quarter Association were allowed a piece of ground in the graveyard for the erection, at their own expense, of a temporary wooden guardhouse, removable at the will of the Magistrates. At Traquair, where watching began officially in 1824, they used a divot hut until it was removed during straightening of the churchyard walls after which they were given the use of one of a group of new buildings being erected close to the churchyard. Forres, Morayshire, had a 'handsome little building . . . furnished with windows looking out in all directions' which presumably saved unnecessary excursions by the watchers into the graveyard. At Oldhamstocks, East Lothian, there is in the graveyard still a nice little watch house with now-defaced wording above the door: 'It shall not be plucked up nor thrown down any more for ever. Jer. 31, 40. Erected by Mrs Agnes Moore, 1824.' (Mrs Moore was the minister's wife.) Another particularly attractive watch tower is at Eckford in Roxburghshire but it is very small and one wonders how the guard avoided being roasted alive, with the inevitable fire in the hearth, because heating for the watchers was regarded as a necessity. Records of the watching society at Traquair show that in 1824 the guard used 12 cwts of coal. Four years later it was decided to employ someone living nearby to put on the fire half an hour before the watch went on duty, for payment of 7d per week, rising to 9d in 1837, and it is this firelighting entry in the accounts which shows how often the guard there was on duty.

Each church laid down rules for the watchers' conduct in the churchyard, forbidding visitors and drinking but at Kirkliston, West Lothian, the Kirk Session's committee on grave-watching decided in December 1818 that those watching in the cold weather should be allowed a glass of spirits and some bread, to be paid out of money in hand. But whether permitted or not, alcohol often accompanied watchers to boost their morale and may well be what lay behind a report at Kirkliston in 1820 that the watchers had broken several of the church windows one night. History does not record whether drink played any part when the watchers at Fala, Midlothian, fired in the darkness at what they thought were body-snatchers, only to find in the morning that the minister's goat was badly wounded. But it was not only drink or sheer nervousness in a graveyard at night that led to accidents. Not all the watchers were used to weapons and inexperience could cause trouble: in 1825 the *Kelso Mail* reported that when a watcher was loading his gun prior to setting off to the graveyard, a shot went off and his fellow watcher died as a result.

Mortality being higher than it is now, no sooner did one grave no longer need to be watched than another did and, even in Traquair, with a small population, in the year 1832 the graveyard was watched for three hundred and twenty-nine nights running – forty-seven weeks – something which must have been very demanding for a small community. The graveyard watch was a very effective method of protecting the dead but a correspondent of the *Kelso Mail* complained in 1826 about the thinking behind it. At that time, various misdemeanours were occurring in Kelso and the writer asked, 'Does it not afford a singular display of civic economy to have four persons set as a nightly guard over the dead while no effort is made to protect the living?'

There were, however, also other ways of protecting the dead. One was to lay a very heavy stone on top of the coffin before filling in the grave. An Aberdeenshire example of one of these mort-stones, as they were called, was ten inches thick. A variation was used at a burial in the Borders about 1823. The inside of the grave was lined with flag stones and when the coffin was let down, it was covered with a certain amount of earth after which two flag stones were laid and closely bound down with iron. The grave was then completely filled up and turf laid in the usual manner. This system was unusual in the area at that time and warranted a report in the *Border Courier*, along with a recommendation that a general adoption of this method would go far to check Resurrectionists in their unhallowed work. Sometimes heavy stones were used in conjunction with a metal mortsafe or cage. The cage went directly on top of the coffin, the stone over that, and then the grave was filled in. In many cases stones were dipensed with and compensated for by the sheer weight of a cast-iron mortsafe beaten into the shape of a coffin. Weighing perhaps as much as a ton, these were lowered into the grave over the coffin although sometimes they were just sunk some two or three feet into the ground. A fine example of this type stands outside the door of Colinton Parish Church, Edinburgh.

A lighter but still effective form of mortsafe was a coffin-shaped iron grill. A wooden base was placed in the bottom of the grave, the coffin was lowered on to it, followed by the mortsafe which was bolted to the wood, after which the grave was filled up in the usual manner. A large 'double bed size' iron grille on four legs which still stands in the graveyard at Dalmally, Ayrshire, may well be an unusual variant of mortsafe although according to local information it was meant to protect graves from wild animals. Mortsafes were intended for re-use and were only left in place for some six weeks, after which the grave was opened up, the mortsafe removed ready for the next funeral, and the coffin left to decay in the grave.

Mortsafes gave excellent protection but they required block and tackle to lower and raise them. Although one can hardly envisage Resurrectionists borrowing this equipment, it was always carefully stored lest it should fall into their hands and at Inverurie, Aberdeenshire, for instance, a most suitable place was found for keeping it – at the bakery, where work went on day and night and it would be difficult for any unauthorized person to make away with it. This set of block and tackle is now in the museum in Inverurie.

Though made of iron, mortsafes seem to have been, to start with anyway, beyond the skill of local blacksmiths. It was a James McGill, a smith from Dalkeith, some twenty-five miles away, who provided mortsafes for Earlston, Berwickshire, and when the first one was to be put to use he came and laid it down himself 'to the entire satisfaction' of everyone present and, when another was shortly needed, he came again and instructed a local person how to do the job.

Mortsafes were not cheap, especially as one was not enough for any parish. At Anstruther, Fife, where they began using them in 1830, they had no less than eight, of different sizes, the largest of which was seven feet long, two feet eight inches wide and three feet deep and cost £4. 11/- stg. At Logierait, Perthshire, there are still to be seen three grilled mortsafes, two of them about eight feet long, and a child's size of four feet long. What brought them within the reach of ordinary people was that they were usually provided by what can only be called co-operative societies. As with watching societies, it was up to individuals to join if they wanted the benefits and most of them did. Whatever voluntary method of protecting the dead was chosen, it was the result of a communal decision usually made after a public meeting of householders and, as methods varied from parish to parish, so did charges and subscriptions. It may be that members of some societies paid their subscriptions and that was that; elsewhere they paid a small charge for use of the mortsafe while non-members could have the use of one for a higher sum. Robert Southey said that in Glasgow in 1819 where, according to him, mortsafes were left in the grave for a month, the charge was 1/- stg. a day, which would come to 30/-, a high cost, so surely a special charge. A press report of the North Quarter Association's operations said that having a watch would avoid relatives having to pay the expense of mortsafes whereas, when mortsafes were introduced at Earlston, Berwickshire, a press report said that the watch had been superseded by mortsafes which were not expensive, all of which shows considerable variations in costing around the country. Some family burying plots were enclosed with iron railings and gates which served the double purpose of fencing off the occupants from the common herd and foiling the body-snatcher as well. Many of these railings were removed for scrap during World War Two.

People began to fear that Resurrectionists might anticipate events and not just steal buried or unburied bodies but commit murder in order to supply the demands of the anatomy schools. This did happen but how often is not known; the only really authenticated instances are the murders by Burke and Hare in Edinburgh and it was their arrest late in 1828 and the subsequent execution of Burke (Hare turned King's Evidence) early in 1829 which caused an extraordinary panic throughout the country about the doings of body-snatchers generally.

While many places had already been taking steps to protect their dead, as already described, others woke up with a jolt at this point and began doing so too. The *Inverness Courier* reported that, 'In almost every town and village in the north nightly watches are appointed over the churchyards', and that was in an area remote from medical schools. Throughout the country more watching and mortsafe societies were formed and everyone was on the lookout for suspicious vehicles or oddly shaped parcels. Very often the fears of the public could only be allayed by opening graves to see if they had been robbed and an inspection at Kirkmichael, Ayrshire, showed twenty-three graves to be empty. Imagine the effect this must have had on that community as the coffins were brought up and the dead clothes laid across the graves while from all parts of the parish relatives came hurrying to know whether or not their loved ones had ended up on the anatomist's table. To have emptied twenty-three graves, although not all at once, and never been detected, says much for the skill of the body-snatchers but it seems that they had had some co-operation from the grave-digger because he promptly absconded and the Sheriff announced a reward for his arrest.

Yet another solution to the problem of body-snatching was the erection of morthouses which were in fact mortuaries or vaults where the coffined body lay until such time as it was of no use for dissection and could be buried. An odd one or two, such as that at Crail, Fife, which was built in 1826, may have been used before the panic of 1828/9 but from the dates of the building most of them it seems that their introduction was a direct consequence of the Burke and Hare terror.

The basic requirement of morthouses was that they should be absolutely impregnable. They might be partly or wholly underground with an immensely solid door. Some were turfed over, some slated; they might be lined with steel and provided with shelves for the coffins to lie on awaiting burial; they might have coffin shelves fitted with rollers. There was considerable variety but the circular granite one at Udny, Aberdeenshire, locally known as the Round House, is unique. A few steps lead down to its outer door, made of oak and studded with about a hundred and forty-four iron studs. The inner door is of iron; it is not hinged but held in slots so that it can drop down to give access and then be hauled up to shut it. Inside is a coffin platform – a circular wooden turntable which revolves on a base of stones or rubble held together with plaster or cement. As each coffin came in it was placed on the turntable which was pushed round to await the next arrival. They were removed for burial in sequence although none was ever allowed to remain there for longer than three months.

It was in 1834 that regulations for its use were laid down and because impregnability was of the utmost importance, instructions for access were strict: 'There shall be four key bearers, members of the committee, who must attend to open and shut the vault at all times necessary but it will be desirable that those wishing admittance will give the key bearers at least twenty-four hours' previous warning – the key bearers to reside as near the church as can be got.' Surprising to say, this Round House received no mention in the *New Statistical Account* for the parish which was written in 1840.

As with watching and mortsafe societies, morthouses were usually co-operative efforts, built by public subscription. The cost of the Round House at Udny was £80 stg. but its use was free to subscribers and their families while it was available to others for a fee. At Culsalmond, also in Aberdeenshire, members had to pay from 3d to 1/- stg. for use of the semi-underground morthouse there while others paid from 1/- to 5/-. This form of corpse-protection seems to have been particularly popular in north-east Scotland. However, what necessitated such extreme forms of protection also ended the need for it. The one benefit of Burke's and Hare's activities was that the resultant publicity and horror led to the passing of the Anatomy (Scotland) Act in August 1832 which regulated the practice of anatomical dissection and made body-snatching unnecessary.

This Act allowed those having lawful custody of bodies (other than undertakers or anyone entrusted with a body only for burial) to permit anatomical examination in certain cases unless the deceased person had previously forbidden this, and a certificate giving essential facts had to be produced along with the body. It ordered that there should be Inspectors of schools of anatomy who had to make quarterly returns and that bodies for dissection should be delivered in a coffin or shell and be thereafter decently buried in consecrated ground or in some public burial ground in use for people of the appropriate religious persuasion, after which a certificate of burial should be sent to the Inspector within six weeks. The Act also dealt with the original source of anatomical subjects, the bodies of murderers.

The Act went a long way to restoring people's confidence, with the result that the morthouse at Udny, for instance, was little used and at one point became an ammunition store for volunteers. Even so, precautions were still taken for a considerable time in many places such as Traquair, where they were still watching graves in 1848. But body-snatching did end and along with it the necessity for using mortsafes and many of them must still be underground as lifting them for re-use was no longer necessary. The style of cast-iron mortsafes made them suitable as watering troughs for stock, once the tackle holes were plugged, and some of these might still be found on farms. Some are still to be seen above ground in various graveyards, but a number of them were removed as scrap iron during World War Two. Watch houses which lent themselves to it became grave-diggers' sheds but others still stand, along with watch towers, as memorials to these anxious times.

Unbaptized Children

Something which seems particularly tragic to modern ears is the old practice of refusing unbaptized children burial in the churchyard and interring them elsewhere. There was a certain element of superstition about baptism; people believed that without a name a child might be taken by the fairies. But this was surely not enough to deny a child proper burial and this denial probably stemmed from a belief that baptism was necessary for salvation, and without any prospect of salvation, what did it matter where burial took place? However, this custom went against Protestant practice which is clear from an order made by the Synod of Fife in 1641 that 'all those who burie unbaptized bairnes apart, be taken notice of and censured'. But the practice went on for many years.

Unfortunately, many children died unbaptized because infant mortality was high and baptism was not always easily obtained. In the Church of Scotland the letter of the law stressed that this sacrament was always meant to be administered in church before the congregation but how did one take or carry a small child miles to church when there were no roads or bridges, especially if the child were ailing or in wintry weather, and how could a mother take a child there if she herself were ill? In the Associate and United Presbyterian Churches these difficulties were recognised and ministers visited their areas at intervals, baptizing as they went, but their visits were not very frequent and death did not always wait for the minister. In later years, many Church of Scotland baptisms did take place in the home as the minister tempered the law with mercy.

These were natural obstacles, but the Church of Scotland put other barriers between children and baptism. It was the practice to refuse it to a child whose parents were undergoing censure for scandal and very often it was only the need for baptism which made the parents ready to undergo public censure. By the time their sin had been investigated by the Kirk Session and they had undergone the appropriate punishment, which was usually standing in church before the congregation for a given number of Sundays, a considerable time could elapse. Gross ignorance on the part of parents was another impediment to a child's baptism and Rev. Andrew Edgar of Mauchline, Ayrshire, quoted an instance of a father being sent away by the Kirk Session to learn the Commandments within a month and also having to pay 10/- as a surety which would be returned to him if he succeeded but not if he failed. Parental misbehaviour of any sort also affected a child's chance of baptism, whether it was a drunken father or Sabbath breaking or violating a Harvest Thanksgiving, even if the two latter were done on the orders of a master. There was reason for this but all the while a little child went unbaptized through no fault of its own and was at risk of being

143

refused a grave in the churchyard. This put these innocents in the same class as suicides, excommunicants and murderers who were also denied Christian burial.

Sometimes parents used devious means to obtain baptism for their children if they thought it would be refused and the Kirk Session records of Inverness refer to this happening and say that parents 'resorted to courses implying some sort of friendly negotiations between them and one or more of the elders'. The Kirk Session as a whole objected to this and in 1695 ordered that no child might be baptized without a Sessional order or at least five elders present at the writing of the order.

Excavation in 1982 of an early manorial churchyard at The Hirsel, Coldstream, in Berwickshire, showed few child burials before the 17th century. In a press report there was speculation as to whether there was less child mortality then or whether people did not give children elaborate burials. A third alternative is that, if unbaptized, children would not have been buried in the churchyard anyway. If a child died unbaptized parents accepted the situation and buried them where they might. When a baby was found buried on the shore near Inverness in 1690, the father was discovered and called before the Kirk Session. He admitted that he had buried it but was able to produce two witnesses to the fact that it had never been baptized, and these people had also helped him to bury it.

Some special areas were designated for the burial of these children but records of them are few and far between. In the 1690s unbaptized children on the Island of Iona were buried along with murderers in a piece of empty ground between St Mary's Church and the gardens. At Watten in Caithness they were buried along with poor strangers – beggars – on the site of a ruined chapel at Scouthal, while in the parish of Nigg, Ross and Cromarty, they were buried around the ancient Pictish Shandwick Stone, along with suicides, until 1790. Interestingly enough each of these sites was in some way special, even if not consecrated ground. In the Torridon area of Wester Ross there were at least three of these burial areas, two of which are marked, 'Infant burial ground, disused' on the 1881 six-inch Ordnance Survey maps of the area but there is nothing on the ground now to show any special significance for the choice of these particular spots. Into the 1880s, an open grassy space surrounded by blackthorn at North Ballachulish, Inverness-shire, had a very eerie reputation among local people even although they had long lost sight of the fact that it was an old burying ground for unbaptized infants and suicides. Rev. Charles Rogers, writing in 1884, said that the practice of separate burial for unbaptized children continued 'till a recent period'. At some point therefore in the late 19th century their burial in churchyards began, but usually only in a special part of them or alongside them, rather than in them, along with the poor, excommunicated persons and very occasionally suicides. In some parishes the remains of unbaptized children were placed under the eaves of the church.

Naturally enough, in view of the attitude to unbaptized children, stillborn babies suffered discrimination also. There was a belief in some parts that they, as well as unbaptized children, must not be buried during daylight hours but between sunset and sunrise. This was thought to be based on verse 8 of Psalm 58 which says: 'As a snail which melteth, let every one of them pass away; like the untimely birth of a woman, that they might not see the sun.' An extension of this belief, although not based on the psalm, was that if buried while the sun was up, these children would find it difficult to get into heaven. According to Alasdair Alpin Macgregor, the practice of burying a stillborn child between sunset and sunrise has been seen this century in Ross and Cromarty and in Sutherland and it is said to have survived till quite recently (from 1965) in the Black Isle of Ross and Cromarty. For a time, in some places such as Berwickshire, stillborn babies were buried on the verge of the graveyard footpath, unmarked by any memorial. Later on, graveyards provided special ground for these infants – the regulations of the Burial Grounds Department in Berwickshire in 1966 gave the following charge, 'Stillborn child in ground for stillborn children, £2.'

Burials of stillborn children are now uncommon as hospitals or health authorities usually dispose of the little bodies themselves. Writing in *Life and Work* in 1982, the Very Rev. Dr John Gray recommends that these babies should always be buried with at least the father present with the minister. He also suggests that the birth should be recorded, under the name it would have been given, in the parish magazine as otherwise the family can be left almost wondering if it ever existed at all. What a different attitude to that of earlier years. Where a family wants such a burial, it takes place now in the family lair or in a new one in which relatives will later join it; but should the local authority be involved such burials take place in free ground.

Suicide

I n most parts of the world, suicide has always produced a feeling of horror. The exceptions include Hindu races who believed it could help in escaping disease and old age; Indian women who burned themselves on their husbands' funeral pyres; and the Chinese and Japanese who see suicide as a virtue in certain circumstances. Although it was occasionally thought of as something good in early Christian centuries, suicide is generally regarded as a bad death and condemned by Christianity. David Hume in his *Commentaries on the Law of Scotland* makes the Scottish position clear: 'Whatever notions may be current among the vulgar, there seems to be no warrant in law or practice for inflicting any indignity on the remains of those unhappy persons who finish their course in this unnatural way.' But legal or not, these indignities did happen in Scotland.

In Birrell's *Diary* he tells how in 1598 the drowned body of a suicide in Edinburgh was 'harled through the town backwards and thereafter hanged on the gallows'. This was the same case recorded in the Burgh records as being put to an assize, convicted and ordered to be 'tayne and drawn throw the toun in ane cairt and hang in the gallows in the Borrow mure'. In 1611 the 'deid corp' of another suicide in Edinburgh was convicted in a court held by the bailies. Much later, in 1769, a particularly unpleasant attitude to suicide, as well as a shocking example of religious intolerance, appeared in Mauchline, Ayrshire. A dissenter committed suicide and the Session Clerk wrote in the Register of Deaths in exultant capitals, 'HUGH CAMPBELL, A SECEDER, CUT HIS OWN THROAT 3rd JANUARY.'

One of the early penalties of murder was confiscation of property and as suicide was self-murder this penalty applied to it also, and even insanity was not an adequate plea in mitigation. This penalty fell heavily not only on the suicide's family but on his creditors as well. In some cases, however, the property was returned to the family – one such was the case of Sibilla Dewar who drowned herself in Edinburgh's North Loch in 1597. Nine years before, her husband had been forbidden to come to her house or interfere with her in any way and one feels that there was perhaps provocation for her suicide, which possibly explains the restoration of her property. Another parallel with murder was that as medical learning developed, the bodies of both murderers and suicides were liable to be handed over for dissection.

Because suicide was regarded as anti-social and unnatural, the church denied suicides burial in consecrated ground. In a country like Scotland where such store was set by burial in the same place as one's forbears and family, this was a terrible thing for the suicide's family to bear and on the west coast especially, the family and friends of such a person also had to suffer the execration of the community; they were regarded with a rather horrified awe and avoided as much as possible. In 1582 the Kirk Session of Perth refused to allow the body of a man who had drowned himself to be 'brought through the town in daylight, neither yet be buried among the faithful . . . ' because it was common practice for suicides to be buried at night. Their bodies were sometimes laid north and south in the grave, not east and west as is usual (apart from some parts of the Highlands.) Even if east and west, suicides might be laid the wrong way round. When workmen were digging just outside the churchyard wall at Balmaghie, Kirkcudbrightshire, in 1894, they found a skull facing west and it was thought that this might have been a suicide, buried outside consecrated ground and facing a different direction to normal.

These unfortunate people were often buried in other strange places, such as the highway and sometimes at cross-roads. The reasons for these two choices are thought to be so that traffic would keep the corpse down, that roads going in different directions would confuse the spirit and prevent it finding its way home and that cross-roads might help to dispel sin. Cross-roads had a bad reputation and burial of suicides at them is one reason for this reputation but, in a vicious circle, by being a place of evil repute they were a natural choice for such a grave. The desire to confuse the spirit and prevent it finding its way home also explains why suicides' bodies were often taken out of the house not by the door but by the window instead, or even through a hole knocked in the wall. Some were buried in woods, also perhaps with the idea that finding the way out of them would be puzzling and difficult. Various suicides' burial grounds around the country have already been mentioned in connection with unbaptized children and poor strangers. There is another one, still spoken of by older people in the parish of Tannadice, Angus, as the 'suicides' burying ground' in which the roadside tradition is evident. It is a small triangle of land in the corner of a field and lies by the side of an old route from Brechin to Forfar which was used until the Finavon bridge was built in 1796; there is however no evidence of a cross-roads.

This burial ground lies on the boundary of the parishes of Tannadice and Oathlaw and apparently a parish or county boundary was also considered as suitable for such burials. In Glen Isla, Angus, there is a cairn on the summit of Mt Blair, an old country and parish boundary, said to mark the grave of a young man who took his own life. Even if not a boundary, a hill top or mountain was often chosen for such burials and in Glen Lethnot, Angus, suicides were buried on the crest of Wirren until 1780, it being the highest hill thereabouts at 2220 feet. Even today people point to its crest and say they can see graves, although there are none to be seen. This hill-top burial seems to spring from a desire to bury suicides out of the way, in contradiction to burial at cross-roads or on the highway, and with this idea of isolation a lonely headland was sometimes chosen too. A suicide's grave in the form of a cist burial has already been mentioned as being on a headland on the north coast. Elsewhere lonely areas were allocated to suicides, such as St Leonard's, Edinburgh, now a built-up area but formerly an unfrequented spot.

There was a tradition on the east coast of Scotland of burying suicides at the water's edge. In 1582 the Kirk Session of Perth insisted that the body of a suicide, the one already mentioned, should be buried 'in the little Inch within the water'. In 1815 some people in the parish of Kincardine, Ross and Cromarty, dug up the body of someone they considered had committed suicide from its burying place and threw it into a hole on the seashore. For this high-handed action and 'riotous proceedings' to do with it they were tried at the Circuit

Court but got off on some technical points.

In 1843 a woman at Hilltown, near Tain in Ross and Cromarty, was believed to have drowned herself in a well although all the evidence pointed to the fact that she had had a fit and fallen in. No one would go near the body but it was suggested that a living dog should be thrown down as the first touch would be unlucky. This was not in fact done but as soon as the husband got the body up, the villagers put it into a coffin of sorts and that evening, presumably with the idea of burial at night, took it some miles to the seashore and buried it in the sand. The authorities obviously did not consider this a case of suicide and had the corpse dug up and given decent burial in the burying ground of St Duthus Chapel.

When someone who was locally thought to be a suicide, was buried in the churchyard of Creich in Sutherland, the men of the district took it upon themselves to dig the coffin up at night and throw it into the firth, only to find it washed up near the dead man's house next day. This happened three times in all but what occurred thereafter is not known. The people were deeply impressed by all this and believed it to be a sign of divine anger with the suicide, not thinking apparently that it might just as well be a sign of God's displeasure with those who treated a dead body in this way. The attitude to the burial of suicides on the west coast was different to that of the east coast, even in the same county. There was the same horror but whereas the corpse was hustled to the seashore as often as not on the east, on the west coast it was removed as far as possible from it because it was believed there that if a suicide's grave was in sight of the sea or of cultivated land it would drive away the fish and no crops would thrive.

The Scotsman of 20 January 1887 reported a sad story from Ullapool, Ross and Cromarty, where a feeble-minded pauper woman drowned herself in a river pool. Although her body could be seen, no one would recover it and even when the police arrived and repeatedly asked for help, still no one would give any assistance. When the body was finally brought to land it was taken to an outhouse belonging to a local gentleman as neither friend nor neighbour would take it in. A coffin was obtained and a horse and cart to carry it to the village burial ground but a crowd of about sixty men – a mob in fact – deforced the police and refused to allow the burial within sight of sea or crops. The horse was unyoked and the coffin carried into the hills for burial some three miles away. The Fiscal at Dingwall was informed and an investigation ordered but it does not seem that this body was brought back.

The horror of suicide extended to articles associated with it. Thus the bier, and the tools used to make a suicide's coffin, were destroyed in spite of the fact that this meant financial loss. In the late 19th century a suicide's body was washed ashore in Little Loch Broom, a sea loch. A rough deal box was quickly made, the body put inside and all the tools then sunk in the sea. The box was towed across the loch and dragged up the hillside to a lonely place where box and ropes were buried. In another case, when a woman hanged herself on her bed posts, the bed was broken to pieces and thrown into the sea. In a case at Lochinver, Sutherland, about 1880, all the spare tools and the remainder of the nails were put into the coffin with the corpse and buried with it and, after the burial, the hammer and anything remaining were thrown into the sea. With such dread on the west coast of burying a suicide within sight of the sea, it seems astonishing that anything to do with the dead person was ever consigned to it. Strangely enough, when Mr Morrison, minister of Kintail, Ross and Cromarty – one of three consecutive ministers of that name there between 1781 and 1898 – insisted on giving proper burial to a suicide the fishing for the next three years was the best for a long time.

People were even unwilling to make a coffin for a suicide. In one instance at Bonar Bridge, Sutherland, the problem was only resolved by the menfolk of the village each driving in one nail. Once made, no place could be found to bury the body until an old soldier offered a corner of his garden and the burial took place under an ancient apple tree there. Just as the minister of Kintail had found, no harm resulted; in fact, the old man used to boast that thereafter he never lacked an apple from that tree.

In former times an unofficial community verdict of suicide seems to have been only too readily given. This happened in the case of the woman who fell into the well, the man whose body kept being washed up at his house, and the body dug up in Kincardine, Ross and Cromarty, and in other cases too. Another instance of a mob interfering with funeral proceedings because they thought the death was a suicide occurred in Cromarty, Ross and Cromarty, in 1807. They 'riotously obstructed' the funeral and even assaulted the mourners and found themselves in court as a result. In the Evanton area of Ross and Cromarty, a tramp drank too much one evening and went over a high bank to his death. No consideration was given to the fact that this might have been an accident; he was refused burial in the churchyard and laid to rest close to where he had died with a pile of stones on his grave – a cairn – on to which any passer-by was expected to put another stone, keeping their eyes closed as they did so. But as with unbaptized children, more merciful and compassionate attitudes prevailed and nowadays suicides are given normal burial and since the Suicide Act of 1961 it has no longer been a crime to commit suicide.

Death is for the Living

T he most striking feature of all this is how constructively death was used to help the
living. The graveyard, which was established for the burial of the dead, became a
meeting place for the living where people met and newsed and craft guilds fore-gathered,
where markets and fairs were held and a variety of other unauthorized activities went on.
During the Clearances, it was in the Highland churchyard of Croik that people evicted from
their homes found refuge and it was not unknown for tramps and vagrants to turn to the
churchyard for shelter in bad weather.

Education was also served by death. In Edinburgh, income from burgh mortcloths, after
originally going to the poor, later went to the Town College to help with the teaching of the
young; so did the fine imposed on a herald painter who used a mortcloth of his own when he
should not have done so. Alloa Colliers Fund or Friendly Society was partly designed for
the payment of schoolmasters and near St Andrews a group of farmers used both hearse
and mortcloth to raise money for the 'encouragement' of a schoolmaster, while in Inverness
a mortcloth given by a provost contributed to the schoolmaster's salary. These are just a
few instances; there must be many more.

But very largely it was the poor who benefitted from the deaths of others. Financial help
for them came from the income brought in from the hire of the parish hearse, of mortcloths,
the mort bell and the tolling of the church bell at funerals. Funerals often gave the poor an
opportunity of a good meal, whether attending as mourners or going as beggars, and if going
as the latter there might be the chance of receiving part of a cash gift. Death of a heritor
often meant a considerable donation or bequest of meal or of money for the poor of the
parish. When a burgh council granted permission for a burial place in the town churchyard,
it was made plain that 'a gratification for the poor' was expected. When the numbers of the
poor increased greatly in Edinburgh in 1691, the way suggested of increasing income for
them was to charge more for burials not at the usual time of 2.00 p.m.

If a corpse was laid in a church overnight, then the poor, too, benefitted. Melrose Kirk
Session records of 1748 say, 'William Douglas of Cavers his corpse from Edinburgh was
lodged in our kirk all tuesdays night last and there were given in for the use of the poor 2
guineas.' Penalties for failure to bury the dead in Scots linen were assigned to the poor and
in 1701 the Scottish Parliament ordered that half the burial fees should go to the poor. Just
as the poor benefitted by the deaths of others, so could the ailing and the cures for several
complaints required the death of someone else. One of these was 'dead water', water over
which the living and the dead pass. This meant water from a stream over which the dead

were carried to burial, something which could be used to relieve various conditions. Even the 'mould' of the churchyards was believed to have special virtues.

Old people in the Seaboard villages of Easter Ross, for instance, still remember how a dead hand was used to cure some complaints. A common disease was King's Evil – scrofula, a form of tuberculosis affecting the neck. It was prevalent even into the 20th century and one cure for it involved taking the patient to a corpse and placing the dead hand on the affected part, something which could also be done to alleviate any ulcer or lump. Another cure for King's Evil, one which is still remembered, was to obtain a little piece of ivory which was 'chapped' between the teeth and put on the affected part. This of course does not involve death but the use of ivory is perhaps what lies behind cures involving skulls.

In view of the great horror of suicide, it is surprising but true that people in the Highlands were prepared to make use of a suicide's skull as a remedy for the 'falling sickness' as epilepsy was often called. It was often thought of as a form of insanity and was a great scourge in the Highlands and Islands. Water from a holy well drunk from a suicide's skull was well known as a cure but was only used after other remedies had failed. If no holy well was available, ordinary water would do.

In the late 19th century, and possibly into the beginning of the 20th, people visited the grave of a suicide near Torridon, Ross and Cromarty, to drink from the skull. There are several accounts from this area of the use of such a skull, all of which refer, it seems, to that of Grant's Wife. Local people kept quiet about it and tried to keep the location of the grave secret from strangers and it was with some difficulty that an Inverness architect, Alexander Ross, managed to persuade someone to take him to it in the early 1880s. The grave was covered by a broken slab which had been some four to five feet long and six inches thick. In a small hollow below it he found part of the roof of a human skull, like a saucer, about five to six inches in diameter. His guide told him that many people from Lochcarron and surrounding districts came there to be cured and judging by the surroundings it had recently been used. One account from the early 1900s of what seems to have been this grave, tells of running water being used, saying that three drinks from the skull, one in the name of each of the Trinity, was a cure. Certainly, when Alexander Ross was there, broken bottles lay close by in which drinking water had obviously been taken to the grave. Another account of the skull speaks on one epileptic frequently drinking from it so it may have been thought of as a regular treatment as well as a cure. Grant's Wife's grave was some way from the graveyard but there seems to have been another suicide's grave in Torridon, just outside the graveyard. This provided a skull which was once taken from its resting place to a gathering of people who were anxious that an epileptic should drink from it. He was blindfolded during the process and a complete cure resulted.

Sometimes drinking from a skull was not sufficient and some of the skull itself was taken in the cure. One case of this occurred in the 19th century in the parish of Nigg, Ross and Cromarty, in an attempt to cure a fifteen-year old epileptic boy. After unsuccessfully trying to cure him with moles' blood, his relatives made a sixty-mile journey to get a piece of the skull of a suicide, although there was a suicides' burying ground no distance away at Shandwick. The bone was scraped to powder and mixed in a cup of water which the boy, all unknowing, had to swallow, but the results, unfortunately, are not recorded.

The *Scottish Antiquary* of 1892, in an article on medical folklore in the Highlands, told of two cases which occurred not long before that date, of the use of skulls as a cure for epilepsy. In both cases, the skulls were of people recently dead, which makes it particularly unpleasant to think that what was being used was the scrapings of the inside of the skull, the directions being: 'Scrab it wi' a knife and tak' it in water, as much as a pooder o't.' One of the skulls was that of an epileptic, the other that of a suicide and in this latter case it was the patient himself who obtained the skull by digging up the body at night. Strangely enough, it was believed that anyone who had been cured of epilepsy might not touch a dead body or even see a funeral without risking a recurrence of the complaint.

While these cures sound horrifying, the fact is that in many areas medical help was virtually unobtainable and too expensive to have anyway so that people had to do the best they could with what they had and if that involved the dead, that was the way it had to be. Education, the poor, the sick all benefitted from the death of others. In the old days death was definitely for the living.

Appendices

'Preparations'.

The word 'corp' was often used instead of 'corpse' in the belief that it was the singular form of the word.

When people progressed from using stone and wooden tools to metal, these metals were thought to be very powerful and it was believed that if properly magnetized they could produce miracles. They appear in several cures such as 'silvered water'. Iron was thought to be able to ward off evil and appears in the phrase 'cold iron'. As a horseshoe, it was doubly effective because it combined iron and the shape of the crescent moon.

Stretching a body was also called striking, straiking, streaking, and was done on a striking board or 'dead deal'.

A cere cloth cost £10. 10/- stg. in 1790. In addition to Lady Mey's cere cloth in 1692, 24 ells of 'fyne linning' and 5 ells of muslin were provided which may have been either for the draping of rooms, or burial linen, or mourning wear for her household. A winding sheet took approximately 4 yards of linen.

In 1684 dead clothes for Mr Philip Nisbet of Ladykirk, Berwickshire, were made by the local sempstress for £60 Scots.

More elaborate dead clothes appeared at a Caithness funeral in 1956 when a woman dressed her daughter's corpse in a specially made pink nightdress.

The church was sometimes used as a mortuary. Records of the Burgh of Peebles in 1631 and of the Church of St Ternan's, Arbuthnott, Angus, 1721, show that drowned bodies were taken to them; and in body-snatching days, when lifted bodies were discovered they were usually taken to the church to await identification.

The only surviving mourning bed in Scotland is at Traquair House in Peebles-shire.

The *Statistical Account* for Stornoway says that when one of a married couple died, it was not uncommon for the survivor to marry again very soon. Some remained in widowhood for just a few weeks, some just for a few days, while one widow arranged her next marriage before her husband was buried and was married the day after his funeral. According to the writer of this Account, grief for the loss of a husband or wife was an affliction little known among the lower classes but it may well be that sheer practical necessity dictated this conduct.

'The Tolling of Church Bells'.

Some charges to do with funeral bell-ringing include:

1720 – Heritors of Galston, Ayrshire, to pay at least 12/- Scots.

1762 – The grave-digger at Galston to be paid '2d each burial for ringing the big bell'.

1773 – At the funeral of the Duchess of Perth the Canongate bellman was paid 2/6 stg.

1830 – The Committee on Public Clocks in the Burgh of Glasgow ordered that 'When bells are tolled one hour at funerals, each bell-ringer receives 1/- stg. from the Session Clerk'.

An article in the *Scottish Antiquary* No. V, says that a large bell at St Giles, Edinburgh, is a recast of an old bell of 1460 which bore a Latin inscription ending with the words, *Defunctus plango; vivos voco; fulmina frango,* meaning 'I mourn the dead' which refers to the passing bell; 'I summon the living' referring to the call to church or to arms; and 'I disperse thunder' from an old belief that thunder could be driven away by making a loud noise with bells.

Church bells could also be used for civil purposes such as the curfew at night and sometimes the bells of a town church belonged to the burgh, as at Montrose, Angus; Lanark; Inveraray, Argyll; and equally a church might be allowed to use the town bell if it had none of its own, as at Tain, Ross and Cromarty.

At some point in the early 19th century, an ancient chapel near Glasgow Cathedral was pulled down; it had a bell which was rung as funerals passed and it was expected that mourners would drop money into an opening in the wall which was surrounded by a Scriptural quotation.

The Scotsman of 5 May 1983 reported the funeral of a Chinese restaurant-owner in Perth when pipers, in lieu of Chinese musicians, led the procession to play and drive the devil away from the body.

'The Mort Bell'.

The mort bell was also called the dead or deid bell, lych bell, little bell, corpse bell.

Thomas Kirke, writing in 1679, gave the following form of funeral announcement, 'Beloved brouthrin and susters, I let you to wot that thir is an fauthful broothir lawtli departed awt of this prisant varld, aut thi plesuir of Aulmoughti Good (and then he vails his bonnet) his naum is Volli Voodcock, third son to Jimoy Voodcok a cordinger; he livs aut thi sext door vethin this Nord Gawt, close on this Nawthwr Rawnd, and I wod yaw gang to hus burying on Thrusdau before twa acloack . . .' (sic)

In some cases the 'bidding to the burial' gave no time, 10 a.m. being understood as the time of assembling and 2.00 or 3.00 p.m. as that of setting out for the graveyard.

The mort bell was referred to in 1621 at Dumbarton and in 1708 in Ayrshire, at Nigg, Ross and Cromarty in 1698 and Stirling in 1741. It was used in Hawick till 1780 and at Tain, Ross and Cromarty, and Bo'ness, West Lothian, until the 1790s. It appears as an emblem of mortality on gravestones from Roxburghshire and Dumfriesshire up to Aberdeenshire and Caithness, although in some places its appearance on gravestones is unusual and may indicate non-use in that district. A mort bell bought by Keith, Banffshire, cost £4. 16/- plus 12/- carriage from Aberdeen. (Scots.)

Hire charges include:

> Burgh of Lanark, 'For once ringing and going out with the bell when the corpse is liftit and for making the grave xs (10/- Scots) ilk persone and any officer he goes with the bell to exact iijs. iiijd (3/4 Scots) each time,' 1655.
>
> 1766, Ordiquhill Church, Banffshire, for the burial of Lady Cowbin's daughter, 8/-, obviously partly a donation.
>
> 1773, Ordiquhill Church, 8d and 3d, with 1/5 as a combined charge for bell and mortcloth. Both lots of Ordiquhill charges are sterling.
>
> 1808, Synod of Ross gave the following charges – digging an adult's grave and use of the bell 3/- stg., and the same for a child under twelve years 1/6 stg.

'Burial Letters'.

The burial letter for the funeral of Rev. John Mackenzie of Redcastle, Ross and Cromarty, who died in 1700 reputedly of witchcraft, read as follows:

> 'The favour of your presence to accompanie the corpes of Mr. John M'Kenzie minister of Killearnan from his Dwelling house ther to his burial place within the church yeard ther, Saturday next, being the twentie sevent instant, be ten a cloacke in the forenoon, is earnestlie intreated.' (sic)

Funeral of Lady Innes, 1786:

> 'The favour of your company upon Saturday the 21st current to mee the corps of Lady Innes, my deceased wife, near Rothiemay, by Twelve o'clock to attend her remains from that to the church of Marnoch, the place of Interment, and thereafter to dine at Kinnairdy, will much oblige, Sir, you most obedient servant, James Innes.'

Funeral of Alexander Milne of Chapelton, 1801:

> 'Sir, the favour of your company upon Monday, the 23rd current, at Twelve O'clock to convey

the remains of Alexander Milne of Chapelton my father-in-law, from this to the churchyard of Keith, the place of Interment, and thereafter to dine at Skinner's Tavern, Keith, is earnestly requested. Alexander Milne.'

Captain Burt, who wrote in 1640 of his travels in Scotland, said that by then when 'people of some circumstance' were to be buried letters were printed.

The collection of burial letters in Inverness Library, which consists of three volumes, has one hand-written burial letter in 1835; and one hand-written death notice in 1849. Some engravings have no wording.

There are examples of mourning cards in Eyemouth Museum, Berwickshire – notification of the deaths by drowning of fishermen in the great disaster of the early 1880s. These give the man's name and date of death, with a short verse below.

'Lykewakes'.

Lykewake – night-watching, wake, wauken, late wake.

The word 'lyke' appears in various forms, i.e. lykestrae, the straw of a deathbed; lyke house, house of death or a mortuary; lykestiggie or leekstiggie, stile in a wall over which a corpse is borne to the graveyard.

Dancing and religion – in November 1982 Spanish choirboys performed a liturgical dance during the Pope's visit to that country.

According to the Ochtertyre MSS (*Scotland and Scotsmen in the 18th Century*) dancing at lykewakes went on 'with great purity' until the late 1860s in some parts of Scotland but the Eastern Highlands had taken it to the same pitch only until about 1820 although strong traces of it remained there and in the bordering Lowlands much later than that.

The *Scottish Antiquary* vol. I gives the Agreement of the Lairds of Lorn to curtail expenses of funerals, 1729: 'Whereas a custom too long observed does more and more prevail in Lorn contrary to the practice of most other parts of Scotland, of commoners conveeing (sic) in great numbers to Latewake and funerals before the day of interment quhich unnecessary formality is often observed likeuayes (likewise) by Gentlemen and Ladies and though we are sensible that this proceeds from the peoples regard for the dead, yet it is obvious that these practices alwise did and if continued will involve the friends and successors of the defunct in considerable charges and trouble and bring the persons Inveeted to inconveniences. Therefore the subscribing Heretors and Gentlemen within the said Division of Lorn resolve and enact that neither Gentlemen nor Commoners upon the death of either Gentlemen or Woman, or upon the death of a Commoner except such as are in the town quhare such person so dying reside, or the nixt neighbouring Town or blood Relations unless Advertized by Letter or otherwise do come present to any funerall or Latewake untill the day of Interment and that none come then but such as are advertized or invited by the Defuncts friends, but in case the person dying be at some considerable distance from the Burial place, that his friends by their Letters or other advertisements give notice to such Gentlemen as are invited to bring quhat number of Commoners shall be thought proper or circumstances requires and no otherwise, and they promise to punish so far as is in their power any within their bounds who shall transgress these rules, and recommend to all people concerned in the management of funerals within Lorn that in the future such persons shall sit unserved on all occasions without allowing them access to any meat or drink as they conveen uncalled, and they appoint that public intimation shall be given after Divine Service within all parishes in the Division of Lorn.'

'Kisting'.

1686, Act anent Burying in Scots Linen – That hereafter no corps of any person or persons whatsoever shall be buried in any shirt sheet or anything else except in plain linen or cloth of hards made and spun within the Kingdom without lace or poynt. Discharging from henceforth the making use of Holland or other linen cloth made in other Kingdoms 'all silk hair or woollen gold or silver or any other stuff whatsoever' than what is made of flax or hards spun and wrought within the Kingdom, under pain of a penalty of £300 Scots toties quoties for a nobleman and 200 lib for each other person, whereof half to the discoverer and the other half to the poor of the parish where the said corps shall be buried; and for the better discovery of the contraveners it is ordained that every minister shall keep a book containing an exact account of all persons buried within the parish, and some one or more of the relations of the deceased or other 'credible persons (tenants in the country and cottars being always excepted)' shall within eight days after such interment bring a certificate upon oath in writing witnessed by 'tuo famous persons' to the minister declaring that the person was wind or wrapt in the manner prescribed herein which certificates are to be received by the minister or reader of the parish gratis without exacting any money therefor. And if no one brings such a certificate within eight days, then the goods of the deceased person are declared liable to the said forfaulter to be pursued at the instance of the minister of the parish before any Judge Competent and if the parties prove litigious, the Judges are empowered to modify expenses as they shall find cause and if such persons die in familia, the father and mother or other relations in whose family they die are hereby declared liable for the said fine, and if the minister is negligent in pursuing the contravener within six months of the burial, he is declared liable for the fine, the one half to the poor and the other half to the discoverer.

1695, Act anent Burial in Scots Linen, ratified Act of 1686 and included the following, 'it shall not be liesum to any person to make or sew any dead linen contrary to the said Act, under pain of 40 merks toties quoties, for the use of the poor'.

1695, Edinburgh Burgh Records show that the Council considered the Act anent Burial in Scots Linen and approved the bailies' recommendation that the elders and deacons should be appointed to take up lists of all persons who trangress the Act and from time to time deliver these to the Kirk treasurer who is to pursue the persons liable or to employ the Town's procurator-fiscal and apply the fines for the use of the poor.

1707, Parliament of Scotland – Our Sovereign Lady for encouragement of the woollen manufacture rescinds Acts of 1686 and 1695 anent burial in Scots linen and ordains that hereafter no corpse of any quality or condition whatsoever shall be buried in Linen, and that where linen has been made use of about dead bodies formerly, plain woollen cloth or stuff shall only be made use of in time coming. Kisting was also called kistan, chesting, coffining.

'Coffins'.

Genesis 50, 26: 'So Joseph died, being an hundred and ten years old: and they embalmed him, and he was put in a coffin in Egypt.'

1563, Book of the Universal Kirk of Scotland (General Assembly):

> 'Twitching the buriell of ye puire in everie parochine to Landward, It is ordaint that a beere be maid in everie parochine to carrie ye deid corps to buriall.' This goes on to say that people in villages or houses where the dead lies, with the next adjacent house, or a certain number of houses, shall convey the dead poor to burial and see him 'eirdit sax futt under ye eird.'

Every Superintendent was to require the Laird and Barons within his bounds to make an Act in their Courts on this subject and to cause officers to warn neighbours of the dead about it.

1568, Edinburgh Burgh Records refer to 'closed biers', i.e. common coffins.

Mort kist, mort chest, mort chist are all words for a coffin.

1602, Perth Kirk Session ordered the Master of the hospital to have 'ane common mort kist' made for the poor.

1673, Edinburgh Burch Records refer to the 'exorbitant pryces takine be the wrights of this burgh for mortkists'.

In some places, lack of a coffin was regarded as a qualification for free use of the mort cloth.

1608/9, Ayr Burgh Accounts: '(For painting) the mort kist in the pest tyme . . .'
1759, the account for the funeral of the Countess Dowager of Traquair is from James Anderson, described as 'Undertaker'.
1711, £180 Scots paid to the carpenter for coffins for the Laird of Balnagown's funeral, possibly two, of lead and wood.

'Funeral Hospitality'.

Edinburgh Burgh Records of 1691 refer to 2.00 p.m. as being the usual time for burials to take place. Early burial letters quoted in the *Scottish Antiquary* and in the Inverness Library's collection show that apart from a few cases, such as one of 1663, when the time is given as between midday and 1.00 p.m., 10.00 a.m. was the usual time for which mourners were bidden. Gradually the time became later and most of the Inverness collection gives 1.00 p.m. while several burial letters of the 1780s give still later times: 1783, 4.00 p.m.; 1783, 3.30 p.m. chesting for 4.00 p.m. burial; 1795, 2.00 p.m.
Various examples of 'services' are given to show how, though different, they were still basically the same:

1. Bread, cheese, ale and porter.
2. Glass of rum with 'burial bread.'
3. Pipes of tobacco.
4. Glass of port wine with cake.
5. Glass of sherry with cake.
6. Glass of whisky.

1. Glass of ale.
2. Dram and piece of shortbread.
3. Dram or other liquor.
4. Piece of currant bread.
5. Dram of wine or spirits.
6. Bread and cheese, pipes and tobacco.

1. Ale.
2. Dram.
3. Shortbread.
4. Dram or other liquor.
5. Currant bread.
6. Dram (spirits or wine.)
7. Bread and cheese, pipes and tobacco.

For people of substance the 'service' might be:

1. Meat and ale.
2. Shortbread and whisky.
3. Wine.
4. Currant bun and rum.
5. Sugar biscuits and brandy.

At the funeral of a seaman in Alloa in 1725, the mourners consumed:

20 pints ale	£13.	6.	–
2 pints aqua (whisky)	2.	–.	–
Bread (shortbread)	2.	3.	6

Tobacco and pipes	–. 10. –	
4 lbs cheese	–. 12. –	(all Scots money.)

A Scots pint equals 2 quarts of present measure so they drank 1 gallon of whisky and 10 gallons of ale.

Shortbread was formerly used in some places for communion – at St Michael's Dumfries, till 1864, and in the parish of Kells, Kirkcudbrightshire, till the late 1870s, and in Dalry, Ayrshire, until about 1887.

The funeral of Hugh Campbell of Calder in 1616 cost £1647. 16. 4 Scots, of which a quarter was spent on whisky.

1684, Funeral of Mr Philip Nisbet of Ladykirk:

Wine, bisquet, tobacco and pipes	£39. –. –	
Bread	9. 3. –	
Ale	10. 9. –	(Scots money.)

From *The Oliphants of Gask* by Graham E. Maxtone, it appears that in 1729 Laurence Oliphant provided the following for his mother's funeral feast:

1 leg of beef	1 ox	1 cow
1 pig	4 sheep	2 doz hens
6 capons	1 doz lobster	3 large cod
crabs	anchovies	capers and olives
6 mangoes	6 ox tongues	bottled cucumbers
1 pint sweet oil	spices	1 pint of walnuts
700 pickled oysters	sweets	1 pot of barberries
2 lbs 'marmallit of oranges'		1 quart bottle good snuff
10 doz strong claret	5 doz 'small'	2 doz cherry brandy

and in addition a barrel and 2 doz ordinary brandy and a selection of other drinks.

An action raised in 1755 by Dr Duncan Ross of Kindeace, Ross and Cromarty, against his sisters for the expenses of their mother's funeral, included:

2 cows slaughtered £4
2 ankers aquavitae (about 8 gallons) £2. 14/-
3 bolls malt £1. 10/-
4 wedders (sheep) 16/-
3 mutchkins white wine (about 3 English pints) 2/-
3 bolls oats for horses £1. 4/- (they had to be fed too.)

Other eatables included sugar biscake, plumbcake, seedcake, almonds, cinnamon, mace, nutmegs, raisins, currants, carvie (carroway) and anise, confected carvie, lemons, and much more besides. There were also costs such as:

To Achanie's servant carrying venison 5/-
To Culcairn's cook for his trouble £2. 2/-
To James Shan, cook, £1. 1/-   (These prices appear to be sterling.)

The word 'dredgy' or 'dredgie' came to mean a funeral feast, but was also used for a funeral service in earlier times, i.e. 'to read the dredgie'. In pre-Reformation times the 'dergen' was a requiem mass. 'Dredgy' was a corrupt form of the old Roman Catholic word and function of the dirge, the office of the dead at matins.

1771, Mauchline Kirk Session Records: 'The Session considering the manner in which the Burying of the Dead is conducted consumes a great deal of time unnecessarily in regard the invitation fixes ordinarily ten o'clock in the forenoon notwithstanding the corpse is not lifted until about 3 or 4 in the afternoon being at the distance of 5 or 6 hours from the time appointed for Neighbours to attend, it is therefore the unanimous opinion of the Session that the Regulations in respect to Burials agreed upon

by the Session of Galston be adopted for this parish which regulations are as follows.'
Unfortunately, they do not follow.

'Burial Services'.

The psalms usually sung in Hawick, Roxburghshire, as a person was dying were Psalms 23, 43 and 118.
A memory of some fifty years ago in Skye tells of how the ministers of the Church of Scotland, Free Church and Free Presbyterian Church all used to go to funerals together but the Free Church minister never entered the graveyard on these occasions lest it should appear that he was taking part in any way in a graveside service. On one occasion, when they came to the point where he always left the procession, one of his clerical friends pointed out to the other, "He'll end up here anyway."

'Mortcloths'.

The mortcloth belonging to Edinburgh Hammermen was free to all members in the 16th century but later on charges came in and by the 19th century there was a distinct difference between the charges made for the best and second-best cloths.
1629, Falkirk Parish Records: 'Quha cumes to buriall with ane kist . . . sall take the mortclaithe for the ordinar price . . . and . . . poore folkes that wantis (lacks) kistis to be bureit with . . . to be servit with the auld mortclaithe gratis.'
1630, a mortcloth gifted to the Burgh of Peebles was of 'fyne blak claith lynit with blak buckasie (a kind of fine buckram) and campassit round about with ane blak silk frenzie (fringe) in the borderis thairof.'
1649, the Deacon of Glasgow Weavers produced two mortcloths with which the brethren 'war content' in which there were 9 ells of velvet and 'of silk to be fassis (tassels, possibly fringing) tua pundis and ane half . . . ane steik of fustian bought for lyning thairof', all coming with making as well to the sum of £203. 14. 4. The Deacon's charges in going to Edinburgh for the materials came to £16, the total £219. 14. 4 Scots.
1695, the minister of Coldingham parish, Berwickshire, and another man were appointed to go to Berwick to get materials for a mortcloth:

14 yards of hair fringe at 10/- per yard	£ 7. –. –
4 yards of fine cloth at £7 10/- per yard	30. –. –
10 drop of silk	–. 15. –
8 ells sarking for lining	3. 4. –
dying of ye forsaid lining	1. 12. –
threed, workmanship and ye tailor's pains,	
in going to Bk. to bring out ye cloth	1. 10. –
Total (Scots)	£42. 41. – (sic)

1737, Old Rayne Kirk Session, Aberdeenshire, obtained a new mortcloth from Aberdeen and the minister produced the account from the merchant and tailor:

To Alexander Christy

7½ yards black plush at £3. 10/- per yard	£29. –. 5 (sic)
3 yards white mantua at £2. 4/- per yard	6. 12. –
3 drops white silk	–. 4. 6
½ yard white buckram	–. 6. –
¾ yard white Sattin	2. –. 6
8 yards of Loupon	–. 12. –
4 yards more of Loupon	–. 6. –
(cord or braid made of loops, used as fastening or trimming)	

Also to Robert Joyner, tailor,

For making the mortcloth	£ 6. –. –
6 ells of (cl)aze at 12/- per ell for lining	3. 12. –
1 ell Sarge (serge) for a Pocke (bag, poke, wallet)	–. 12. –
Dying the Sarge	2. 4. –
Lettering the Belt	1. 4. –

The total came to £52. 10/- Scots.

1765, Old Rayne Kirk Session obtained another mortcloth:

5 yards fine Genoa velvet at 21/- per yard	£ 5. 5. –
6 yards glazed linnen at 16d per yard	–. 8. –
6 yards Shalloon at 22d per yard	1. 11. –
2 ozs of Thread	–. –. 6
5⅛ yards of white mantua at 15/- per yard	1. 6. 10½
24 yards of waling at 1d per yard	–. 2. –
11 drop Black Silk at 2d per drop	–. 1. 10
7 drop white at 2d per drop	–. 1. 2
¾ yard white Buckram at 16d per yard	–. 1. –
2 yards Shalloon at 18d per yard	–. 3. –
2 yards of Tep (patterned material)	–. –. 2
½ oz of Threeds	–. –. 1½
	£ 8. –. 8
To making the mortcloth	–. 12. 6
	£ 8. 13. 2 stg.

Although this itemised report given by the minister to the Kirk Session is in sterling, the cost of the mortcloth appears in the accounts as £103. 18/- Scots; the price of a wallet for holding it was £1. 12/- Scots.

1752, a mortcloth for the parish of Arbuthnott, Kincardineshire, came to:

7 yards Genoa velvet	£ 5. 12. –
6 yards shalloon (woollen lining)	4. 4. 4
Silk fringe	
Silver lace	1. 7. 6
Silver cord and thread	
Payment to the tailor	–. 17. –

The total came to £12. 19. 10 stg.

Channelkirk, Berwickshire, 1804:

To velvet etc for the new mortcloth with expense of buying	£ 3. 7. 5
To the tailor for making the new mortcloth and mending of two old ones, with silk and thread	–. 18. 6
	£ 4. 5. 11

1839, St Cuthbert's Church, Edinburgh – Inventory of Mortcloths:

First size: 2 As, 2 As, 1 B, 1 C, 1 D, 1 F (almost new).
            (NB. There are two lots, as said, of 'a As.')
Second size: 2 As, 1 A, 1 B, 1 C, 1 D.
Third size: 1 A, 1 B, 1 D, 1 E.
Poors' cloths: 2 first size, 1 old first size, 1 second size, 2 third size.

The *New Statistical Account* of the 1840s records the use of the mortcloth in various of the Northern Isles:

> Evie and Rendall, Orkney, where mortcloths brought in about £1. 17/- stg. as against £15 from collections annually; Lerwick, Shetland, where mortcloths raised about £2. 12. 6 per annum as against about £74 from collections; and Nesting, Shetland, where the figures were about £1. 8/- as against about £14.

Hire Charges of Mortcloths:

Date	Owner of Mortcloth	Best	Second-Best	Child's	Outside Parish
1593 Archibald Roger, Edinburgh bellman (private cloth)		½ merk			1 merk
1603 Masters of Trinity Hospital, Edinburgh		£6 Sc.			£12 Sc.
1611 Glasgow Weavers (for unfreemen in burgh)		13/4 Sc.			20/- Sc.
1621 Dumbarton Burgh Records		20/- Sc.	12/- Sc.		
1649 Glasgow Weavers (for freemen)		12/- Sc.		6/- Sc.	
1681 Glasgow Weavers (for freemen)		20/- Sc.	10/- Sc.	10/- Sc., 5/- for old one	
1693 Fowlis Easter and Lundie, Angus, Kirk Session		14/- Sc.			£2 Sc.
1730 Nigg Kirk Session, Ross and Cromarty		2 merks Sc.	1/- stg.		
1736 Corstorphine Kirk Session, Edinburgh		£4 Sc.		£1. 10/- Sc.	
1740 St. John's Clachan, Dalry, Ayrshire, Kirk Session		£1. 10/- Sc.			
1752 Channelkirk Kirk Session, Berwickshire		£2. 2/- Sc.	16/- Sc.	6/- Sc.	
1756 Cromarty Kirk Session, Ross and Cromarty		1/- stg.		6d stg.	18d and 9d
1765 Old Rayne Kirk Session, Aberdeenshire		£1. 4/- Sc.	12/- Sc.		
1773 Ordiquhill Kirk Session, Aberdeenshire		1/5 incl. bell, stg.			
1775 Channelkirk Kirk Session, Berwickshire		5/- stg.	2/9 stg. litter		
1804 Channelkirk Kirk Session, Berwickshire		6/- stg.+1/- for dykes	3/2 stg.+6d for dykes	16d stg.	7/- stg., best 3/2 stg., 2nd 16d stg., small cloth
1821 Edderton Kirk Session, Ross and Cromarty		5/- stg.	3/6 stg.		
1826 Nigg Kirk Session, Ross and Cromarty		5/- stg.	3/6 stg.		

1630, details of hire charge for mort-cloth belonging to Burgh of Peebles:

> 13/4 in burgh or more at their pleasure.
> 20/- out of parish, or more, + caution for return.
> 30/- in four named parishes, + caution for return.
> 5 merks in other parishes, or more according to distance and quality.

% Income from Mortcloths – taking the parish of Edderton, Ross and Cromarty, as an example:

Income	If original cost	£10 stg.	or	£12 stg.
1824 – £ 2. 9. 6		24.75%		20.5%
1831 – –. 17. 6		8.75%		7.3%
1833 – –. 3. 6		1.74%		1.45%
1842 – £ 1. 3. 6		11.75%		9.75%

In fact, a mortcloth bought in 1781 cost £11. 8/- stg. At 5/- stg. per hire in 1785 it brought in £1. 15/- or 14.8%. That year, the second-best mortcloth and bells brought in £1.

Interest rates: 1731, the Bank of Scotland offered 3% or 4% on deposits for six or twelve months. In 1819 John Maberley offered 4% on deposits for a reduced time of thirty days; his bank failed in 1833. 1824, Royal Bank offered 3½% and in October that year all the Scottish banks reduced their deposit interest to 2%; in 1875 eleven Scottish banks offered 2½% on deposits over one month.

In some places, the elders expected the use of the mortcloth free for themselves, perhaps as a final reward for service to the church.

The *Statistical Account* for Newton, Edinburgh, describes how the colliers had a 'box' to support their ill members. Some years before the *Account* was written, they bought a set of mortcloths, to be used free of charge by contributors. The carters followed their example and the Kirk Session realized that, as the parish consisted largely of these two groups, the practice would soon mean that the parish mortcloths would bring in no income. They and the heritors decided to settle the point in court and the neighbouring parish of Liberton, who were in the same position, joined in the action. A decree of the Court of Session dated 30 November 1792 was obtained, prohibiting the use of all but parish mortcloths. However, the Kirk Session were well aware of the help given to the needy by the 'boxes' and with the agreement of the heritors, they decided to be lenient: they allowed the two groups to use their own mortcloths for the next twenty years, by which time it was likely that the cloths would be worn out, on condition that each time they were used, the Kirk Treasurer should be paid 4/- for the benefit of the poor. It was expressly stated that this indulgence would continue only so long as the colliers and carters continued to give out aid from their 'boxes'.

'Walking Funerals'.

Genesis 47, 30: 'But I will lie with my fathers, and thou shalt carry me out of Egypt, and bury me in their burying-place.'

The 'resting cairns' at Murlaggan, Inverness-shire, are on the hill above the small church and churchyard of Cille Choireill; there are memorial cairns by the track up to the church from the main road. The carrying of a coffin shoulder-high is still a mark of respect. A memory from early this century is of Black Bobby who lived in a Border town and loved funerals; he used to go to every one, hanging about outside or near the graveyard gate. He got his nickname because he used to put coal into people's coalsheds after coalmen had dumped it outside and, as he never washed, his face was always black. In 1956, an elderly piper who was unable to attend a friend's funeral, went instead into the hills near his home in Sutherlandshire, at the time of the service, and played a lament for his friend, all alone.

'Great Funerals'.

The Act restricting the exorbitant expense of Marriages, Baptisms and Burials, 1681, begins by saying, 'Considering the great hurt and prejudice arising to this Kingdom by the superfluous expense bestowed at Marriages, Baptisms and Burials . . . '

Funeral of Countess of Traquair, 1759 – account of James Anderson, undertaker:

> To a frame for an Escutcheon 10/6.
> To hanging 2 rooms in black for 2 nights @ 21/- each, £4. 4/-.
> To hanging a passage in black for 2 nights @ 10/6, £1. 1/-.
> To 2 doz. plate sconces (candlesticks) for 2 nights @ 1/- each per night, £2. 8/-.
> To 6 large place candlesticks with long wax candles for 2 nights @ 1/6 per night each, 18/-.
> To 6 common sconces for the passage for 2 nights per piece each, 6/-.

Dowager Duchess of Perth's funeral, 1773:

> To a passage hung with blacks 5/-.
> To 2 rooms hung with blacks one night £2. 2/-.
> Use of 12 silver sconces 12/-.
> Use of 12 wax tapers 12/-.
> 16 Tind (? tinned) sconces with candles 8/-.
> 6 ushers @ 5/-, £1. 10/-.
> 8 Baton men @ 3/-, £1. 4/-.
> Housekeeper £1. 1/-.

Lady Margaret Stuart's funeral, 1791:

> 4 ushers £4. 4/-.
> 4 horses for ditto £1.
> Use of a State Bed £1. 1/-.

The above prices all appear to be sterling.

At the funeral of Mrs Elizabeth Dunbar at Greyfriars Churchyard, Edinburgh, there were the following payments to the poor:

> To the Poors' box 2/-.
> To the common poor at the lodging 1/-.
> To the common poor and blew gowns (licensed beggars) at Greyfriars 1/-.

For the funeral of Lady Margaret Stuart in 1791, £10. 10/- for horses and servants' entertainment at Peebles appears in the accounts; this appears to have been at an inn.

1839, Inventory of St Cuthbert's Church, Edinburgh, of funeral equipment includes batons with green baize covers to be used by baton men.

Very large numbers attended important funerals, such as 3,000 at the funeral of Sir James Gordon of Fassifern who was buried at Corpach, Inverness-shire, in 1828; and 8,000 at the burial of the Duke of Gordon in 1836.

Funeral gatherings could be used for political purposes.

The funerals of all landed gentry were not necessarily expensive: that of John Munro of Novar, Ross and Cromarty, in 1735 cost £38. 11. 7d and that of David Macculloch of Mulderg, in the same county, in 1755, £100, both Scots.

'Handspokes and Hearses'.

Handspokes might be called spakes, spaiks, spikes, specks.

1709, Session Book, Glasserton, Wigtownshire. 'The Session appoints Patrick McKie, treasurer, to provyde a box for keeping of the mortcloth and sufficient handspecks as soon as possible.'

1744, Melrose Kirk Session, Roxburghshire: 'Everyone using the litter within the parish shall pay 8/- Scots beside 2d Scots to the Beadle and the people out of the parish shall pay 16/- Scots and 2d to the Beadle.'

1691, Edinburgh Burgh Records: Because the poor had so increased in the burgh, it was suggested that income should be increased by exacting more for funerals 'and a committee appointed to consider the same reported that it was their opinion that for every person carried on Spokes who was not buried at the ordinary time a dollar could be exacted, and for a child half a dollar, for those carried on a hearse 2 dollars, and for a child carried in a coach, one dollar, all which to be collected by the Kirk treasurer for the use of the poor. Also in future, the price or hire of each coach attending any burial within the city should not exceed twenty shillings Scots and the price of each horse in the hearse should not exceed half a crown – public intimation to be made to the grave-diggers.'

Income of the hearse and mortcloth might be put together as at Kirkliston:

> 1833 – £17. 4. 6
> 1834 – £12. 9. 6
> 1835 – £10. 13. –
> 1836 – £13. 18. 6
> 1837 – £13. 9. 6

1929, At the funeral of a Fife man, out of a total expense of £25. 8/-, the cost of motor hearse and three cars was £4. 15/-.

1791, Funeral of Lady Margaret Stuart:

> A hearse with 6 horses to Traquair £6. 6/-.
> A coach with 4 horses to Traquair £4. 4/-.

The coachmen 10/-.
Cash paid for tolls £1.
Stamp duty on hearse and coach, 7/-.   All prices are sterling.

'Graveyards'.

The *New Statistical Account* for Urquhart and Glenmoriston, Inverness-shire, mentions a number of burial grounds in the parish – one at Kilmore, the main burial ground at the parish church; one at Temple; one a little west of Drumnadrochit and another in the 'height of the country'. In Glenmoriston there were two, one at the top and the other at the foot of the valley. The *New Statistical Account* for Barvas, Lewis, lists four former small Roman Catholic chapels near villages, with surrounding graveyards which were then still in use.

Act of the Parliament of Scotland, 1457 – Wapinshaws to be held by lords spiritual and temporal four times a year, and bowmarks and a pair of butts to be made at each parish church where shooting should take place every Sunday. Edinburgh Burgh Records, 1609, show that weapon-showing was to be held in the Greyfriars kirkyard on 10th June at 10.00 in the morning. The Statistical Account for Kincardine, Ross and Cromarty, says 'Nigh to the church there is an alley, walled in and terminating in a large semicircle, appropriated to that ancient military exercise and discipline, known by the name of weapon shawing.'

Act of the Parliament of Scotland, 1592: 'Forasmeikle as crueltie and bluidsched is cumit to sik ane heicht whithin this land that the house of the Lord his sanctuary is not fre but filthely pollutit and defylt thairwith in sik sort that comounlie all revenges of querrellis and deidlei feidis, Is now execute in kirkis and kirkyards at the tyme appoyntit to the service of God . . . whoever slauchters in any kirk of kirkyard during the service time shall he declared rebels or fugitive and the king shall have power to confiscate their moveables.'

Numbers 35, 11 and 12: 'Then ye shall appoint you cities to be cities of refuge for you; that the slayer may fly thither, which killeth any person at unawares. And they shall be unto you cities for refuge.'

Act of Parliament of Scotland, 1503, fordbidding markets and fairs to be held in kirkyards, was ratified in 1579.

1578, Records of Burgh of Glasgow: Provost, Bailies and Council appoint a new person to the job of upholding 'of the kird yard deyk and keiping furth thairof of all bestiall for reverens of the burial . . .';

In 1600 a man went surety for another man's wife, and three other people, that their animals would not go into the kirkyard in future.

In 1595, 'The poynder ordained to poynd every beast that comes into the kirkyard, to pay iiijd ilk futte, and if he suffers any to be thairintill he is to pay xvs for ilk falt.'

1579, Edinburgh Burgh Records: Walter Hagy, a flesher, promised not to put sheep in the kirkyard ever again under threat of £10 fine to be given to the common works.

1632, Culross Kirk Session, in Fife, ordained that if any man's horse, cow or beast should be found eating grass by night or day in the kirkyards of the west church or the Abbey, the owner was to pay 8/- Scots 'and for this cause the dykes to be repaired with diligence'.

1581, Edinburgh Records – Trees having been planted in a graveyard, a tailor was ordered to pay the Dean of Guild 10/- Scots for 'raising and drawing' one of them; he was forbidden to do the like again 'under the paynes of gritt punishment'.

Anstruther Church in Fife formerly had a lych-gate; and Chapel of Garioch, Aberdeenshire, has an entrance gateway in the west wall of the churchyard, dated 1626, which was said in 1878 to have been 'until lately a funeral porch' under which the bier had been set down during the burial service. It is thought probable that it was built as a gate but an old inhabitant who came to the chapel in 1874 as a bride, agrees with its use as a lych-gate although she never saw it in such use. She had been told that the coffin was laid below it on an iron framework.

Aberdeen Burgh Records, 1647: The Bailies and Council appointed the master of the kirkwark 'to go about the repair of the said kirkyard dyke and stylls, preparing of the ground and making of the same in the form of ane houff, for the more decent burieing of defunct persons . . .' and ordered that everyone be convened by tuck and drum within the tolbooth on the 2nd April so that intimation might be made to them 'so that none may pretend ignorance'.

Yird swine – also called yird pig, earth hound, earth hun.

1696, Edinburgh Burgh Council, considering that several people had been granted burial places in Greyfriars kirkyard for erecting and building tombs for themselves and their successors, realized that several of them had not yet erected monuments which was the reason for which they were granted the ground, and enacted that thereafter they would only give grants for the space of a year.

A table stone in Nigg graveyard, Ross and Cromarty, dated 1690, is inscribed as being the possession of David Rose 'by act of session', i.e. by authority of the Kirk Session. An extract in the Nigg Session Minutes is from a transaction of 1705, in which a man claimed the right to 6' x 12' in the graveyard and one gravestone, which the Session granted him and his heirs 'so that no other person can claim right to the foresaid burying ground, being his right by Heirdom . . .' An entry of 1810 shows that a man, on leaving to live in Inverness, granted a 7' x 7' burying ground with two headstones to someone else.

Six years later, a burying ground was granted to a man with a reservation that Roderick Ross, mealer, Rarichy, and his son should have 'the liberty of interring one Corps therein if necessity requires'. In 1829 one man made over to another the burying ground devolved on him by his ancestors, 'the dues of which are to be paid by him' and that year too, a burying ground was assigned to a man 'or any of his legitimate descendants'.

1784, Tarbat Kirk Session, Ross and Cromarty: Two groups of people were in dispute about ownership of a burying ground. One side cut out a capital letter from the stone so that 'I' appeared instead of 'K' to suit another woman's name. The Session had previously passed a sentence to do with this case and 'finding that the affair as it now came before them turns upon some points of law of which they do not sustain themselves competent to judge, they therefore decline judging in it, leaving it to the parties concerned to terminate the difference amongst themselves . . .'

A committee reporting in 1856 to the Kirk Session of St Cuthbert's Church in Edinburgh proposed that 'with a view of inducing sales' in a particular part of the burying ground the plots should be 8' long, and 3, 6, 9 or 12 feet wide as required, that a gravel path 4' wide should be made in front and a flower border 3' wide as well. They were sure that these improvements and the situation of this particular part of the burial ground would be very good and they anticipated a ready sale of plots at £6. 6/- for 3' wide, and an equal sum for each additional 3', irrespective of the usual fees. Three years later, the Recorder of graveyards who appears to have been the keeper of records, asked for a percentage of sales arranged by him and was allowed 2½%.

In St Duthus graveyard, Tain, Ross and Cromarty, new regulations were drawn up in 1874. They describe the division of the graveyard into Old and New Ground, within which there were two classes – Free, for paupers, and Select for others. People could buy an exclusive right in perpetuity of one or more lairs of Select ground on payment of the appropriate charges, although it was carefully stated that the ground must be for burial purposes only. These lairs varied in price from 10/- to £3 stg. according to locality in the graveyard. In the Old ground there was a uniform charge of 10/- to those with relatives or friends buried there and £1 for others wishing a lair there. A certificate of registration was provided at a fee of 1/6 if the price of the lair was under 30/- and 2/6 above that. Although this gave perpetual rights in the grave specified, if no burial took place in it for forty years or more, then the ground reverted to the Parochial Board, although it was ordered that no memorial erected by the original owner would be interfered with.

Humpy graves may be seen at Cille Choireill, near Murlaggan in Inverness-shire; Old Annat at Torridon, Wester Ross; and Melness, Sutherland; and elsewhere too.

Regulations of Nithsdale District Council, Dumfriesshire, in 1983: A proprietor shall not be entitled to sell the Right of Burial in any vacant lair belonging to him except to the District Council who may, if they agree, buy it for a mutually agreed price but not more than 75% of the price paid by the original purchaser. The proprietor shall not transfer his right in a lair except to a cousin or nearer relative or nominee, and only with the consent of the District Council. After the death of the purchaser of the Right of Burial in a lair, his wife and lawful children living in family with them, shall have the right of burial in the lair for themselves only. Where the Right of Burial has been specially bequeathed, on producing written evidence of the right of succession, a person will be entitled to have his/her name entered on the Certificate of Right of Burial.

'Church Burial'.

Mr William Birnie, who became minister of Lanark in 1597 and later Dean of the Chapel Royal, issued a publication called *The Blame of Kirk Burial* (Edinburgh, 1606) deprecating intramural burial.

1573, the mourners burying Sir William Hamilton of Sanquhar broke into Mauchline Church, Ayrshire, on the day on which Holy Communion was being celebrated, and threw over the 'table boords' and buried him in their place. The Kirk Session complained to the General Assembly who ordered those concerned to submit to discipline from the Kirk Session.

1653, Aberdeen Burgh Records – Act anent bureing in the churche: '. . . any who sall burie in the church sall pay the pryces following, towitt ane abortive child, thrie punds Scotts money; ane child not borne vpoun staves, sex punds; ane child borne vpon staves, within fourteen yeeres of age, ten punds. Item, men and women above the aige of fourteen yeeres of aige, twentie pounds.' (Scots money.)

In 1978, in Nigg, Ross and Cromarty, the boiler room which was part of the church, was altered to receive the Nigg Stone, and twenty-four skeletons were found which were re-buried in the churchyard. In the church of Tulliechetil, near Comrie, Perthshire, five slabs lay on top of one another in the church.

'Grave-making'.

Cist burial, normally regarded as belonging to the Bronze Age, appeared occasionally in northern districts of Scotland until nearly the end of the 18th century. One such was the grave of a suicide on a headland in the north, made of small slabs from the beach and covered with a single slab seven to eight feet long. By working out the ages of the suicide's descendants, the date of this grave was established as about 1800 or so.

1687 – Act of Privy Council stated that it was His Majesty's pleasure that Clerks of Kirk Sessions, other church officers like Readers, precentors, beadles and others who serve the clergy, should not lose their accustomed fees for baptisms, marriages and burials, the ordinary means of their subsistence. Aberdeen Burgh Council laid down the following burial charges for St Nicholas Church in 1603, ratified 1643:

> For each adult inhabitant buried in the south side, over 20 years, £10.
> For each unmarried person between 14 years and 20 years, £5.
> For each child, under 14 years, with a coffin, £3.
> For young children with no coffins, 20/-.
> Strangers – A baron or his wife in the south side of the churchyard, 40 merks.
>   Gentleman or his wife in the south side, £20. All Scots money.

The money had to be paid before the ground was broken and was to be used for maintenance of the church.

1860s, Regulations for Edrom Churchyard, Berwickshire:

> Digging, filling up and finishing grave, and grave-digger's attendance, to depth of 5' . . . 5/-.
> Ditto, to depth of 6' . . . . 6/-.
> Ditto, to depth of 7' . . . . 7/6.

Ditto to depth of 8' . . . . 9/6.

Recording death and interment . . . . -/6.

1922, Chapelhill Cemetery, Nigg, Ross and Cromarty:

Graves for children under 7 years . . . . 3/6.

Ditto over 7 and under 14 years. . . . . 7/6.

For each foot over 5' and not more than 8' . . . . 2/3.

Farm servants, labourers etc. . . . . 5/3.

Paupers from other parishes . . . . 3/3.

1966, Burial Grounds Dept, Duns, Berwickshire:

New fees:

Adult graves at permissible depth . . . . £8.

Children under 15 years . . . . £5.

Stillborn children in ground for stillborn children . . . . £2.

Cremative remains . . . . £3.

Persons living outwith landward area of the county
without a right to a burial ground . . . . Add 50%.

Persons outwith landward area of the county who are not ratepayers. . . . . Add 50%.

Beadle/grave-digger's wages:

1583/4, Burgh of Edinburgh – 2/- out of every grave that paid 8/-, and the fourth penny out of
those paying less, Scots money.

1676 – Galston Kirk Session, Ayrshire – a groat (4d Scots) for digging a pauper's grave.

1687 – Borgue Kirk Session, Kirkcudbrightshire – 2/6 per quarter and 6d. for digging each
grave, Scots money.

1804 – Channelkirk, Berwickshire – 1/6 stg. for big graves, 9d for small.

1837 – Channelkirk's beadle's wage was £2. 2/- per year, stg.

1847 –   ”   ”   ” £3. 3/- per year, stg.

1855 –   ”   ”   ” £2. -/- per year, stg.

1873 –   ”   ”   ” supplemented by heritors to £6 per annum.

1922 – Nigg Parish Council, Ross and Cromarty – Grave-digger and keeper of the cemetery
received £25 per annum.

Regulations of Nithsdale District Council, Dumfriesshire, in 1983:

No coffin is to be laid nearer the surface than 3'.

Not more than 3 adult interments allowed in any one lair.

No coffin to be removed to make room for a fresh interment.

In the Shetland Isles, 1983 – burials are cheaper than on mainland Scotland; there is a standard fee of
£12 for opening a lair at any cemetery. The only cemeteries where a fee is paid are the Lerwick new
Cemetery, Tingwall Cemetery and Gott; the fee charged is £5 for a new plot of ground.

'Gravestones'.

In a few graveyards, ancient stones may sometimes be found but they do not come within the scope of
this book. Some examples of early gravestones include the Groat stone found about 1894 under the
floor of the church at Canisby, Caithness, and dated 1568. In the churchyard of the old church at
Aberdour, Aberdeenshire, closed in 1818, the oldest flat stone, now broken, is dated 1593. Three
other tombs are in memory of three lairds, the Baird of Auchmedden one being dated 1593. It is a panel
stone and on the other side of the entrance another panel is said to have been dated 1420 but it is now
completely weathered.

J. Weever, in his *Discourse of Funeral Monuments*, (London, 1631) says that tombstones should be
made with regard to the quality and degree of the dead person – lower gentry might have a flat stone,

gentry of more importance might have effigies but no arms displayed, noblemen and royalty and their families might have raised tombs with carvings. Epitaphs were only for those of virtue, wisdom and valour; needless to say the common people should have none at all.

Although three gravestones with Gaelic inscriptions are said to exist at Rosehall, Sutherland, they are not visible now; there is one at Tutim, not far away, however. At Nigg, Ross and Cromarty, a gravestone in memory of a couple who died in 1828 and 1863 respectively, is worded in English but has twelve lines of Gaelic verse in praise, not of the departed, but of a former parish minister, Rev. A. McAdam (1788-1814.) Gaelic inscriptions are, of course, more common in the Islands.

The records of Berwickshire Naturalists' Club, 1923-5, have an interesting breakdown of types of gravestone carvings.

Paint was sometimes applied to gravestones. A large box tomb in the graveyard at Fogo, Berwickshire, is one of the few remaining on which traces of paint may still be discerned.

The *Daily Record* of 7 January 1982 reported the theft of tombstones from several Aberdeenshire and Kincardineshire graveyards, saying that the police believed the stones are being refaced and sold as new, or else as fireplace bases.

'Mourning Apparel and Keepsakes'.

Funeral of Lady Margaret Stuart, 1791:

> 'A suit of fine crapes £6 stg.
> 12 pairs of gloves and stamps £1. 1/-.'

The wearing of bright clothing at funerals – was this purely a matter of wearing one's best or was it folk memory at work, because evil spirits are believed to find red and yellow most obnoxious; and they also detest black which helps to explain its choice for so much to do with funerals.

'Death Registration'.

The office of keeping a register of those buried in Greyfriars Churchyard, Edinburgh, was a desirable one and in 1701 a merchant, Thomas Trotter, petitioned the Council for it. This was granted, with the requirement that he noted the age of the deceased, time of death and burial, their sickness and quality, and place in the churchyard, for which he was to be paid 5/- for each person carried on handspokes or in a hearse, and 3/- for children, while pensioners, the poor and those dying in hospitals or who used mortcloths – presumably without coffins – were free.

Dowager Duchess of Perth's funeral, 1773, shows a charge of 'Recorder £1. 1. 6'.

'Executions'.

Edinburgh Burgh Records, 1553/4: 'For twa hors to cary the fals cunyers (counterfeiters) to the gallows and hame bringing of thair legs and heids and eirding of thair bodeyis...' In 1583/4, the Burgh Treasurer was ordered to 'caus hing up at the Nether Bow and other patent pairts, the heid and certane of the legs and airmes of two men' who had been executed for murder. In 1584, the Treasurer was ordered to 'send west to Stirling the legs and arms of umquhile David Home lately executed...'

'Epidemics'.

An early entry in Edinburgh Burgh records describes how a cleaner was sent to all infected houses to cleanse them at night time, between 9.00 p.m. and 5.00 a.m., 'and that siclyke all deid cors deand in the said seikness be eirdit (buried) at the same tyme.' Furthermore, if he found clothing etc. it was lawful for him to intromit with the same as his escheat, or burn them.

A large cairn erected at Easdale, Argyllshire, over a common grave during the Seven Years Famine, may have been as much a sealing-in of disease as a memorial, for all that it was a traditional form of burial monument.

The *Scots Magazine* of June 1983 carried a photograph of a 'Pest House' as it was called, where cholera victims were nursed in the mid-19th century. It stood at the end of the village of Kilmaurs, Ayrshire, and was demolished only two or three years ago.

Cholera seems to have killed about a third of those getting it:

Date	Place	No. of cases	No. of deaths
Mar. 1829	Campbelltown	34	11
Sept. 1832	Inver	100	53
Sept. 1832	Inverness	409	136
Oct. 1832	Cromarty	30	10

In spite of many early deaths, there were also striking examples of longevity:

100 years – The *New Statistical Account* for Kilmuir, Skye, reported that three or four people had lately died aged 100; also Lady Louden, Ayrshire, in 1779; Jean Miller, Moy, Inverness-shire, 1828; Euan Macmillan, Fort William area of Inverness-shire, 1837; and a man in Kiltearn, Ross and Cromarty, 1775.

103 years – A woman died aged 103 in Irvine, Ayrshire, in the 1830s.

104 years – A man in Irvine, Ayrshire, died aged 104, and another at Maybole, Ayrshire.

105 years – George Swan, a cooper, died 1781 at Langholm, Dumfriesshire (uncorroborated); Rev. Mr Gordon of Alvie, Inverness-shire, died 1787, reputed to be 105; Christopher Macrae, Kintail, Ross and Cromarty, a Chelsea out-pensioner, died at Fort George, Inverness-shire, aged 105.

106 years – Two Ross and Cromarty men, one from Culrain and the other from Kiltearn, died aged 106, in 1841 and 1782 respectively.

107 years – John Macdonald from Skye died in Edinburgh at 107 years in 1827; William Fraser, from the Highlands, died at Teviothead, Roxburghshire, in 1760.

108 years – John Munro died near Dingwall, Ross and Cromarty, 1817 aged 108; Duncan Munro, Inveraray, Argyllshire, died 1841 aged 108.

109 years – Donald Ross, Nigg, Ross and Cromarty, died 1774 aged 109; Mrs Batchen, Elgin, Morayshire, died 1840, said to be 109.

110 years – A Chelsea pensioner died in Edinburgh in 1825 aged 110; Mary Innes from Ross and Cromarty died in Skye aged 110 about the 1830s.

111 years – Alexander Urquhart, Brora, Sutherland, died 1826 aged 111.

112 years – John Martin, Isle of Harris, died 1846 aged 112.

113 years – The *Statistical Account* for Balmaghie, Kirkcudbrightshire, reported that about 1770s a woman died aged 113.

116 years – A woman died in Kiltearn, Ross and Cromarty, about 1706 aged 116.

120 years – John Mowat, surgeon from Aberdeenshire, died about the 1700s, at the reputed age of 120 years; about the same date, a man in North Yell, Shetland, died at the same age.

124 years – Thomas Wishart died at Kirkpatrick-Fleming, Dumfriesshire, in 1759 aged 124 years.

The *Statistical Account* for North Yell and Fetlar, Shetland, claims that this was the most healthy spot in the country and that one man reached the age of 139 years, having married in his 100th year.

'The Poor'.

Burgh of Peebles, 1650: 'For the half pryce of ane dead kist to ane poor soldier . . .'

Rayne Kirk Session, Aberdeenshire, 1750, 'for a winding sheet £1. 7/- Sc.'

Inverness Kirk Session 1688, 'paid for a poor woman who came from Aberdeen and died here 4 ell Linen to be her winding sheet.'

St Ternan's, Arbuthnott, Kirk Session, 1771, '£2. 12/- for some spirits and ale needed at the burial of . . .'

Nigg Kirk Session, Ross and Cromarty, 1782, 'To poor object to help bury her daughter, 1/- stg.'

Penpont Kirk Session, Dumfriesshire, in the 1790s allowed 14/- stg. for a pauper's funeral.

Coffin prices for paupers – adults unless otherwise stated:

> 1641-75, Galston Kirk Session, Ayrshire, 30/- Scots.
> 1672, Glasgow Weavers, £2. 8/- Scots.
> 1679, Mauchline Kirk Session, Ayrshire, £3 Scots.
> 1688, Inverness Kirk Session, 3 merks Scots.
> 1696, Ashkirk Kirk Session, Selkirkshire, To a man for a coffin for his wife, £3 Scots; for a child £2. 8/- Scots.
> 1689, Ashkirk Kirk Session, 'For a cheast and a winding sheit to . . . a poore and decripit old man, £3 Scots.'
> 1703, Carstairs Kirk Session, Lanarkshire, '. . . a chist for a child 3/4 Scots.'
> 1706, Mauchline Kirk Session, 30/- Scots.
> 1733, Channelkirk Kirk Session, Berwickshire, £3 Scots.
> 1741/44, Drainie and Lossiemouth, Morayshire, £1. 4/-, £1. 10/- Scots.
> 1747, Mauchline Kirk Session, 40/- Scots 'and not any more'.
> 1755, Channelkirk Kirk Sesssion, 5/- stg.
> 1766, Drainie and Lossiemouth Kirk Session, 5/- stg.
> 1770, Tarbat Kirk Session, Ross and Cromarty, 4/- stg.
> 1781, St John's Clachan, Dalry, Ayrshire, 7/- stg.
> 1796, Channelkirk Kirk Session, 9/- stg.
> 1797/1812, Sorbie Kirk Session, Wigtownshire, 12/-, 13/- stg.
> 1804, Channelkirk Kirk Session, 12/- stg.
> 1826, Resolis Kirk Session, Ross and Cromarty, 12/- stg.
> 1830, Edderton Kirk Session, Ross and Cromarty, 10/- stg.
> 1846, Inspector of Poor, Tain, Ross and Cromarty, 10/- stg.

These paupers' coffin prices may be compared against those of other people:

> 1692, coffin for Lady Mey, Ross and Cromarty, £30 Scots.

About 1855, coffins could be made and mounted in Kincardine O'Neil, Aberdeenshire, for 10/- to 18/-, a few costing £1; but with extra mountings it was not thought an overcharge to pay £5 stg.

Graves:

> 1676, Galston Kirk Session, 1 groat (4d) Scots.
> 1696, Ashkirk Kirk Session, 6/-.
> 1699,   ”   ”   ” 'For Marrion Durrand's grave 12/- Scots.'
> 1699,   ”   ”   ” Graves for a stranger and an idiot, 8/- each, Scots.
> 1702,   ”   ”   ” John Botch the orphan's grave, 8/-, Scots.
> 1763, Melrose Kirk Session, Roxburghshire, 1/4 stg. for an adult, 1/- stg. for a child over 8 years and 8d. stg. for a child below 8 years.
> 1797-1812, Sorbie Kirk Session, Wigtownshire, 1/6 stg.
> 1810-40, Nigg Kirk Session, Ross and Cromarty, 3/- stg. for an adult, 1/6 stg. for child under 12 years.
> 1834, Edderton Kirk Session, 1/8 stg.
> 1847, Inspector of Poor, Tain, Ross and Cromarty, 2/6 stg.
> 1922, Chapelhill cemetery, Nigg, 3/3 per grave for paupers of other parishes.

Many Friendly and Benefit Societies were formed all round the country, some of which are:

> 1670, Anstruther-Wester (Fife) Mortcloth and Benefit Society, re-established 1819.
> 1763, Dirleton, (East Lothian) Friendly Society, open to tradesmen, servants and others

between sixteen and twenty years, for 'the support of those members under affliction and for the decent interment of themselves and their wives.'

1782, Langholm (Dumfriesshire) Friendly Society.

1813, Tain (Ross and Cromarty) Friendly Society.

1814, Alloa (Clackmannanshire) Friendly Society for Funerals.

1818, Parish of Crichton (Midlothian) Whipman Society for ploughmen etc.

1827, Eastwood (Renfrewshire) Funeral Friendly Society.

1829, Burntisland (Fife) Funeral Insurance Society.

1830, Avoch (Ross and Cromarty) Friendly Society, to pay funeral expenses of members and their wives and to make allowances to invalid members and their widows.

1831, Rosemarkie (Ross and Cromarty) Friendly Society – 'promises to benefit the poorer classes of labourers and mechanics therewith connected.'

1834, Bonhill (Dunbartonshire) Funeral Society, dissolved in 1894.

1837, Alexandria (Dunbartonshire) Funeral Association, still in existence 1912.

'Body-snatchers'.

About 1895, while a man was away from home and staying at Invergarry, Inverness-shire, he had to have his leg amputated but the leg was taken to the family burying ground and buried there to await his ultimate arrival. In the very early years of the 20th century, a workman's hand was amputated in the farm house at Tarrel, Ross and Cromarty; it was briefly laid down on the floor where a dog got a hold of it, so it was quickly buried outside. Shortly afterwards, the man's family came to ask for it so that it could be buried in the family lair to enable him to go to Heaven in a state of completeness. The minutes of the watching society at Traquair, Peebles, are at Register House, Edinburgh, among papers of Strathearn & Blair, W.S., ref. GD 314, item 114.

Architecture of Scottish Post-Reformation Churches, by George Hay lists places where watch towers, mortsafes and morthouses etc. may be seen.

To protect coffins – two sleepers or blocks of wood could be laid in the bottom of a grave at right angles to the position of the coffin. The coffin was put in and the wooden base screwed to it by long upright bolts which were double-locked. A description of use of a grilled mortsafe says wood was placed in the foot of the grave and four strong rods, hinged near the upper ends, screwed into it, two on each side. The coffin was lowered in, then the cage-like mortsafe placed on top of it, and the hinged rods, the tops of which interlaced, were bent over and padlocked, and the key given to the nearest relative and turned in the presence of the mourners.

A grave opened for burial at Legerwood churchyard, Berwickshire, in the early 1940s was found to have a layer of tarmacadam over an earlier burial.

In Fife, three nearby villages each chose a different method of protecting their dead – by an armed guard at Pittenweem, with mortsafes at Anstruther and at Crail with a mortuary or morthouse. Records of St Cuthbert's Church, Edinburgh 1843: 'The Inspector and Manager for the Edinburgh Schools of Anatomy to the Kirk Session of St Cuthbert's for coffins furnished and interments in the Burying-ground of St Cuthbert's, of bodies which had undergone anatomical examination in the Edinburgh Schools of Anatomy.' This is divided into columns and begins in 1836, giving the deceased's name, and from whose anatomy classroom he came; age; coffin price; a column for what appears to be 'gravedigger' which was not used till 1841, and a column for the total. Coffin prices vary from 3/4 to 4/10 to 6/10 stg., totals coming to just shillings. In 1841, it became more expensive as the column for the gravedigger was used with entries of 2/- to 3/- to 5/- in it, and the total then comes, for one burial at a time, to anything up to 11/10. In 1841, there were fifteen dissected corpses so buried and in 1843, twenty-two.

'Unbaptized Children'.

The usual approach to a church was from the south and it was natural that burials should be on that side of the church so that those coming to worship might pray for the souls of the departed as they walked past their graves. Equally, it was natural for the less fortunate to be buried in the less desirable north side of the churchyard and for outcasts, such as suicides and unbaptized children, to be put out of sight altogether. The nearer the altar the holier, so the farther away such burials were the better.

It was probably due to transport difficulties that ministers appear to have visited different areas and baptized all the members of their flock requiring it. More than one child in a family might be baptized at the same time – in 1896 the U.P. minister in Nigg baptized four children of one family on the same day. Delayed baptisms were not uncommon; the Nigg, Ross and Cromarty, records show that someone born in 1860 was only baptized in 1880 and in 1925 an illegitimate child of twelve years old was baptized.

Adult baptism only took place after certain consideration; in 1867, the following entry in the Nigg Free Church minutes is taken to refer to an adult who after being 'dealt with for a considerable time, was refused baptism on account of ignorance and ill conduct'. A young woman adherent of that church wished baptism and, with a view to checking up on her conduct, she was 'left under the notice of the elder of the district' who must have reported favourably as later that year she was baptized.

In the Associate Church in Nigg, the minister baptized area by area at the outset but a different system came in about 1807. Thereafter, baptism took place from the third or fourth day of life, up to about a month old, and this is written into the Register. From 1860, it appears that the child was almost certainly taken to the church.

Kirk Session records show various cases of delayed or refused baptism but a kinder attitude occurs in the records of Edderton, Ross and Cromarty, in 1908. The minister had baptized a very ill illegitimate child which had died the following day; he asked the Kirk Session to endorse what he had done as owing to the child's state of health there had been no time to consult them.

Bibliography

Allan, Rev. Archibald, *History of Channelkirk* (Edinburgh, 1900)

Allardyce, A. (ed.) *Scotland and Scotsmen in the 18th Century* 2 Vols. (Edinburgh, 1888)

Allardyce, John, *Bygone Days in Aberdeenshire* (Aberdeen, 1913)

Anson, Peter, *Scots Fisherfolk* (Edinburgh, 1950)

Barron, James, *The Northern Highlands in the 19th Century,* 3 vols. (Inverness, 1901-1913)

Beeton, Isabella, *The Book of Household Management* (London, 1861)

Bentinck, Rev. G.D., *Dornoch Cathedral and Parish* (Dornoch, 1926)

Brown, P. Hume, *Early Travellers in Scotland* (Edinburgh, 1891)

Carruthers, Robert, *Highland Notebook* (Edinburgh, 1843)

Chambers, Robert, *Domestic Annals of Scotland* (Edinburgh, 1858)

Chambers, William, *Exploits and Anecdotes of the Most Remarkable Gypsies in the Southern Counties of Scotland* (Edinburgh, 1821)

　　　　　　　　History of Peebles-shire (Edinburgh, 1864)

　　　　　　　　Book of Scotland (Edinburgh, 1880)

Cohen, Daniel, *The Body-Snatchers* (London, 1977)

Cramond, W., *Presbytery of Fordyce* (Banff, 1886)

　　　　　Church and Churchyard of Rathven (Banff, 1885)

　　　　　Church and Churchyard of Fordyce (Banff, 1886)

　　　　　Church and Churchyard of Ordiquhill (Banff, 1886)

　　　　　Church and Churchyard of Deskford (Banff, 1885)

Craven, Rev. J.B., *Church Life in South Ronaldshay and Burray* (Kirkwall, 1911)

Dalgetty, A.B., *History of the Church of Foulis Easter* (Dundee, 1933)

Davey, Nancy, *The Howff* (Dundee, n.d.)

Dinnie, Robert, *An Account of the Parish of Birse* (Aberdeen, 1865)

　　　　　History of Kincardine O'Neil (Aberdeen, 1885)

Dixon, J.H., *Gairloch* (Edinburgh, 1886)

Dunbar, Edward, *Social Life in Former Days* (Edinburgh, 1865)

Duncan, James, *Fala in Former Days* (Edinburgh, 1920)

Edgar, Rev. Andrew, *Old Church Life in Scotland* (Paisley, 1886)

Ferguson, Thomas, *Scottish Social Welfare 1864-1914* (Edinburgh, 1958)

Forsyth, W., *In the Shadow of Cairngorm* (Inverness, 1900)

Galt, John, *Annals of the Parish* (London, 1821)

Gardner, Alexander, *History of Galston Church* (Paisley, 1909)

Geikie, Sir Archibald, *Scottish Reminiscences* (Glasgow, 1904)

Gillies, Patrick, *Netherlorn, Argyllshire and its Neighbourhood* (London, 1909)

Godsman, James, *Glass, Story of a Parish* (Aberdeen, 1952)

Gourlay, George, *Anstruther, or Illustrations of Scottish Burgh Life* (Anstruther, 1888)

Graham, H.G., *Social Life in Scotland in the 18th Century* (London, 1937)

Grant, I.F., *Highland Folkways* (London, 1961)

Grant, James, *Old and New Edinburgh*, 3 vols. (London, 1880)

Green, G.G., *Gordonhaven* (London, 1887)

Haldane, E.S., *Scotland of our Fathers* (London, 1933)

Harrison, John, *Oure Tounis College* (Edinburgh, 1884)

Hastings, James (ed.) *Encyclopaedia of Religion and Ethics*, 13 vols. (Edinburgh, 1926)

Hay, George, *Architecture of Scottish Post-Reformation Churches* (Oxford, 1957)

Henderson, G.A., *Kirk of St Ternan, Arbuthnott* (Aberdeen, 1962)

Inglis, Rev. W.M., *Annals of an Angus Parish* (Dundee, 1888)

Keith, Agnes, *Parish of Drainie and Lossiemouth* (Inverness, 1975)

Kinna, J.G., *History of the Parish of Minnigaff* (Dumfries, 1904)

Laing, David (ed.) *The Diary of Alexander Brodie of Brodie* (Aberdeen, 1863)

Lindley, K., *Of Graves and Epitaphs* (London, 1965)

Logan, James, *The Scottish Gael or Celtic Manners* (London, 1831)

Lumsden, Harry, *History of the Skinners, Furriers and Glovers of Glasgow* (Glasgow, 1937)

Macdonald, Colin, *Echoes of the Glen* (Edinburgh, 1936)

McEwan, R.D., *Old Glasgow Weavers* (Glasgow, 1905)

Macgregor, A.A., *The Western Isles* (London, 1949)
                        Land of the Mountain and the Flood (London, 1965)

Mackay, William (ed.) *Records of Inverness and Dingwall Presbytery 1643-1688* (Inverness, 1896)

Mackenzie, Osgood, *A Hundred Years in the Highlands* (London, 1921)

Maclaren, A.A., *Religion and Social Class in Scotland* (London, 1974)

Miller, Hugh, *Scenes and Legends of the North of Scotland* (Edinburgh, 1835)

Mitchell, Alexander (ed.) *Inverness Kirk Session Records 1661-1800* (Inverness, 1902)

Nicolson, Alexander, *History of Skye* (Glasgow, 1930)

Paton, James (ed.) *Scottish History and Life* (Glasgow, 1902)

Paton, Rev. J., *Book of St Michael's Church, Dumfries* (Dumfries, n.d.)

Pennant, Thomas, *A Tour in Scotland* (London, 1771)

Plant, Marjorie, *Domestic Life of Scotland in the 18th Century* (Edinburgh, 1952)

Ramsay, E.B., *Reminiscences of Scottish Life and Character* (Edinburgh, 1871)

Rea, F.G., *A School in South Uist* (London, 1964)

Reid, Rev. H.M.B., *The Kirk above the Dee Water* (Castle Douglas, 1895)
                        About Galloway Folk (Castle Douglas, 1889)

Robertson, Rev. A.E., *Old Tracks, Cross Country Routes and Coffin Roads of the North West Highlands* (Edinburgh, 1945)

Scott, Sir Walter, *The Antiquary* (Edinburgh, 1820)

Smout, T.C., *A History of the Scottish People* (London, 1969)

Somerville, Rev. Thomas, *Scotland in My Early Life* (Glasgow, 1861)

Sprott, G.W., *Worship and Offices in the Church of Scotland* (Edinburgh, 1882)

Strawhorn, John, *On an Ayrshire Farm* (Edinburgh, 1951)
                        A New History of Cumnock (Cumnock, 1966)

Westcott, W.W., *Suicide* (London, 1885)

Willsher, Betty and Hunter, Doreen, *Stones* (Edinburgh, 1978)

Also consulted: Acts of the Scottish Parliament; Berwickshire Naturalists Club Records; Burgh Records of Aberdeen, Edinburgh, Glasgow, Lanark, Peebles, Stirling; Burial Ground Regulations of Edrom, Nithsdale, Tain; Burial Letters of Inverness (3 vols. in Inverness Public Library); *Directory of Worship; Fasti Ecclesiae Scoticanae*; Inverness Scientific Society Records; Kirk Session Records; *Layman's Book of the General Assembly*; *New Statistical Accounts*; Press, the archives of *Home and Country, Inverness Journal, Kelso Mail, Life and Work, The Scotsman*; Pamphlets of St Michael's Parish Church, Linlithgow, Linlithgow History Society, Incorporation of the Hammermen of Edinburgh; Presbytery Records; Proceedings of the Society of Antiquaries of Scotland; *Statistical Accounts*; Traquair Watching Society Minutes, 1824-1858 (Papers of Strathearn and Blair, Register House, Edinburgh).